The Book of Sodom

The Book of Sodom

◆

PAUL HALLAM

VERSO

London · New York

First published by Verso 1993
Collection © Verso 1993
All rights reserved

Verso
UK: 6 Meard Street, London W1V 3HR
USA: 29 West 35th Street, New York, NY 10001–2291

Verso is the imprint of New Left Books

ISBN 0–86091–476 3

British Library Cataloguing in Publication Data
A catalogue record for this book is available from the British Libary

Library of Congress Cataloging-in-Publication Data
A catalogue record for this book is available from the Library of Congress

Typeset by Type Study, Scarborough
Printed in Great Britain by
Bookcraft (Bath) Ltd

Contents

Acknowledgements

For help along the way I would like to thank Charles Adam, Patrick Cardon, Philip Derbyshire, Martina Dervis, Constantine Giannaris, Kate Pullinger, Stuart Richmond and Vron Ware.

Carol Clark generously provided a fresh translation of Vigny and assistance on other French texts.

Sue Golding brought 'The Address Book' to the anthology and kept me going when the circuit-walk got tiring.

Bernard Walsh provided all kinds of cover.

Thanks also to the staff at Verso and particularly to my editor, Malcolm Imrie, who has been enthusiastic and supportive throughout.

I welcome the opportunity to thank the following for their help and friendship over the years: Hilary Boyd, Keith Cavanagh, Howard Hodgkin, Antony Peattie, Ron Peck, Mandy Rose, Judie Sandeman-Allen, Richard Taylor, Bernard Walsh, my sisters, Chris and Sue, and my brother, Kev.

The book is for them.

Introduction

Bound into my bruised and damp-stained King James Bible there is *A Historie of the Bible, Briefely collected by way of Question and Answer* by Eusebius Pagit 'and by him corrected' in 1627. There's a preliminary Pagit poser:

Q. Why is this booke called the Bible, which is a common name for all bookes?

A. Because this is the Booke of bookes, and all other bookes, in respect of it, are but waste paper.

Pagit's own breezy contribution to the world's waste paper comes in at a modest forty-six pages. It takes the Reverend Thomas Stackhouse forty-three pages to reach the 'pack of outrageous Sodomites' and their 'unnatural and preposterous deeds' in the *second* volume of his *A New History of the Holy Bible from the Beginning of the World to the Establishment of Christianity with Answers to Most of the Controverted Questions, Dissertations upon the Most Remarkable Passages . . . Reconciling Seeming Contradictions. The Whole Illustrated with Proper Maps* (1764).

The commentaries on any single Bible tale extend well beyond the concision of Pagit and the Stackhouse stodge.

The short, stark story of Sodom has certainly generated its share of waste paper. I admit a fondness for this Sodom waste in all its variety. I've found Sodom in theological and scholarly tomes; in slim tracts, weighty archaeological investigations and old reference books; Sodom in sermons and in scandal-sheets. Sodom in death sentences and laments, Sodom in school textbooks and in trash.

I am more a Sodom obsessive than a Sodom scholar. The idea of this

1

city has long intrigued me. It's a bold and rounded name, easy to spot, and I've seen it in all manner of books. As a result my selected Sodom writings are not always respectable, not always of the finest quality. There is some pompous and verbose prose, some clumsy poetry in this book, alongside writing I greatly admire, some of it stunning. It's a rough assembly of texts, printed much as found. Not necessarily the most classic writing, the definitive text or, in the case of Victorian material, the finest translation. My concern has been with distinct authorial tone. The writers' visions of Sodom are frequently condemnatory, sometimes celebratory and often simply bawdy. To savour the diversity of tones I've opted for chunkier Sodom texts. I soon lost interest in Sodom snippets, Sodom one-liners; I prefer lengthier, more self-exposing explorations.

The arrangement of the anthology is deliberately loose. I've tried to cover the stories of Sodom's citizens, as depicted at all times and in all places; the city itself, which has come to be a byword for all the world's 'wicked' cities; and some acts, trials and tortures, real and fictional, which have been inspired or informed by the image of Sodom. Finally there's a range of unclassifiable stories, some strange Sodom texts. The anthology rests with a Sodom rumour. The ordering will, I hope, provide a more interesting, if sometimes disorientating, Sodom experience than would, say, a chronological arrangement or a division of the book into types of Sodom studies. I hope the reader will share my pleasure in the criss-cross and collision of times, styles and approaches to Sodom.

My own two-part guidebook and autobiographical essay, 'Sodom: A Circuit-Walk/Looking Back', enfolds the anthology. It is not meant to be a conventional introduction. It is rather a personal exploration of the city and refers to many a version, including celluloid Sodoms and Sodoms in newsprint, that seemed inappropriate to the anthology. It is my way of approaching the city, of reaching into these disparate Sodom texts.

Most of the stories of Sodom are in some way a comment on my life, and the lives of countless others deemed citizens. I've tried to resist some of the attacks on the city I think of as my own, a city I find pleasure and a comfort in. I wanted to explore some of the metaphorical uses to which the city has been put, to tease out the essential Sodom, and rescue, or at least reinvestigate, Sodom's reputation. I've attempted to assess some of its attractions for residents, would-be residents and the curious visitor alike. The whole illustrated with word-maps, proper and improper.

I hope my essay, together with the anthology, will provide a rough and sometimes startling guide to Sodom. A city about which *only* the accumulated waste paper can tell us. For clues about the city in the original, not to say strange story, are few . . .

Genesis 18–19

AND the LORD appeared unto him in the plains of Mamre: and he sat in the tent door in the heat of the day;

2   And he lift up his eyes and looked, and lo, three men stood by him: and when he saw them, he ran to meet them from the tent door, and bowed himself toward the ground,

3   And said, My Lord, if now I have found favour in thy sight, pass not away, I pray thee, from thy servant:

4   Let a little water, I pray you, be fetched, and wash your feet, and rest yourselves under the tree:

5   And I will fetch a morsel of bread, and comfort ye your hearts; after that ye shall pass on: for therefore are ye come to your servant. And they said, So do, as thou hast said.

6   And Abraham hastened into the tent unto Sarah, and said, Make ready quickly three measures of fine meal, knead it, and make cakes upon the hearth.

7   And Abraham ran unto the herd, and fetched a calf tender and good, and gave it unto a young man; and he hasted to dress it.

8   And he took butter, and milk, and the calf which he had dressed, and set it before them; and he stood by them under the tree, and they did eat.

9   And they said unto him, Where is Sarah thy wife? And he said, Behold, in the tent.

10   And he said, I will certainly return unto thee according to the time of life; and lo, Sarah thy wife shall have a son. And Sarah heard it in the tent door, which was behind him.

11   Now Abraham and Sarah were old and well stricken in age; and it ceased to be with Sarah after the manner of women.

12   Therefore Sarah laughed within herself, saying, After I am waxed old shall I have pleasure, my lord being old also?

13   And the LORD said unto Abraham, Wherefore did Sarah laugh, saying, Shall I of a surety bear a child, which am old?

14   Is any thing too hard for the LORD? At the time appointed I will return unto thee, according to the time of life, and Sarah shall have a son.

15   Then Sarah denied, saying, I laughed not; for she was afraid. And he said, Nay; but thou didst laugh.

16   And the men rose up from thence, and looked toward Sodom: and Abraham went with them to bring them on the way.

17 And the LORD said, Shall I hide from Abraham that thing which I do;

18 Seeing that Abraham shall surely become a great and mighty nation, and all the nations of the earth shall be blessed in him?

19 For I know him, that he will command his children and his household after him, and they shall keep the way of the LORD, to do justice and judgment; that the LORD may bring upon Abraham that which he hath spoken of him.

20 And the LORD said, Because the cry of Sodom and Gomorrah is great, and because their sin is very grievous;

21 I will go down now, and see whether they have done altogether according to the cry of it, which is come unto me; and if not, I will know.

22 And the men turned their faces from thence, and went toward Sodom: but Abraham stood yet before the LORD.

23 And Abraham drew near, and said, Wilt thou also destroy the righteous with the wicked?

24 Peradventure there be fifty righteous within the city: wilt thou also destroy and not spare the place for the fifty righteous that are therein?

25 That be far from thee to do after this manner, to slay the righteous with the wicked: and that the righteous should be as the wicked, that be far from thee: Shall not the Judge of all the earth do right?

26 And the LORD said, if I find in Sodom fifty righteous within the city, then I will spare all the place for their sakes.

27 And Abraham answered and said, Behold now, I have taken upon me to speak unto the Lord, which am but dust and ashes:

28 Peradventure there shall lack five of the fifty righteous: wilt thou destroy all the city for lack of five? And he said, If I find there forty and five I will not destroy it.

29 And he spake unto him yet again, and said, Peradventure there shall be forty found there. And he said, I will not do it for forty's sake.

30 And he said unto him, Oh let not the Lord be angry, and I will speak: Peradventure there shall thirty be found there. And he said, I will not do it, if I find thirty there.

31 And he said, Behold now, I have taken upon me to speak unto the Lord: Peradventure there shall be twenty found there. And he said, I will not destroy it for twenty's sake.

32 And he said, Oh let not the Lord be angry, and I will speak yet

but this once: Peradventure ten shall be found there. And he said, I will not destroy it for ten's sake.

33   And the LORD went his way, as soon as he had left communing with Abraham: and Abraham returned unto his place.

19

AND there came two angels to Sodom at even; and Lot sat in the gate of Sodom: and Lot seeing them rose up to meet them; and he bowed himself with his face toward the ground.

2   And he said, Behold now, my lords, turn in, I pray you, into your servant's house, and tarry all night, and wash your feet, and ye shall rise up early, and go on your ways. And they said, Nay; but we will abide in the street all night.

3   And he pressed upon them greatly; and they turned in unto him, and entered into his house; and he made them a feast, and did bake unleavened bread, and they did eat.

4   But before they lay down, the men of the city, even the men of Sodom, compassed the house round, both old and young, all the people from every quarter:

5   And they called unto Lot, and said unto him, Where are the men which came in to thee this night? bring them out unto us, that we may know them.

6   And Lot went out at the door unto them, and shut the door after him,

7   And said, I pray you, brethren, do not do so wickedly.

8   Behold now, I have two daughters which have not known man; let me, I pray you, bring them out unto you, and do ye to them as is good in your eyes; only unto these men do nothing; for therefore came they under the shadow of my roof.

9   And they said, Stand back. And they said again, This one fellow came in to sojourn, and he will needs be a judge: now will we deal worse with thee, than with them. And they pressed sore upon the man, even Lot, and came near to break the door.

10   But the men put forth their hand, and pulled Lot into the house to them, and shut to the door.

11   And they smote the men that were at the door of the house with blindness, both small and great: so that they wearied themselves to find the door.

12   And the men said unto Lot, Hast thou any here besides? son in law, and thy sons, and thy daughters, and whatsoever thou hast in the city, bring them out of this place.

13   For we will destroy this place, because the cry of them is waxen great before the face of the LORD; and the LORD hath sent us to destroy it.

14   And Lot went out, and spake unto his sons in law, which married his daughters, and said, Up, get you out of this place; for the LORD will destroy this city. But he seemed as one that mocked unto his sons in law.

15   And when the morning arose, then the angels hastened Lot, saying, Arise, take thy wife, and thy two daughters, which are here; lest thou be consumed in the iniquity of the city.

16   And while he lingered, the men laid hold upon his hand, and upon the hand of his wife, and upon the hand of his two daughters; the LORD being merciful unto him; and they brought him forth, and set him without the city.

17   And it came to pass, when they had brought them forth abroad, that he said, Escape for thy life; look not behind thee, neither stay thou in all the plain; escape to the mountain, lest thou be consumed.

18   And Lot said unto them, Oh, not so, my Lord:

19   Behold now, thy servant hath found grace in thy sight, and thou hast magnified thy mercy, which thou hast shewed unto me in saving my life; and I cannot escape to the mountain, lest some evil take me, and I die:

20   Behold now, this city is near to flee unto, and it is a little one: Oh, let me escape thither, (is it not a little one?) and my soul shall live.

21   And he said unto him, See, I have accepted thee concerning this thing also, that I will not overthrow this city, for the which thou hast spoken.

22   Haste thee, escape thither; for I cannot do any thing till thou be come thither. Therefore the name of the city was called Zoar.

23   The sun was risen upon the earth when Lot entered into Zoar.

24   Then the LORD rained upon Sodom and upon Gomorrah brimstone and fire from the LORD out of heaven;

25   And he overthrew those cities, and all the plain, and all the inhabitants of the cities, and that which grew upon the ground.

26   But his wife looked back from behind him, and she became a pillar of salt.

27   And Abraham gat up early in the morning to the place where he stood before the LORD:

28   And he looked toward Sodom and Gomorrah, and toward all the land of the plain, and beheld, and, lo, the smoke of the country went up as the smoke of a furnace.

29   And it came to pass, when God destroyed the cities of the plain, that God remembered Abraham, and sent Lot out of the midst of the overthrow, when he overthrew the cities in which Lot dwelt.

30   And Lot went up out of Zoar, and dwelt in the mountain, and his two daughters with him; for he feared to dwell in Zoar; and he dwelt in a cave, he and his two daughters.

31   And the firstborn said unto the younger, Our father is old, and there is not a man in the earth to come in unto us after the manner of all the earth:

32   Come, let us make our father drink wine, and we will lie with him, that we may preserve seed of our father.

33   And they made their father drink wine that night: and the firstborn went in, and lay with her father; and he perceived not when she lay down, nor when she arose.

34   And it came to pass on the morrow, that the firstborn said unto the younger, Behold, I lay yesternight with my father: let us make him drink wine this night also; and go thou in, and lie with him, that we may preserve seed of our father.

35   And they made their father drink wine that night also: and he perceived not when she lay down, nor when she arose.

36   Thus were both the daughters of Lot with child by their father.

37   And the firstborn bare a son, and called his name Moab: the same is the father of the Moabites unto this day.

38   And the younger, she also bare a son, and called his name Ben-ammi: the same is the father of the children of Ammon unto this day.

Sodom: A Circuit-Walk

There is no Sodom, there are only Sodom texts.

Stories of Sodom, commentaries, footnotes, elaborations and annotations upon Sodom.

* * *

Go where we will, at every time and place
Sodom confronts, and stares us in the face.

Charles Churchill, 'The Times', 1764

Churchill, loathing Sodom, was far from pleased at this prospect. I, a citizen, look eagerly, but find the city at once ubiquitous and elusive. In the eighteenth century a guide to a city might append a 'circuit-walk' of its boundaries. Taking in churches, the writer would select the most comic, the sad, the most splendid of monuments and memorials to the dead. My walk is in London, but I drift across time, across place. It could be a walk in almost any city. Any city worth its salt has been called, at one time or another, Sodom.

I regularly wander Clerkenwell in search of Sodom. It's the part of London I'm most at home in. I like its day-for-night inversions. The hospitals and the meat market. The shift workers, the uniforms of the porters and the nurses, the doctors' coats and butchers' aprons. On weekdays there's the added attraction of city boys in their suits and ties.

Parked in the road that dissects the hook-lined Smithfield Meat Market there are huge lorries. The cabins at the front might have their curtains drawn, the driver asleep after a long haul. A curious mix of temporary home and den, these trucks. Some display car toys, window-sticker slogans and family photos. Others look less homely, rougher. Homes that move, dens that can be closed off, in the middle of the city. The older lorries have slightly rusted, chrome-plate door handles. I want quietly to press a handle down, to climb in. Closed, these cabins, as sometimes are the other temporary dens of this city, the builders' huts, the canvas and metal meshed tents of gas, electricity and telecom men. Huts, tents, dens; always loved them.

I'll pass the lorries, cross over to the church of St Bartholomew-the-Great, once part of a twelfth-century Augustinian priory. The priory was founded by Henry I's court jester, following a vision in which St Bartholomew saved him from a winged monster. A fresh-faced couple might think twice about marrying in this dark crumbling, blackened stone interior. Too grim and encrusted with memorials. It feels like, and is, a place for the performance of Bach *Passions*. In bad weather I might rest here. In good, I'll head towards St Paul's, sit instead in Postman's Park, with its ludicrously sweet Victorian monument to ordinary heroes. Like the railwayman, who, surprised by a train whilst gauging a line, 'hauled his mate out of the track'. Daniel Pemberton saved his mate's life at the cost of his own. The nearby Post Office was the work-and-play place of boys charged in connection with the late-nineteenth-century Cleveland Street scandal. A young clerk named Newlove hung around the basement lavatory and there introduced telegraph messengers Messrs Wright, Thickbroom and Swinscow (I've made none of these names up) to pleasures later made plain and dry in their statements to the police. 'He put his person into me, that is to say behind only a little way and something came from him.' The police were eliciting the exact nature of the acts to decide on the exact nature of the charges. Newlove told the boys how they might augment their meagre wages by performing similar acts with toffs in the plusher surrounds of 19 Cleveland Street, up West. Newlove was pimping, and, given that he took Swinscow into the lavatory lock-up more than once, he clearly enjoyed the perks of the job. Not that the boys objected. No money exchanged hands in the basement. Wright was well-rewarded in Cleveland Street, by a gentleman: 'We got into bed and played with each other. He did not put his person into me.' Wright added, 'I treated Newlove to a drop of beer.' Newlove's reward for the introduction.

When Lord Arthur Somerset, superintendent to the Prince of Wales's stables, was widely rumoured to be a Cleveland Street client, he took sudden leave of absence. A poem appeared in the *North London Press*:

My Lord Gomorrah sat in his chair
　　Sipping his costly wine;
He was safe in France, that's called the fair,
　　In a city some call 'Boo-line.'
He poked the blaze, and he warmed his toes,
　　And as the sparks from the logs arose,
He laid one finger beside his nose –
　　And My Lord Gomorrah smiled.

He thought of the wretched, vulgar tools
　　Of his faederastian joys, [sic]

How they lay in prison, poor scapegoat fools!
  Raw, cash-corrupted boys.
While he and his 'pals' the 'office' got
  From a 'friend at Court', and were off like a shot,
  Out of reach of Law, Justice and 'that – rot',
    And my Lord Gomorrah smiled.

Anon., *North London Press*, 1889

'Gomorrah', rather than Sodom, was chosen by Anon., perhaps for reasons purely metrical. Or perhaps 'Sodom' was considered too disturbing a word for this radical paper's readership. Or Gomorrah, sometimes seen as Sodom's sister, the girls' place, might be a way of effeminising the Lord. The interesting mis-spelling of pederastian in the poem might be a printer's error, or it too might be an example of press prudence. The *North London Press* pursued the scandal and named a second lord, Lord Euston, as a regular customer. Euston sued its editor, Ernest Parke, for libel. The French press showed no hesitation in describing London as 'Sodome' when a complex scandal and classic establishment cover-up unfolded. Euston admitted visiting the house, once. He expected, he explained, to see an artistic exhibition of *poses plastiques* (female strip-tease). When he discovered the true nature of the house, he left in disgust. A contemporary wit suggested that Euston had sought a game of 'poker' but found the game to be 'baccarat'.

A witness in the trial was John or Jack Saul. Saul claimed that he had personally escorted Lord Euston to the house and that Euston was a regular visitor. In his summing-up, the judge asked whether the jury could possibly take the word of a 'melancholy spectacle', a 'loathsome object' such as Saul against the oath of a lord. Parke was found guilty of libel and imprisoned.

Saul was the author of a rare piece of Victorian porn, *The Sins of the Cities of the Plain; or the Recollections of a Mary-Ann with short essays on Sodomy and Tribadism*. The book cost four guineas so you'd need to be a lord to afford it. *Sins* purports to be Saul's erotic autobiography as related, at a price, to a gentleman. It opens with a street-cruising and pick-up scene. The gentleman's attention is caught by Saul's manner and attire, but mostly by his extraordinary 'appendage', his 'manly jewel':

He was dressed in tight-fitting clothes, which set off his Adonis-like figure to the best advantage, especially what snobs call the fork of his

17

trousers, where evidently he was endowed by a very extraordinary development of the male appendage; he had small and elegant feet, set off by pretty patent leather boots, a fresh-looking beardless face, with almost feminine features, auburn hair and sparkling blue eyes which told me that the handsome youth (ah youth no longer) must indeed be one of the Mary-Annes of London.

Saul, Adonis in Sodom, the first of many classic guest appearances in the Bible town, introduces himself:

> 'Saul, Jack Saul, Sir, of Lisle Street, Leicester Square, and ready for a lark with a free gentleman at any time.'

The gentleman is much taken by the attributes of Adonis, and desires to know him better.

> 'You seem a fine figure and so evidently well hung that I had quite a fancy to satisfy my curiosity about it. Is it real or made up for show?'
> 'As real as my face sir and a great deal prettier. Did you ever see a finer tosser in your life?' he replied, opening his trousers and exposing a tremendous prick, which was already in a half-standing state. 'It's my only fortune, sir; but it really provides for all I want, and often introduces me to the best of society, ladies as well as gentlemen.'

Saul's narrative is curious on several counts. Explicit and almost exclusively gay content was rare in Victorian erotica. Saul's adventures reveal an expensive and exclusive Victorian gay underworld. There's a drag ball on at Haxell's Hotel in the Strand in this Sodom. 'Transports of delight' available in the back dressing-rooms. There's also a lengthy digression on the recruitment of soldiers into prostitution. Having learnt to goose-step, they soon learn to be 'goosed'. Prostitution, like pugilism, is seen as a way 'for a boy to make his way in this world'. 'Although of course we do it for the money, we also do it because we really like it,' declares Fred Jones, the book's principal soldier boy. Saul certainly really liked it too, and *Sins*, for all its incidental information, is much more a leisurely tour of intertwined men's bodies than a Sodom/London guide.

> I got bolder and generally my bedfellow would turn over and reciprocate my dalliance till we joined in a mutual fuck between each other's thighs,

belly to belly. My favourite idea was to pull back the skin of my foreskin, and doing the same to my bedfellow's prick, bring the nose of his affair to mine, then draw the skin of mine over the heads of both cocks, and fuck each other gently so. What delicious thrills we had when spending, the seed seeming to shoot backwards and forwards from one to the other.

A state of perpetual 'spending crisis' where 'the creamy essence of life' freely flows. The reader coaxed to that same delicious crisis. The language of old porn, an erotic relation with its characters' timeless deeds yet dated words, I always find it oddly moving.

The occasional unstimulating character detail suggests that these are the authentic, if elaborated, memoirs of an actual Mary-Ann. Saul is offered a trip to meet the best of German society, but 'not caring to leave Good Old England, I politely declined his overtures'. But though *Sins* is a portrait of a city seen as Sodom, the reference ends almost with the title. Acts concern Saul; his is no exploratory vision of Sodom. The book does, however, have 'Private Case' status in the British Library. I sat and read it about ten years ago, close to the librarians' desk, as required. I made pencil notes (pens are proscribed), as part of my research for a film script on the Cleveland Street scandal. I smiled at the bookplate, 'In Honour Bound, George 2nd Marquess of Milford Haven. Royal Navy'. I thought at the time that *Sins* was worthy of republication. Recently I noticed two books with that code-for-Sodom title. The first *City of the Plain* turned out to be a history of twentieth-century gay life in Sydney. The second, an American import, had the twin-town title, *Sins of the Cities of the Plain*. A handsome very 1990s-style shirtless male model adorns its cover. The author is 'anonymous' and *Sins* is republished as an 'adult fiction BADBOY book' by Masquerade Books of New York. Cheekily, Masquerade claim 'copyright'. Inside there's a taster quotation from the book: 'My name is Saul, Jack Saul, sir, of Lisle Street, Leicester Square, and ready for a lark with a free gentleman at any time.' Jack Saul, a hundred years after the Cleveland Street scandal, back to entertain a new bunch of badboys and at a more affordable price. I was pleased to see it. At first the Masquerade edition follows the original text with reasonable care, but my suspicion was aroused when Saul's 'appendage' was compared to a 'tremendous length of sausage'. A graceless addition. Modern phrases creep in: 'I would set about proving my daft theory of Jerry's sexuality', 'You were such a tit then', 'I will bet you are right indeed, cuz. Have you given thought to a regimen of calisthenics or some other form of exercise?' I won't go on. Perhaps the adulteration gives Masquerade some kind of copyright. *Sins* still works as a handbook, and that was always its main intent. But the linguistic and historical interest is confused by the Masquerade edition being precisely that – modern porn masquerading as 'a classic'. This is a familiar story in the world of sodomitica. Books are copied, added to, excised and mistranslated prior to their under-the-counter circulation. Sodom spawns some strange mutating texts.

*

Long before the Cleveland Street scandal, in the 1720s, Clerkenwell/ Farringdon was the area where 'molly houses' flourished. Gay meeting places that fell foul of the Society for the Reformation of Manners and were raided. The mollies stood trial close by, round the corner from the post office, at the Old Bailey. The trial reports were published as *Select Trials*. Such books were the forerunners of our ubiquitous 'True Crime' series, and about as reliable. Select trials for murder, robbery, rape, sodomy, coining and fraud were the public's favourites then as now. Unreliable, these accounts, but they're almost all we have of molly voices. And the records of moments ring true.

From the trial of George Duffus, for sodomy, December, 1721:

> . . . as soon as we were got into Bed, he began to hug and kiss me, and call me his Dear. I asked him what he meant by it? He answer'd, *No Harm, nothing but Love*, and presently got upon me, and thrust his Tongue into my Mouth.

From the trial of John Dicks, for sodomy, April, 1722:

> . . . we went to another Alehouse, in *Chancery-lane* where he treated me with hot Ale and Gin; and from thence he carried me to the *Golden-ball*, near *Bond's-stables*, near *Fetter-lane*, where we drank more Ale and Geneva 'til I was so drunk and sick that I vomited, and lay down to sleep. The Prisoner unbutton'd my Breeches, and turn'd me on my Face, and try'd to enter my Body, but whether he did it or not, I was not sensible enough to be certain.

The molly men met to dress up, drink and dance. They devised extraordinary mock-wedding and mock-birth rituals. Last year I was mooching after molly lives, at work on another script; at the same time, it turned out, as Rictor Norton was finishing *Mother Clap's Molly House*, his book on them. On my Sodomite trails, I might cross the paths of other researchers. Records of gay history are scarce, students of Sodom are bound to bump into each other sometimes.

Some of the mollies were imprisoned in Newgate, others were fined, pilloried and carted through central London to be hanged at Tyburn. Clerkenwell was Sodomite territory. There is no memorial.

More recently Clerkenwell housed the London Lesbian and Gay Centre. Somehow the words don't have quite the appeal of 'molly house'. A somewhat dull building, the Centre was like a students' union, but cleaner, with one of my least favourite city structures, the membership desk. Such desks always put me off being a member. The Institute of Contemporary Arts has one, and it too seems too clean a place for its purpose, the promotion of the new, the subversive. The Centre, recently closed, was handy for picking up the free gay papers – *Capital Gay*, *Boyz* and the *Pink Paper*, which you could take with no obligation to enter. I pass by it on the regular walk to Clerkenwell, in search of Sodom.

It's a leisurely tour, there's an alternative to the Postman's Park. I might take a bench in Clerkenwell Square, facing the locked-up 'Gentlemens', a notorious cottage once, with my back towards the Marx Memorial Library. It's not a place I've ever been a member of, the library that is, but it's an exile's monument, and I'm glad it's there. One particular Saturday there's a sign, a booksale at 11 a.m. It's early yet, but I'll come back. I'm looking for socialist versions of the Sodom story still. You never know . . .

Turning a corner, Turnmills is turning out. It looks like a wine bar for business boys, and a chalked sign promises early evening office-party karaoke. But some nights Turnmills turns Sodom. Turnmills was the home of the original ff club. ff ads featured a hand clutching a crucifix, and asked, 'where else on a sunday?' It promised hard music, ten hours of dance. It delivered. White sheets hung from ceiling to floor, created closed-off corners; the club was packed, small, dry-iced and sweaty. It was, for a while, the best club in London and the ff crew created a smart, comic-style, alternative gay magazine, *ff*. A caustic view of the 'straight' gay scene. Sixteen thousand copies of the magazine, or 'zine' as they're called now, were recently seized by police officers of the

Territorial Support Group. Officers were particularly offended by a safe-sex image, a man about to penetrate another, which accompanied an article subtitled 'Rubber Fuck'. A rubber-fuck report is being prepared for the Obscene Publications Squad.

The mollies got into trouble, not least for choosing, just a few minutes' walk from here, to gather at Mother Clap's molly house on Sundays. This at a time when Sabbath-breaking was in the serious sin category. The Society for the Reformation of Manners saw an England sliding towards Sodom:

> O how dreadful it is to relate our deplorable case. Where are the Mourners? Would to God England (England most especially) could weep day and night, and be in bitterness of grief; and that all our eyes might send forth streams like many Rivers, and make our barren unfruitfull earth a Bochim. We have been planted a noble vine, a vineyard of God's own watering, and defence from Age to Age: But how have we degenerated into the Plant of a Strange Vine, even since our late miraculous EXODUS? Have we not brought forth Apples of Sodom, and four Grapes of Gomorrah? Thorns and thistles instead of Figs?

The anonymous 1698 pamphlet appended 'A Black Roll Containing the real (or reputed) Names and Crimes of Several Hundred Persons that have been Prosecuted by the Society, this last Year, for Whoring, Drunkenness, Thefts, Sabbath-breaking, etc. as Delivered unto Them by their Clerk: And been published for the Satisfaction of many who have been desirous to know what progress we have made in this Reformation of Manners'. Anon. appended 'For the more Effectual Promoting the Design of this Book' a list of offences, statutes and penalties to enable any would-be reformer to be constantly on the look-out for offence.

> All laws in force concerning the observation of the Lord's-Day shall be put in execution: This day is by every one to be sanctified and kept holy; and all persons must be careful herein to exercise themselves in the duties of piety and true religion, publickly and privately; and every one on this day (not having a reasonable excuse) must diligently resort to some public place, where the service of God is exercised, or must be present at some other place, (allowed of by Law) in the practice of some religious duty, either of prayer, preaching, reading or expounding of the Scriptures, or conference upon the same.

Sodomites weren't of course the only Sabbath-breakers, nor were they the sole target of the Reformers. Among those condemned are 'Such as meet or assemble out of their own parish upon the Lord's-Day for any sports or pastimes whatsoever', any butcher selling victuals and anyone guilty of drunkenness, 'a crime from which the ancient Britons were free'. Blasphemers are especially to be watched for. A blasphemer is defined as any Christian-educated person who 'within this realm, shall, by writing, printing, teaching, or advised speaking, deny any one of the persons in the Holy Trinity to be God, or shall assert or maintain there are more gods than one, or shall deny the Christian religion to be true, or the Holy Scriptures of the Old and New Testament to be of Divine Authority'. Adultery and all acts of bawdry are breaches of peace. Whore-masters, whores and 'Strangers, or others, that are suspicious, that walk by night, especially if they haunt lewd houses, or keep ill company, or commit outrages' must be pursued. 'Idlers that refuse to work, and disorderly persons, Wandering rogues' are to be committed 'to the house of correction, whipped, and sent to the place of birth'. And 'If any woman shall have a bastard child which may be chargeable to the parish . . . she shall get the House of correction for one year' etc., etc.

A 1730 pamphlet declares:

> Without this care at home, it is vain to hope for a thorough, public reformation; the Kingdom will never grow good, till private families become, what they ought to be, seminaries of religion and virtue – and if it be apparent, that of late years these have much declined in this great and populous city; the mischief, I believe, is owing to nothing more, than the too visible neglect of parents and masters in these respects; who, many of them, when the business of the day is over, make a constant practice of spending whole nights in gratifying their vices or their pleasures, entirely neglecting family devotion and order, and oftentimes leaving their apprentices, if not their children and servants, to go even where, and to do even what they please; to drink, to game, and to frequent the play-houses, where the entertainments are now become a reproach to common sense and decency, as well as the chief sources and encouragements to all manner of impiety, iniquity and lewdness – and when young and giddy persons, whose age disposes them to be lovers of pleasures, are thus prepared, what wonder is it that they wax wanton . . .

The SRM were never modest about their achievements. In the *35th Account of the Progress of the Societies* they boast:

Multitudes, for more than thirty years last past, have been prosecuted. . . . Great numbers of bawdy-houses and other disorderly houses
have been suppressed and shut up, and the streets very much purged
from the wretched tribe of night-walking prostitutes and most detestable
sodomites.

The said Societies have prosecuted and been assisting in prosecuting,
from 1st December 1728 to the 1st December 1729, a considerable
number of persons for the following crimes and offences, viz.

For sodomitical and other disorderly practices; for keeping disorderly
houses; profane swearing and cursing, and exercising their trades or
ordinary callings on the Lord's Day.

The total number of persons prosecuted in or near London only for
debauchery and profaneness for 38 years last past, are calculated about
96326.

They have been assistant in bringing to punishment several sodomitical
houses, as well as divers persons for sodomy and sodomitical practices,
who have been prosecuted by the direction, and at the charge of the
government.

The company we Sodomites keep, and the glorious number of that
company. The figures represent those *caught*. So, if we multiply that
figure by a speculation on the numbers that weren't, we'd be in danger
of losing our minority status. In the SRM target list, as in so many,
Sodomites form part of the whole panoply of perversion. You'll hear
the panoply attacked, with great relish and to great applause, in 'little
list' speeches at Tory Party conferences; in those tired old homilies on
family values, Victorian values. Single mothers, lesbian mothers,
sodomites, gypsies, blasphemers, whores, social security scroungers,
New-Age travellers and Sunday traders. Pick and mix across the
centuries, the litanies remain the same.

*

The boys of Turnmills, night-dancing Sodomites, stumble out into the
brightness of the morning, dazzled. They'd be on any Reformer's list.
The club is high on the local police chief's. Chief Inspector Derek
Talbot has waged a relentless campaign to get the club's rare-in-
London and much cherished twenty-four-hour licence revoked.

Many doe so debauch their lives with odious drunkennesse, cosenage, lying, swearing, Sabboth breach, with other abominations, proclaiming their sin as *Sodom*, abhorring the light, and maintaining their lusts and pleasures against it, that their hearts are poured out as water; and there is no heart left in them to looke after the Sacrament: They tell themselves in secret, That such holy things are not for dogges: Swine more become the trough than the Table: The Devill also takes on and torments them (if they dare look toward the Sacrament,) and tells them, They have another trade to thrive upon, their whoring, their riot, their roaring, and emptying themselves into their lusts without all controll, and stabbing all that give them a crosse word, must be their joy and delight, and in stead of all Word and Sacrament. And thus they desperately go on saying, There is no hope, Jeremy 3:25. The remedy is, That they submit to God's terrors, and stop their ungodly courses, and try if the terrors of God can tame them, and bring them into some generall compasse.

The Second Part of the Treatise of the Sacrament by
D.R.B. in Divin. and Minister of the Gospell. London, 1633.

The ff boys, in their sweat-soaked tops, emptied of their riot and their roaring, hearts poured out in water, blink in ordinary daylight. They will probably go home, and make drowsy love, or take a bath and sleep.

A short quotation from a bulky book, two treatises on the sacrament bound in with D.R.B.'s *A Practicall Cathechisme*, the second edition, 'corrected, enlarged, and restored to order'. I wonder about the chaotic catechism, the first edition. The note conjures up an image of inversions, a less well-mannered list of dos and don'ts. A catechism that might challenge, not slip into the weary list of sins begetting sins. I've always preferred a well-written questioning to a badly written celebration. I've little time for the dictates of the 'positive image' merchants. Attacks, stirred and fascinated by what they condemn, can be exploratory. Certainly they're there to be explored. There's much in this catechism and meditation on the sacraments that catches my curiosity, that I find affecting, but once in Sodom the catechist slips into the loose and sloppy list offensive. Think of a sin, say debauchery, sprinkle in lying, cozenage, swearing. The result: Sodom. In the end the writing winds me up, provokes my jibes. *Jeremy* for me was the coy title of an early gay magazine, replete with pin-ups. One of the first I ever bought. Unlike D.R.B.'s Jeremy, my *Jeremy* did offer hope. A cheap stab, that, at a cross word.

*

25

There are two kinds of Sodom lists, the black list (the SRM Black Roll) and the pink. Learned divines versus the divine learned (Proust, Gide, Cocteau and Co.).

In the pink corner there are Pink Plaque guides to where gay gurus lived. And a list can also mean a pleasure, a joy, a delight; or again, a boundary, an edge, a strip. A Bob Damron or a Spartacus list might direct you to these edges, our strips, and hopefully to pleasure. For rainy days there are the easy-digest reads, Gay Books of Lists, Gay Books of Days, Famous Fags, the Great and the Gay. Consider the Kinsey lists, take your place on the Hetero–Homo Rating: Active Incidence scale; or select a position from the 'On Sodomy and the Tricks of the Sodomites' chapter available in unexcised editions of *The Perfumed Garden*. No time for elaborations? Pick up the handkerchief colour code chart: Greek Active/Greek Passive, Has 8-inch plus/Wants 8-inch plus, Has Uniform/Wants Uniform, Whipper/Whippee . . . I get colour confused, I can never remember these cotton Likes to blow nose/Likes to be blown distinctions.

In the black corner, the Inquisition lists, FBI pinko-commie-faggot hit lists, police lists, penalty lists and penitentials.

The end-list, easy, bold and simple as a baby toy, the kill list of coloured triangles.

One of the strangest of the black lists is discussed in Joseph Dean's *Hatred, Ridicule or Contempt: A Book of Libel Cases*. Dean quotes a 1918 newspaper:

> There exists in the *Cabinet noire* of a certain German prince a book compiled by the Secret Service from the reports of German Agents who have infested this country for the past twenty years, agents so vile and spreading debauchery of such a lasciviousness as only German minds could conceive and only German bodies execute. The officer who discovered this book while on special service briefly outlined for me its stupefying contents. In the beginning of the book is a précis of general instructions regarding the propagation of evils which all decent men thought had perished in Sodom and Lesbia [sic]. The blasphemous compilers even speak of the Groves and High places mentioned in the Bible. The most insidious arguments are outlined for the use of the German agent in his revolting work. Then more than a thousand pages are filled with the names mentioned by German agents in their reports. There are the names of forty-seven thousand English men and women.

It is a most catholic miscellany. The names of Privy Councillors, youths of the chorus, wives of Cabinet Ministers, dancing girls, even Cabinet Ministers themselves, while diplomats, poets, bankers, editors, newspaper proprietors, and members of His Majesty's household follow each other with no order of precedence. . . . The story of the contents of this book has opened my eyes, and the matter must not rest.

The Imperialist, January 1918

The war wasted on. The article appeared after the German counter-attack that followed Passchendaele. There seemed no end in sight, who was to blame? Noel Pemberton Billing, Independent Member of Parliament, purity campaigner and editor of *The Imperialist*, had the answer: the Hun had the strategy of Sodom. Contaminating Britain, rendering the great, but not-so-good, vulnerable to blackmail. The classic gay spy scare. *The Imperialist* had a limited, subscriber-only circulation. No names were named, and no one sued for libel, but there's an odd twist to this story, which might otherwise have been forgotten as the mad ramblings of a Sodom-obsessed purity campaigner.

J.T. Grein, drama critic and impresario, planned to stage two private performances of Wilde's *Salome* – of necessity private, the play had been banned by the Lord Chamberlain for public performance. Maud Allen was to appear in the revealing title role. Salome is damned in the play as the 'daughter of Sodom', by, it must be said, an understandably irate John the Baptist. Pemberton was incensed. A *German* to stage a play by that notorious Sodomite, Oscar Wilde. Or posing 'Somdomite' as the Marquess of Queensberry spelt it on the bitter scribbled calling card that triggered Oscar's downfall.

'Lesbia' for Lesbos in *The Imperialist*, 'Somdomite' for Sodomite, 'faederastian' for pederastian in the Lord Gomorrah poem, and recently I saw a clip from a Bible Quiz Show, aired on American cable TV. The contestants were hopelessly at sea spelling Gomorrah. Can there be a connection between Sodom and an ability to spell?

In the next issue of *The Imperialist*, now renamed *The Vigilante* (to attract a more active readership?), Billing declared, 'If Scotland Yard were to seize the list of these members [i.e. the subscribers to the performance], I have no doubt they would secure the names of several thousand of the first 47,000. Allen and Grein sued for libel. In the event the case centred around the article's suggestion that Maud Allen

27

was 'a lewd and unchaste and immoral woman . . . about to give private performances of an obscene and indecent character so designed as to foster and encourage lewd and immoral practices'. Billing pleaded not guilty to libel, asserting that the play was an 'open representation of degenerated lust, sexual crime and unnatural passions . . . an evil travesty of a biblical story', and its performance could only be prejudicial to public morality. This was all very confusing. *Salome*, after all, was a story of *heterosexual* passion; or rather, as Allen argued none too convincingly, the story of the awakening of Salome's soul to the voice of God. Witnesses testified to the existence of the Black Book, many a prominent person was outed, Mrs Asquith and Lord Haldane to name but two. The case got more and more bizarre and distinctly undignified. Doctors, drama critics, an array of reverends and the repentant sinner Lord Alfred Douglas solemnly testified to Oscar Wilde's perversion. Douglas, who had in his youth translated the play from Wilde's French, called Wilde 'the greatest force for evil that has appeared in Europe during the last 350 years'. This in 1918! Sadly Oscar couldn't be there to reply.

After four days, the judge declared the Black Book irrelevant to the case, Billing withdrew the charge of lesbianism aimed at Allen, and in a way it was Oscar and his *opus* back on trial again. Billing was found not guilty of libel, the mob outside cheered. As for the Black Book, it never turned up. Some, Dean suggests, said it was merely a list of potential customers for Mercedes cars.

J. Edgar Hoover, the ultimate list man, if recent revelations are to be believed, liked to drag up and wrestle with rent. The boys would pepper the proceedings with choice readings from the Bible. Genesis 19? There are names you wish you could erase from the pink list. Hoover's name apparently made the Mafia records of the sexually irregular; it helped keep Hoover off their backs.

Martin Duberman, in his excellent exploration of the gay past, *About Time*, unearthed a Sodom list from 1960. One Countess Waldeck reflected on the recent ousting of 119 homosexuals from the State Department. Her musings were aired in an article on the 'Homosexual International' in the 29 September 1960 issue of *Human Events*, a magazine for business leaders and politicians.

> . . . the main reason why . . . the elimination of the homosexuals from all
> Government agencies and especially from the State Department is of

vital urgency is that by the very nature of their vice they belong to a
sinister, mysterious and efficient International . . .

. . . this conspiracy has spread all over the globe; has penetrated all
classes . . .

. . . members of one conspiracy are apt to join another conspiracy. This is
one reason why so many homosexuals from being enemies of society in
general, become enemies of capitalism in particular. Without being
necessarily Marxist they serve the ends of the Communist International
in the name of their rebellion against the prejudices, standards, ideals of
the 'bourgeois' world.

Homosexuals as a race apart, as rebels. She reflects on their 'passion for
intrigue', the disturbing nature of their 'social promiscuity' and 'the
fusion it effects between upperclass and proletarian corruption'.
Cash-corrupted boys again. But she doesn't mince words, the Countess; nor will she opt for the softer sound of Gomorrah.

With fascination I watched the little Sodoms functioning within the
Embassies and foreign offices. Somehow homosexuals always seemed to
come by the dozen . . . homosexuals really do look after their own.

. . . a complicated mass of obscure hates, frustrations, inferiority feelings
and guilt feelings mark [the Sodomite's] humiliated soul.

They also make natural secret agents and natural traitors. She has it
on the authority of Proust, no less, that the homosexual is forced to live
'in falsehood and perjury'. This naturally made the Sodomite a bad
security risk.

Sodom is a kind of constantly exposed secret. All those archaeolo-
gists, like Duberman, exploring, tracing carefully within. Outside,
Waldecks poised and watching, cool lenses trained on Sodom. I'd like
to think in some ways she was right, that we'd look after our own in the
face of threat or danger. In the Aids years many have done just that.
'With fascination' the Countess watched the never-ending Sodom
party. The view never changes. Sometimes, she might be surprised to
hear, even Sodomites can tire of Sodom.

I'll take a different walk, at dusk, before the curtains close. Glimpse a
couple on the sofa, a family meal, a child's red ball as it rolls across a
living-room floor. Sometimes I'm shocked how this can catch me by the

throat, how suddenly I'm lost. Sometimes, of course, a plate is hurled, I'll hear a shout, see the child clouted and left crying. I'll hurry awkwardly by. Mostly though, at dusk, I'm just watching, with fascination, as a father changes his sweat-damped shirt after work, his chest caught in light.

*

Strange the catechist's and countess's list. Purity Pemberton's and the SRM. All feature the familiar features of the Sodom myth. Sodom as the vice of the 'other', the enemy, the wicked foreigner or worse, the enemy within. Sodom as an unwelcome guest, the import of impurity. The rabid taint of Sodom, its contagion. Waldeck watching all the time, yet oblivious to detail, no distinctions made. Word upon word they stack their Sodom pyres. There's a comedy to their Sodom concoctions and solemn certainties, there's also paranoia. Sodom fears and fantasies have forever informed the liquidation lists of Bible-bashing and Bible-burning states alike.

They have to be watched for, these lists, tempting as it is to smile at and dismiss them. It's not enough to say Michelangelo was 'so' and so was Leonardo, to oppose with pink. Some don't care much for art anyway. A new kind of list has appeared in the past ten years, the list of Aids-related deaths. This list too has its variations, sometimes subtle. The popular press scarcely conceals its joy at the latest star name added. Drool at the death toll. The slightly more 'respectable' press prints photograph after photograph with the 'tragic loss to the art world' caption. Faces arraigned in mug-shot fashion. A kind of 'outing' retrospective, even when they include the odd rumoured-to-be hetero-sexual.

There has been a very different visual response to Aids in the 'names' projects, the quilts to commemorate those who have died. A list of tender opposition and memorial. I admit an aversion to home embroideries, to most types of tapestry. And yet, looking at these soft cloth gravestones, the efforts of friends and sometimes, but not always, family, I'll end up choked.

*

When I last went to the ff club, I was feeling my age. Just a little slow, certainly not up to all-nighters, well, not often. Time, at forty, to retire gracefully from disco Sodom, I thought. Pleased to leave it in the nineties with what seemed like the energy it began with in the seventies. I'm content now to watch the boys leaving. Some head for the ubiquitous mini-cabs. The drivers standing around outside chatting, or smoking, waiting in their cars. At the end of their shift? Or just starting? Ready to ferry the exhilarated and the exhausted, the sometimes bizarrely dressed, the newly formed couples, the loner-types and the lonely back to their flats. I watch the boys climb into the cabs. It's a strange moment, seeing them slide in beside the driver. Coming out of a gay club is coming out. You know, the cab driver knows. You might simply want a cab, he might simply want your fare. You might both want each other, and after all, he has *chosen* to be outside a gay club. There's always a chance ... A sweat-soaked, T-shirted boy slipping into the car, driven off ... The Clerkenwell truck fantasy again.

The bag-gentleman side of me can't resist the pavement confetti, flyers for other discos that litter the streets. Taken by boys from other boys as they leave the club, and quickly discarded. Offers of 'free entry with this flyer'. Promises of flesh. Clubs for the club cognoscenti, some of the clubs are *only* advertised this way. Clubs competing for custom, with ever-sexier graphics, wilder names. More songs, more sweat, more Sodom. Loaded, Sweat, Shaft, Trade, Strip-Search at Customs. I lie, I made the last one up.

*

I turn the corner, to continue the Sodom search and head for the Farringdon Road bookstalls; there, or at bookshops later in the day, I'm bound to find fresh Sodoms. The bulk of cheap second-hand books are religious; in posher shops they're pricier and called 'theological'. So many verbose vicars, whingeing from their country parishes on the sins of far-off cities, especially the cities of the plain. All had their day on Sodom. I'd always ignored the theology sections of bookshops, now I'm addicted.

Bibles themselves, even seventeenth-century ones, are not hard to come by, and they're surprisingly cheap. I must have flicked through dozens in the past year. Letters, sentimental prayer-cards and hand-stitched markers slip their pages as you pick them up. Unsexy confetti. I look to see if there's a family tree inscribed on the Bible inside cover. Often there is. A book that has been handed down, generation to generation, but at some time recently, the handing stopped, someone

flung the Bible. My copy belonged once to the Shorters. I know the date
of the Shorter unions, their births. I notice some Shorter branches that
stop short as others multiply. I wonder about that bachelor boy Shorter
and his spinster sister. A Sodom family tree should be started. I'm
grateful to Gregory Woods for a footnote in his *Articulate Flesh: Male
Homo-Eroticism and Modern Poetry*. He drew my attention to a *Gay
Sunshine* interview with Allen Ginsberg in which he 'established, as a
kind of Apostolic succession, his own homosexual descent from
Whitman, by pointing out that he (Ginsberg) slept with Neal Cassady,
who slept with Gavin Arthur, who slept with Edward Carpenter, who
slept with Walt Whitman himself'. Ginsberg added that this was 'an
interesting sort of thing to have as part of the mythology'. I started to
play this game, thinking of friends who'd slept with friends who used to
know and maybe met . . . Perhaps I should start a page to rival the
pages of the Shorters, or patent this as a Sodom software game.

Even cheaper, and more plentiful than the Bibles, the commentaries. Annotations, questions and answers, radical reinterpretations,
revisions, dissertations, speculations; some as never before illustrated
throughout 'with proper maps'. Before starting this book, I'd never
thought to look at them. They range from the massive, multi-volume
and serious tomes, by indisputably learned divines, to little books of
homely homilies. There are endless Bible Picture Books, Bible Tales
Re-told, Characters from the Bible and Guide Books to the Bible Land.
Within their pages there are running commentaries, free-wheeling
footnotes on just about anything the reverends care to mention. I've
found many an attack on the French Revolution, as foreseen in
Revelation.

I enjoy the details of the books, the vanities of the divines, the listing
of their qualifications. The number of the edition sold. *Portraits from
The Bible* (Old Testament Series) is by the Right Rev. Ashton Oxenden,
D.D., Bishop of Montreal, and Metropolitan of Canada. It was
published by Hatchard's of Piccadilly in 1876, and was on its thirty-four
thousandth. The Preface is classic Victoriana.

> It is hoped that this Volume may be used by *Heads of Families*, who wish to
> give some short simple instruction to their Servants and Children; and
> also by *Cottagers*, as a book to be read on Sunday Evenings.

(I hope cottagers enjoyed the experience.)

The Author has aimed at nothing new. Neither has he sought for difficulties with the view of removing them. But his desire has been to bring before the reader some of those Portraits which are sketched in the Sacred Volume for us to gaze upon. And he trusts that he may have succeeded in drawing attention to the prominent features in these characters. . . . May God, who has seen fit to teach His people by example, as well as by precept, enable us to profit by the living Pictures which He holds up to us in His Word, leading us 'to refuse the evil, and choose the good!'

Worth risking 25p on, for an essay on Lot aimed for the family reader, to instruct the children, not forgetting the servants. How will he deal with the sins of Sodom? Lot's incestuous union with his daughters? Though aiming at 'nothing new', he promises not to remove the difficulties. The reader may judge, his essay on Lot appears in *The Book of Sodom*.

Another 25p-priced earnest reverend, the Rev. J. Paterson Smyth, B.D., LL.D., LITT. D., D.C.L., Late Professor of Pastoral Theology, University of Dublin, sets tests for his young readers in *The Bible for School and Home: The Book of Genesis*. Smyth swears by tests. So did my religious instruction teacher at secondary school. He could, and frequently did, reduce many a test-failing fourteen-year-old boy to tears.

Questions for Lesson VII
Who was Lot?
He treated Abram rather selfishly?
His choice led him into a dangerous place? How was it dangerous?
What did he gain and what did he lose by going there?
What happened to Sodom?
What happened to Lot?

Such questions, the Reverend suggests, might be asked at home, in school and at Sunday school. Unfortunately there is no upside-down list of answers to see how well you've done. It would be interesting to try this out on schoolchildren. I should have sent out a questionnaire, I'd like to know what children make of Sodom.

It isn't only quality writing about Sodom that interests me. I enjoy the authoritative tone of old encyclopaedists. I find myself drawn to cheap educational books, whatever their perspective. Not simply to smile at them, though sometimes the digs are hard to resist. I wonder how many people read such books? How many of them found their way into working-class homes? And I wonder whether books like them became as important to their readers as *The Book of Knowledge* became to me? *The Book of Knowledge* was the one set of books we had at home. The Dead Sea must have lain somewhere between the covers of the volume CRU–GERA. I remember the clusters of letters on these reference book spines, as if they were proper nouns. A source book for countless homeworks, a book I pored through with Mum. She loved the pages on Egypt and the picture-story ruins of Rome. My mother, Kathleen (not that I'd ever have called her by her first name), Kathleen, who never went out of the country, but saved hard for my school-trip to Rome.

In seeking Sodom, what reference was there for a young, latent resident? Many must have had picture books of the Bible in their homes. Most such books leave the reader with a very vague impression of Sodom's sins. I certainly never connected the swear-word with any story. 'Sod, as in grass sod', you'd add, to distinguish it from a word more wicked and mysterious. 'As in grass sod', you'd say, to show you weren't really swearing! 'Sod' was on the select list of acceptable swear-words at home. There was a definite list of words you could use, and ones that would end with a clip round the ear. I was allowed a party piece, a sentence-long flourish: 'Bloody 'ell fire Jack, bugger and blast'. Which contains enough biblical reference to deserve a commentary of its own. I didn't know then, admired by aunts for childish cheek, that 'bugger' was a racist corruption of *bougre* and referred to Bulgaria, where Manichaean and Albigensian heresies flourished. Heretics everywhere supposed to be buggerers. You could spend a whole Book of Buggery unravelling the word. I knew none of this then. Neither, I suspect, did my aunts.

The images and colours of Sunday school picture books remain with me. Deep-blue skies, the shepherds' crooks and their fabulous outfits. The stars in the skies, like those given for good work at school. I didn't have many books then, and I didn't hang on to them, I'm re-supplied now by bookstalls and jumble sales. I've picked up at least five *Look and Learn*-style archaeology books. *Look and Learn* was an educational picture-book magazine, it arrived weekly through our letter-box at home, at my request. My childhood assertion that I was getting too grown-up for comics. The archaeology books, the odd volumes of encyclopaedias, are often at odds on Sodom. All affirm its former existence, but some assert that it stood at the north end of the Dead Sea, others are certain it was at the south. My undated, circa 1920, two-volume *The Story of the Bible* (Amalgamated Press) is a tale told by 'Living Writers of Authority' (Revds, Very Revds, prebs, canons and the odd Sir) and is copiously illustrated with 'famous masterpieces of religious art *and* Modern Camera Pictures from the Lands of the Bible'. A photograph of neatly arranged artefacts is captioned: 'RETRIEVED FROM THE DESTROYED "CITIES OF THE PLAIN". This array of stone mortars, pestles, and other tools, was found on what may be the site of Sodom. Research and excavation have established that this part of Palestine was peopled and prosperous when Abraham came there shortly before its destruction.' As a child, and this book was meant for the edification of children, I would scarcely have noticed the 'may'. I would have been fascinated by the pictures of the inhabitants of the Bible lands, still living, it suggests, as in Abraham's time. The stress throughout is on the unchanging, the timeless nature of life in Palestine. The photographs, striving to authenticate, are black and white and bizarrely tinted in a range of orange and blue.·

The Story is cautious on the sins of Sodom; the men, young and old, 'made an onslaught on the house to ill-treat the two messengers'. No photograph or painting here to aid the puzzled reader, unless you count the preserved pestles. They're still pressed out, these Bible books for all the family. *Stories and Legends from the Bible* (1988) by K. McLeish offers, according to its jacket, Bible narratives with no 'interpretation or aside'. In McLeish the Sodomites know precisely what they want of the angels: 'We want to rape them,' they declare. No exclamation mark, I called back at the remainder bookshop to check.

Approaching Sodom this way, wondering how the idea of the city first entered people's lives. Looking for books that might have been given by aunts at Christmas, or as free introductory offers by missionaries. In the revised edition of John Stow's massive *Surveys of the Cities of London and Westminster and the Borough of Southwark* (1598, 'very much enlarged' in 1720 by John Strype and sundry 'careful hands') there's a chapter on 'The Spiritual Government of London'. It gives the latest on the progress of the Society for the Reformation of Manners. After approving the progress in closing the 'Sodomitical Houses' there's a report of a book bonanza.

> . . . on *Good Friday*, 1704 were given away at the Churches of *London* and *Westminster*, and several other Parishes near *London*, many Thousands of such good Books, *viz.*

A Pastoral Letter, being an earnest Exhortation to take Care of the Soul.
The Necessary Duty of Family Prayer.
An Account of the Progress of the Reformation of Manners.
The Present State of the Charity Schools.
The Representation of the Immorality of the English *Stage.*
There are also printed, for these religious Purposes, Books of Prep-
aration for the Receiving the Holy Sacrament, small books for the Use of
Seamen in their Voyages, and Soldiers in their Camps and Services.

Many a Sodom would have been found in the *Account of the Progress*,
with its 'desire to prevent the Spreading of the Leprosy of Sin', and you
would almost certainly find it on the English stage. But most could read
neither free books nor fine bound; they'd be more likely to hear of
Sodom in a sermon. Those who *were* struggling to read would probably
have come across Sodom in the Bible, the one book likely to be found in
the house. If they began in the Beginning they would not have had far
to go. Around the time of the revised Stow, *Select Trials* were becoming
popular; you might read of Sodom there, if, that is, you selected
Sodomy.

*

Some days I'll wander from the stalls to bookshops, looking for
second-hand Sodoms, for more obvious and directly related books, for
Sodom studies. Enough of the cut-price clergy. One of the slightly chill
experiences of late is the sometimes obvious explanation behind the
bulging 'new in stock' shelves. New stock after deaths. My local
second-hand bookseller confirmed what I'd already suspected: the
sixties porn that he'd like to clear had belonged to a man who had
recently died. No more spending, no more the creamy essence. Once
cherished pin-ups now dumped in the corner, unadmired. Gay's the
Word bookshop recently replenished its second-hand stock after a
funeral. Not that this puts me off, collectors have to follow hearses, it's
part of the course. I wonder about the books, though, the magazines.
Were they bundled off before the descent of family, to spare their
sensibilities? I've known it happen. Henry C. Ashbee, obsessive
collector of erotica, and of rare first editions and translations of
Cervantes, stipulated in his will: take one book, take them all. A
spirited and shrewd move, for this is how the British Library came to
possess such a precious 'Private Case'. The porn would have been
rejected but for the value of Cervantes. Without that clause in Ashbee's

will, this book, and many before it, would have been that much more difficult to research. The provenance of the literature of Sodom. In Southend once I picked up most of my second-hand Gide and several biographies of Cocteau. Inside the covers, the black-ink stamp 'Salvage'. The books discarded from the USAF Bomb Division, Upper Heyford. Every time I open one I think about the man who selected these books for the edification of bomber pilots. I enjoy this second-hand Sodomite relation with the bomber boys' librarian. Sodom salvaged.

Also flown in from the States, at Gay's the Word, a shelf of Sodom studies, hot off the university presses. University studies weren't like this in my day, I find myself reflecting as I take in the latest titles. Three catch my eye. Barry Burg's *Sodomy and the Pirate Tradition: English Sea Rovers in the Seventeenth Century* is the oldest (1984) and the easiest read. There's scarcely any starting point for Burg's speculations on widespread buccaneer buggery, few pirates kept notes. All-male expeditions over periods of three to four years at sea, with stop-offs on isolated Caribbean islands, a subject ripe for scholarly fantasy. Burg did, however, uncover two Sodoms. Thomas Walduck, a Barbadian colonial, wrote, in 1710, of the Caribbean:

> All Sodom's Sins are Centered in thy heart
> Death is thy look and Death in every part
> Oh! Glorious Isle in Vilany excell
> Sins to the Height – thy fate is Hell.

And earlier, in 1655, Madam Margaret Heathcote wrote to her cousin John Winthrop Jr about life in Antigua: 'And truely, Sir, I am not so much in love with any as to goe much abroad . . . they all be a company of sodomites that live here.' Burg asserts that Port Royal was seen as 'the Sodom of the Universe' by those who visited and exploited it. With a different title, the Burg would be fine as a general introductory study of seventeenth-century sodomy, with a digression on the buccaneers. But with a different title, would it sell?

More complex than Burg, the recent studies in the realm of 'sodomy, that utterly confused category' of Foucault. Foucault's line always finds a place in these new Sodom texts. Gregory W. Bredbeck's *Sodomy and Interpretation: Marlowe to Milton* sets off with a trawl of sixteenth- and seventeenth-century dictionaries, like Florio's *A Worlde of Wordes, or*

Most Copious and Exact Dictionarie in Italian and English (London, 1598), and finds:

> Sodomia, the naturall sin of Sodomie.
> Sodomita, a sodomite, a buggrer.
> Sodomitare, to commit the sinne of Sodomie,
> Sodomitarie, sodomiticall tricks.
> Sodomitico, sodomiticall.

The later *Glossographia: Or a Dictionary Interpreting the Hard Words of Whatsoever Language, Now Used in our Refined English Tongue* (1670) by Thomas Blount, is more complicated and cross-referenced. A conflation of Sodomites, inglers, catamites, buggerers and Ganymedes. For example:

> Ingle (Span. from the Lat. Inguen, i. the groin) a boy kept for Sodomy. See *Ganymede*.

Bredbeck shifts from these definitions to a meticulous exploration of Renaissance texts, and sometimes crosses paths with Jonathan Goldberg. Goldberg chooses for his title a word absent from Florio's flourish, *Sodometries: Renaissance Texts, Modern Sexualities*. *Sodometries*, from Stanford University Press, has a delicious detail from Ghirlandaio's *Visitation* on the cover. Three boys, leaning over a parapet, look down on a city. And in so doing they present three choice, contoured bums, bent for the viewer to admire. 'Sodometries', splendid sound, was once a portmanteau word for all manner of perceived villainy and vice. I first came across it in Thomas Nashe's *The Unfortunate Traveller* (1594):

> Italy, the paradise of the earth and the epicure's heaven, how doth it form our young master? It makes him to kiss his hand like an ape, cringe his neck like a starveling, and play at heypass, repass come aloft, when he salutes a man. From thence he brings the art of atheism, the art of epicurising, the art of whoring, the art of poisoning, the art of sodomitry. The only probable good thing they have to keep us from utterly condemning it is that it maketh a man an excellent courtier, a curious carpet knight; which is, by fine interpretation, a fine close lecher, a glorious hypocrite. It is by now a privy note amongst the better sort of men, when they would set a singular mark or brand on a notorious villain, to say he hath been in Italy.

A list, the sheer linguistic vigour of which I can't help but admire. There are dozens of such Sodom jibes at Italians, more vicious ones at Turks. And sometimes, as Goldberg relates, there was genocidal 'justification' in the labelling of the native populations of the New World as Sodomites. Goldberg leaps deftly between modern Sodoms, Renaissance literature and stories of conquests and colonisation. What I didn't expect was for this book to begin with an analysis of an ad for a T-shirt. On the T-shirt in question (Goldberg reproduces it) we see the back-view of a camel. Saddam Hussein's face stares out from the camel's arse. The advertisement invites Americans to 'Make A State-ment . . . Express Your Patriotism.' The 100 per cent cotton, top quality American Made T-shirt (MasterCard, Visa accepted) bears a message: 'America Will Not be Saddam-ized.' I discover from the footnotes that this T-shirt, along with other Gulf War tack, has been widely discussed among American academics. Rightly so, for Saddam was a fortuitous name, it could help whip up American fears and loathing, help justify the far-off war. Similar fears informed many a European Renaissance text. Surprisingly, the ad is taken from *Rolling Stone* magazine and not a K.K.K. bulletin. What does this say about the paper's rock-fan readers? Would they wear it as a serious statement? Or in ironic play? The Goldberg variations on the theme of the T-shirt are startling and, if you can settle into the language of theory, witty and worthwhile. It encourages you to look more closely at the earlier Sodom texts.

Three Sodom studies, all important, all undeniably of interest. But they don't affect me, these scholarly Sodoms, in quite the same way as the simple Sodom reference in an old, discarded textbook, or a Bible tale retold and newly illustrated in living colour.

*

On the bookshop trail I've noticed a lot of classic Marxist texts about of late, shelves and stacks of them. Evidence of socialist spring-cleans? Like the porn, another embarrassment in front of family, in front of friends? Clear-outs, perhaps, after the Wall? I remember the book sale at the Marx Memorial Library, surely they can't be flogging off *their* stock? I'm still looking for socialist versions of Sodom. There's a tendency to skip biblical reference in the volumes I've scanned. The authors prefer to have a go at Greek gods, those decadent Athenians.

Thus Engels in the *The Origin of the Family, Private Property and the State*:

> . . . this degradation of women was avenged on the men and degraded them also, till they fell into the abominable practice of sodomy and degraded alike their gods and themselves with the myth of Ganymede.

Ganymede, in his Zeus suit, stars in the myth of the upwardly mobile. Ganymede, shepherd-boy, carried off and abused by a Sodomite god.

As it turns out the library is discarding a bunch of bourgeois novels, books and pamphlets on the Communist rebuilding of postwar Eastern Europe (optimistic new townscapes featuring handsome, hunky builders on scaffolding) and a quirky selection of sideline socialisms. The standard texts have stayed, as they should. I pick up a slim volume with the library bookplate, it features an etching of Marx and a Lenin quote, 'Without a revolutionary theory there cannot be a revolutionary movement'. It's pasted into 'Human Origins' by Samuel Laing, revised by Edward Cloud, a book issued for the Rationalist Press Association in 1903. In his introduction, Laing hopes for success in 'stimulating some minds, especially those of my younger readers, and of the working-classes who are striving after culture . . .' In attempting to demolish one set of prejudices, fundamentalist interpretations of the Bible, Laing slips easily into others. In a chapter on 'The Historical Element in the Old Testament' he suggests that

> When we arrive at Abraham we feel as if we might be treading on really historical ground. There is the universal tradition of the Hebrew race that he was their ancestor, and his figure is very like what in the unchanging East may be met with to the present day. We seem to see the dignified sheik sitting at the door of his tent dispensing hospitality, raiding with his retainers on the rear of a retreating army and capturing booty, and much exercised by domestic difficulties between the women of his household. Surely this is an historical figure.

Surely not, Laing answers himself. 'Doubts and difficulties appear.' He's suspicious of Abraham's ability to have lived to the ripe old age of 175, and to have had a son by Sarah when she was ninety-nine and he'd reached a hundred!

> Nor can we take as authentic history Abraham talking with the Lord, and holding a sort of Dutch auction with him, in which he beats down from

fifty to ten the number of righteous men who, if found in Sodom, are to save it from destruction.

About the story of Lot's wife, Laing is quite clear. Centuries of pious pilgrims, he relates, until quite recent times, 'saw, touched, and tasted' the pillar of salt supposed to be Lot's wife (a particularly bizarre kind of necrophilia Laing evokes here). There is a perfectly rational explanation:

> . . . the volcanic eruptions were of an earlier geological age . . . the story of Lot's wife is owing to the disintegration of a stratum of salt marl, which weathers away under the action of wind and rain into columnar masses, like those in a similar formation in Catalonia described by Lyell.

Lot's wife, Laing adds, was variously described by the pilgrims:

> Some saw her big, some little, some upright, and some prostrate, according to the state of disintegration of the pillars, which change their form rapidly under the influence of the weather; but no doubt was entertained as to the attestation of the miracle. It turns out, however, to be one of those geological myths of precisely the same nature as that which attributed the Devil's Dyke near Brighton to an arrested attempt of the Evil One to cut a trench through the South Downs, so as to let in the sea and submerge the Weald.

That story nailed, the pillar of salt as much a myth as a South Downs dyke, Laing hastens to consider the incest. I can't pass by quite so easily. Lot's wife turned to salt. It has to deserve more than a Rationalist Press dismissal or a grounding by geology. Salt, common and cheap. Salt as a commodity, salt as symbol. A preservative yet something that changes the flavour. Lot's wife, turned into salt, unable ever to change, a frozen figure, sadly and for ever looking back. Salt, plentiful yet prized. A magic, transforming ingredient, yet basic. Salt of the earth. There's something barren about salt, a suggestion of sterility. Yet salt is the covenant between God and the Jews. Salt is a symbol of hospitality. It suggests, to sound like a soap ad, a touch of luxury. Rabbinical speculations suggest that Lot's wife popped round to the neighbours to borrow salt for her guests. Unintentionally, or with malice, she might, by so doing, have betrayed the presence of the guests to the Sodomites. Her fault, then, that the neighbours rushed round 'to know' the strangers. Lot's wife commits a salt crime, and salt is her punishment. In other stories she's seen as a mean and inhospitable woman, tight with the salt.

Salt in our tears, our blood, our sweat, salt in our urine and saliva. Margaret Visser, in her *Much Depends on Dinner*, notes that:

> Sodom, in the neighbourhood of which Lot's wife turned into a pillar of salt (petrification, turning into stone, is a common story-punishment for looking back when you shouldn't – but then, salt is 'rock'), was near to the Dead Sea and to numerous salt mines. Its name is probably a contraction of *Sadeh Adom*, meaning 'red field' or 'field of blood.' The reason may be that when solar salt is evaporated from brine springs and lakes, the concentrate often turns bright red because of bacterial action.

There are many stories of the pillar of salt. Among them that Lot's wife, after petrification, continued to have her periods. Reddened salt. The menstruation seen by gloating misogynists as another example of Sodom's uncleanness. You might see this intriguing woman in a different light, as the Sodomites' friend, unable to bear the thought of their burning. Madonna, Liz, Dionne, Barbra – they could all be up for the part. Or perhaps, in secret, she leaned to Gomorrah. Lot's wife, a south (or north) Dead Sea dyke. Jodie, maybe?

It endlessly confuses me, this example of God's punishment. I settle on the cleanness theory. Her punishment, as a friend of the unclean, to be turned into a scouring block. Sometimes, reading the story, and the stories of the story, I smile. There's another image of her, I can never quite escape it. I loved the large plastic tapering table-salt cones that stood on the kitchen table at home. Doll-like, with grand names like Cerebos or Saxa. I keep seeing Lot's wife as one vast, grand cone . . .

Laing, geology lesson over, turns his attention to the incest. A great many painters did the same. Sodom burns on canvas, but this most visual of events is often relegated to the background. The painters' attention would focus rather on the story of an ageing Lot made drunk by his nubile daughters. Laing brushes quickly past the scene. The story's end is:

> . . . clearly a myth to account for the aversion of the Hebrew to races so closely akin to them as the Moabites and Ammonites, and it could hardly

have originated until after the date of the book of Ruth, which shows no trace of such a racial aversion.

As to Sodom itself, the supposed sins, Laing, author of *A Modern Zoroastrian*, says nothing. Perhaps to spare the sensibilities of his ideal young reader. The language of the introduction, the stepping round that awkward business with the angels, the over-use of 'surely' and 'surely not', the proudly displayed knowledge, not to mention the sweeping racial stereotypes. This is all familiar. Laing's tone is much the same as that of my 25p reduced-to-clear vicars. I admit, however, an affection for his book; it might well have found its way into those hotbeds of socialism, warm libraries of self-improvement, the Working Men's and Mechanics' Institutes (more fantasy locales). Questioning Genesis at all, it always involved a risk. None of my other cheap educational books of the period dared or desired to go so far.

Laing's wasn't exactly the socialist commentary I was hoping for. But at least I picked up a Marx Memorial bookplate, the cover stamped 'Marx House', and an unexpected Sodom. Eventually I *was* directed to a fuller and less guarded Engels on ingles invective. Not quite socialist Sodom stories, but references to sodomy that draw on the Sodom image repertoire. Engels wrote to Marx ('dear Moor') from Manchester, in chummy club-man tone. Karl had sent Friedrich a copy of the work of pioneering gay theorist Karl Heinrich Ulrichs. Friedrich:

> Well, that is a most curious 'Urning' that you've sent me. These are indeed exceedingly unnatural revelations. The pederasts are beginning to stand up and be counted and discovering that they are a power in the state. All they lacked was organization, but to judge by this it seems already to exist secretly. And since they include such important men, in all the old and even the new parties, from Rösing to Schweitzer, they cannot fail to be victorious. 'War to the front apertures, peace to the rear apertures of the body', will be their slogan now. It is fortunate that we personally are too old to have to worry that, at the victory of this party, we might have to pay physical tribute to the victors. But the young generation! Incidentally, only in Germany is it possible that a chap comes along and transforms this filth into a theory and then invites: Join us, etc. Unfortunately he still lacks the courage to declare himself openly as 'that' and still has to operate before the public 'from the front' though not, as he says in one place, by a slip, 'in from the front'. But just wait till the new North German Criminal Code recognizes the rights of the posterior, then he'll talk quite differently. And we poor frontal chaps, with our

childish inclination towards women, we'll have a very thin time then. If that man Schweitzer were any use he might lure this strange solid citizen into disclosing the identities of those prominent and most prominent pederasts – which surely should not be difficult for him as a kindred spirit . . .

Yours, F.E.

The Sodomite conspiracy, the Sodomite threat to the young, Sodomite organisation and the assumed freemasonry. You could marry the words of Engels and Countess Waldeck. Left and right, their insults interchangeable. They can't both be correct about Sodomites, surely? And why is it that the most unattractive of 'frontal chaps' always voice fears of a threat to the rear? If not their own (as if . . .) then the rears of the young. There's always this knowledge of the attraction of men, many of the elaborations on Sodom stress the angels' beauty, many paint them young. Our frontal Friedrich at least concedes that the posterior rights brigade might have a use, they could help draw up a list, expose Sodomites in High Places, name names . . .

It's the 'filthy' in this letter that stops me short. I've always cared for the slightly soiled, the worn, the frayed, found comfort in the chipped and the rusting. I've seen 'filth' used so often, it has to be seen as our Sodomite mark, our emblem. You don't need a Freud Memorial Library to dream up connections. I'll accept the dirt tattoo. I can't imagine a world without dirt.

It might explain why I find the mushrooming of smart gay café bars in Soho so alarming, a gay village (small town, Zoar) that looks less and less like Sodom, more and more like the cleaned-up Covent Garden. A sanitised Sodom. Sodom clean and cold, with fake class. Out, the decay, the smutty and the sleaze. The fashionable club night, Village Youth, I find a stress on either word alarming. I like the slightly scarred, the bruised. The clean attractive only when it's obsessively, fetishistically so. Clean governed by a rule book of cleanliness, sailor spruce, soldier smart, their ritual of spit and polish. The fantasy, then, is to soil, to lay waste to regulations. Strewn uniform.

I can't rejoice at the brave new world of television sanitary sex guides. These too are essentially clean. Spruce young presenters look intensely interested as guests reveal the secrets of their S/M parties. Cut to: an alternative comedian in a condom sketch. Cut to: the video guide to lovers in a Laura Ashley setting. Sometimes there's an orgasm guide from a brash older woman; preferably she speaks with a cockney or a Liverpudlian accent. The voice of the no-nonsense working class. Sometimes there's even a drag queen, to rough the programme up a little, give it extra credibility.

No darkness, no mystery here, gays fully included, even fashionable. In Berlin, ten years or so ago, I was excited by the glass-fronted gay bars, open to the streets, no curtains necessary. I couldn't believe it, I thought it could never happen here. There'd be bricks through the windows. Now it has happened I'm not so sure about the triumph of style over Sodom. It has to be good that a Queer Carnival can parade through Soho, christen it Queer Town. But the ever-so-educated English voices declaring themselves 'queer' made me wince. It's not the politics of 'queer' that bothers me, it's the arrogance of English arts and media queens thinking themselves queerer than anyone else. Nothing very queer about making gay programmes for Channel 4, I know, I've done it myself.

I want neither bricks nor brimstone. No return to the fears of the fifties, the closed-curtain clubs. It's just that I miss Satyricon Sodom. Sodom circuit-walks should take in alleyways, dark passages, stone steps down. I'm wary of the clean and pure, and all that is done in their name. Leave a few corners dark, not designer dark, but plain.

If I wallow in nostalgia for seedier, smokier Sodoms I'll confirm some of John Evelyn's early eco-fears. He complained in his 1661 *Fumifugium or the Inconveniencie of the Aer and Smoak of London* that the 'horrid smoak' imparted 'a bitter and ungrateful Tast to those few wretched Fruits, which never arriving at their desired maturity, seem, like the Apples of Sodome, to fall even to dust, when they are but touched'. I should have checked Green lists for Sodom, I didn't think . . .

I leave the Marx Memorial Library, pass the cottage, overgrown with weeds, council-closed, padlocked with rusty chains. I hope that socialist trysts were once kept there. Picture scholars, relaxing after a long day's sweat, engaged with the Electro-plate boys, men of neighbouring light industries. A Sodomite solidarity.

I've read many an explanation/apologia for the Marx/Engels position on Ganymede, how they couldn't be expected, at that time, to take up the Uranian cause. 'In fact, the conceptual vocabulary to enable rational discussion of sex did not exist in Marx's time,' etc. This is usually accompanied by a gentle knuckle-rapping (they were forward enough on other fronts, these frontal men, after all). Polite apologias, historically inaccurate. They clearly knew the Ulrichs argument, and simply mocked. They must have known about the revocation of anti-sodomy laws that followed from the French Revolution. The later apologias are more devious than the letter itself. What does surprise, though, is the seeming lack of socialist interest in the Jewish stories of Sodom, wonderfully written up in Louis Ginsberg's *The Legends of the Jews*. Sodom's judges named as Liar, Arch-deceiver, Falsifier and Perverter of Judgement. Strangers in Sodom tortured or deviously offered money but no food, and left to starve. The richer the man of Sodom, the more the law favoured him. Talmudic commentaries, wonderfully bleak and often funny tales that repeatedly expose the iniquities of greed, skip past the 'to know' business, past the fears of the frontal men.

Time to move on. One last look back at Turnmills. Ginsberg tells how Lot's disbelieving sons-in-law called Lot a fool for believing the grim warnings – after all, 'Violins, cymbals, and flutes resound in the city'. House, Homocore and Techno resound in ours, but there are warnings. Cries against ff.

*

Back past the London Lesbian and Gay Centre, it too in line for the padlock, closed. There was no accolade of a police raid, unlike Turnmills, 'Britain's most disgusting disco' (*News of the World*), which has survived more than one. The cry against the LLGC was really not so great. Rumours of financial 'mismanagement', committee wranglings. I have to go elsewhere for the free gay papers now. It's only a short walk to King's Cross.

According to Neil Norman, writing under the headline: 'The fear that stalks the Twilight Zone' in the *Evening Standard* (25 February 1992), by walking this way I'll reach my destination. Darren, a newspaper seller, tells Norman how the area used to be 'full of wogs': 'One geezer got stabbed up the arse. They're like animals, they should all be caged up. They'd supply drugs to anyone, any age, twenty-four hours a day – crack, skag, cocaine, all the Class A drugs . . .' He knows his drugs, does Darren. Neil Norman sees King's Cross as 'blighted', a 'place to pass through as quickly as possible to somewhere less insalubrious'. He gets quite carried away on the subject:

A hinterland of seediness, illuminated by the headlamps of kerb-crawling cars, King's Cross has long needed to clean up its act. Despite the best efforts of the police, there is a feeling that it is all too late. What was once the received image of Soho, the Apocrypha of inner urban sleaze, is still the reality of King's Cross.

King's Cross makes Soho seem like a playschool for fashion victims. Unlike the purifying fires of the Old Testament which visited Sodom and Gomorrah, the King's Cross inferno had the opposite effect. In its wake emerged all manner of nocturnal denizens and crawling slime – crack dealers, junkies, pimps and whores. The area became so casually vicious that even the streetwalkers walked on some place else, somewhere safer. Somewhere less diseased.

The disease, the leprosy of sin, the easy lumping together of prostitutes and drug dealers who stab and kill, in one of the tackiest metaphoric uses of Sodom I've come across. To mix up the King's Cross fire, thirty-one people burnt to death, with a cheap exposé of a red-light district is beyond bad taste. It's a familiar plea for purity, for purifying fires, an SRM-style purge of the detestable tribe of night-walking Sodomites. People as dirt. 'Whores' and 'foreign' people especially. The ugly racist remarks are Darren's, of course, not Norman's.

Company here for James Anderton, Chief Constable of Manchester, paid-up, fully frontal man, whose speech given at a conference on Aids and hepatitis at Manchester's police training school in December 1986 should never be forgotten. Surely he was seeing, if not directly mentioning, Sodom:

> Everywhere I go I see increasing evidence of men swirling about in a human cesspit of their own making. . . . Speaking as a man, Christian, husband, police officer, lover of the human race, believer in God's creation, and above all someone who wants to see a future for children born today, we must ask why homosexuals engage freely in sodomy – let's be blunt about it – and other obnoxious sexual practices, knowing the dangers involved. We must ask it head on, challenging them to answer it.

or the 'eighty-nine-year-old grandmother', quoted approvingly in a *Daily Express* editorial (13 December 1986):

> Yesterday an 89-year-old grandmother from Solihull rang us: 'The homosexuals who have brought this plague upon us should be locked up.

Burning is too good for them. Bury them in a pit and pour on quick-lime . . .' The majority of Britons would appear to be in agreement.

*

The Scala Cinema in King's Cross is the nearest thing London has to a Sodom Odeon. Here you can see the best in the old underground and the new cult cinema. As I write the Scala is threatened with closure following a court case over an alleged illicit screening of the still-banned *A Clockwork Orange*. The sort of screening that adds to the cinema's Sodom credentials. You can pick up the gay papers from the foyer, buy a *Save the Scala* T-shirt, contribute to their Fighting Fund, or purchase a Scala orange, price £1. There's the requisite air of seed about the Scala, it's not for the Neil Normans of the world. Not specifically a gay cinema, it nevertheless programmes numerous gay films and events. Unsurprisingly, the local council didn't take to its all-night, hugely popular film and dance mixes. Scala parties have been stopped.

The Scala's August 1992 programme included SODOM ALL: GAY EROTIC SHORTS. Shorts such as Luther Price's 1991 film *Sodom*:

> The film that was banned from the New York and San Francisco Lesbian and Gay Film Festivals as homophobic but defended by gay film maker Michael Wallin. Price's film uses found footage from gay pornography of the seventies manipulated through optical printing to give an horrific yet beautiful vision of Hell.

(Scala programme note)

A short, burning vision that offends. Why do people so love to be offended? This presumably was censorship in the name of Aids, a recent and particularly unwelcome branch. Such censorship confuses fact and fiction, life and film; acts and representations of acts. It stifles debate in much the same way as traditional censorship. Luther's sex footage has clearly passed its sell-by date, and not quite reached connoisseur/collector status. You can tell by the haircuts, even if you're unfamiliar with that seventies porn film colour, the murky greens and browns. Something about the film stock and the favoured colours of the decade combined to hideous effect. What upset the festivals? We're clearly not talking 'unsafe' sex here, either real or represented (there were dangers even then, of course, but nothing that couldn't be handled with regular check-ups). So I guess it got the 'homophobic' label for its conjunction of fire, sex and church music. The title probably didn't help. Not positive enough. Was Price being simplistic? Unsafe sex, as represented by old footage = Death; or, taking part in group sex was a bad thing and ultimately led to deaths? Perhaps he was saying that, or perhaps the film is simply a lament. *Sodom* is fast, fragmented, ambiguous cinema. I find it extraordinary that anyone could have been so certain of a single meaning. It's a good deal more challenging than many of the bland 'Gays and . . .' documentaries turned out of late. Gays and gardening, gays and the church, gays and fostering, gays and food. *Sodom* is moving and hypnotic, really not homophobic at all. It doesn't have a happy ending, but then I've never been big on those, quite irrespective of the sex lives of the characters. Imagine Romeo and Juliet if they'd *lived*, settled down and bought a maisonette on the outskirts of Verona, *King Lear* with a happy family reunion.

Sodom has not, on the whole, been well served by celluloid. Robert Aldrich's *Sodom and Gomorrah* features a vicious and vaguely lesbian Queen of Sodom, played by an acid Anouk Aimée. Her favoured slave ends up as the widower Lot's second wife. The slave comes to adore Lot, but is forever torn between the slit silk dresses of Sodom and her newly acquired, humble Hebrew tribal-wear. 'You Hebrews confuse clothes with tents,' she declares. But if she comes to believe in the good Lot, she can never quite embrace that Jehovah of his. Sodom never fully loses its appeal to a once-pampered slave.

It is given to Lot, following a vision of two bearded patriarchal-style angels, to make an intervention on behalf of any good men left in Sodom. This was meant to be Abraham's job. I know screenplays sometimes involve the 'doubling' of characters, but this goes a bit far. Doubling Lot and Abraham is much like doubling Cain and Abel. It tends to defeat the point of the story.

The decision appears to have been to make *sadism* the major sin of Sodom. The city's fun-fair boasts a big and fire-fringed wheel. Strapped-on, recaptured, renegade slaves are turned and dipped in a bath of oil. The Queen loves this. For 'Next only to the pleasure of giving death, is the excitement of watching it'. The censor denied the audience any such excitement, the climactic wheel scene was mauled. The result of the film-maker's or film-backer's reluctance to tackle sexual sin, and the censor's decision to spare the audience unnecessary violence, is that you might leave the cinema wondering why on earth

God was so miffed. What was the sin of Sodom, Mary? Did I miss it? There's some slave-bashing and confused tribal warfare, heroic dam-building and dam-busting, traditional epic set-pieces all. And there's one exceptionally good outfit, the ultimate in S/M wear, a metal breastplate, with holes. When the wearer breathes out, spikes emerge. If the wearer happens to be hugging you at the time, you meet a particularly nasty end. Another entertainment, this outfit, for that lesbian bitch of a Sodomite Queen.

In her weekly 'epistle' to Paul, enclosing a ten shilling 'donation' towards my university grant, my mother, who'd just, in 1973, got a colour television, remarked:

> I too watched both films mentioned and enjoyed both. When I started watching *Sodom and Gomorrah* I had your Dad, Susan, Neil and Kevin for company. From one o'clock to 2 o'clock I was on my own. But I really enjoyed those sort of films (especially in colour, especially the bit where they were cooking the men on the wheel and basting them in oil).

So something of the culinary sadism did get through on late-night television. There is some choice dialogue, I particularly liked the warning 'Beware of Sodomite patrols'. And Sodom is impressively and expensively smote (smitten, smited?). The Queen shrugs off the lightning storm, 'nothing to worry about'. Sodom shakes. 'It's an earthquake, we've had them already,' she remarks prior to her palace and the picture tilting. There's also one remarkable kiss in the film, albeit a heterosexual one (this *was* a 1962 film, intended for a mass audience). As their city crashes around them a couple rush to each other's arms for a final death-defying clinch. A Sodomite farewell to the world, quite touching really. And though the sceptical wife is turned to salt, her 'lucky comb' escapes God's wrath. She'd used it as 'bait' to catch Lot's attention. At the end of the film it's all Lot has left of her.

If, as we're constantly told, though I have my doubts, children don't read much now, but watch the video, and if they rent *Sodom and Gomorrah* from the local store, they'll get a very curious impression of the city. Those who wish to whitewash Sodom, purge the story of its sexuality, might be pleased to hear it.

John Huston fared little better in the Sodom section of *The Bible* . . . *in the beginning* (1965). To get to the Sodom story you must sit through an interminable, cutesy *Zoo Time* special, featuring John himself as Noah, ambling round the Ark, smiling at the animals, two by two by two by two . . . and all the beasts expected to turn out straight. The next set arrives as a welcome relief. Dark passageways, vague shadows, the sense of dark deeds in dirty places. Promising this, compared with anything in Aldrich, there's an effort at least to suggest sex. Screams and grunts on the soundtrack and the clashing of cymbals. Peter O'Toole, visiting Abraham, plays all three angels, one of him sports a beard. Two of him turn up in Sodom. If you've got Peter O'Toole in a bit part, use him, I say, and he was undeniably handsome back then. Though the Sodomites' demand to 'know them' (the 2 × Peter O'Toole) is understated, sophisticates in the audience might catch the meaning. There are subtle clues, the phallic battering-ram at Lot's door, the heavy Bible badboy make-up of the Sodomites, and their spectacularly bizarre hair-styles. There's also a hint of bestiality (goat-worship), and a nasty-looking black queen sashaying around the place. But if the sin of Sodom is sexual, Huston, like Aldrich before him, shirks the other major sex angles. The mostly unnoticed story hint that the Sodomites might rape Lot, and of course, the final incest. The destruction of Sodom takes place off-screen. I suspect he went badly over-budget on the beasts.

Pasolini's *Salo: or the 120 Days of Sodom*, Sade adapted, updated and relocated to the fascist republic of Salo, leaves little out. It's a film I wanted to be brilliant. Pasolini is my favourite film-maker. *Theorem* was a turning-point discovery in my adolescence, and later, by chance, I think I was the first person in England to hear of Pasolini's murder. I took a telephone message for someone else, from an Italian journalist, anxious that the *Guardian* should know that Pasolini's death might be suspicious. That the state might have been at work under cover of a rough-trade killer. I was hugely upset.

I first saw *Salo* in a Berlin porno house, where the film played in so many countries, banned as it was almost everywhere they banned things. A shady-looking audience, me included, and the film shook me up. I couldn't understand the dialogue, Italian with German sub-titles, I just had to watch. It certainly plays the Sade game well, arousal, and horror at arousal. Stories of the uncut versions of this film have an urban legend quality about them: 'Did you see the bit where . . .?'. You wonder whether people are adding fantasy tortures of their own. In England the film was seized, in 1977, by Scotland Yard's Obscene

Publications Squad (*ff* is with them now), following a raid on the Compton Cinema Club in Soho, old-style Soho. The Director of Public Prosecutions threatened to prosecute the management for 'keeping a disorderly house'.

A scratched and scarred print (who knows what raids and old police projectors it has been through?) resurfaces at the Scala from time to time. The scratches a part of its history. It begins with a tacked-on health warning-style voice-over. Required, I presume, by the DPP or the censor. An authoritative British male assures you of Pasolini's artistic stature, his absolute integrity; he insists that nothing at all gratuitous has been added to the Sade text. Everything you are about to see is true, true to Sade, true to the terrors of fascist Italy. An odd combination of truths. This whets the appetite, raises expectations. The opening of the film, the gorgeous landscape, the house you'd die for, a line-up of boys to be toyed with and tortured, all bodes well, a promise of a complex audience complicity in the horror. The ad for the American videotape splatters 'Now Available' as a fig leaf over a picture of a naked youth giving the fascist salute, and sells the video with a glowing review by Leonard Maltin, 'Controversial and disturbing! Sadism, scatology and debauchery galore!'

But the women narrators are weak, the scatology galore embarrasses the audience. Hard to make it work, I think, on film. I've seen a more effective scat home movie. At least I think it was more effective, a friend assured me it was, I had to fast forward.

Watching the Pasolini for the second time, I was mainly watching the wallpaper, looking at the clothes, the paintings, the furniture, the artefacts. All stunning. I got tired, and not in any blasé kind of way. That is until the final sequence, when the two soldier boys waltz, at first falteringly, then beautifully, whilst in the courtyard outside, torture follows torture (censor permitting). For the boys dancing, I'd watch the film over and over. It's a complex image – tender, callous, excluding; yet intimate, sexy, sick and human.

By far the best Sodom on film is a real curiosity, the 1933 Doctor James Sibley Watson/Melville Webber film *Lot in Sodom*, the first underground gay movie, years ahead of Kenneth Anger and every bit as wild, sexy and provoking. Underground maybe, but it apparently had a successful film run, pre-Hay's Code, in Times Square. I caught a rare screening of the film in 1976 at the Electric Cinema in the Portobello Road. Another cinema once as adventurous in its programming and as seedy as the Scala. I don't remember much about the film, except that Lot was presented as a crabby old patriarch and the Sodomite tribe was a bevy of doomed but beautiful boys. Like ff-ers, they wore few clothes and danced all night. Multiple images of boys dancing, nude-descending-staircase-style, very sexy, even those in camp badboy make-up. The stunning montage effects impressed British critic Norman Wilson, 'even though we deplore the choice of theme, and the decadent artiness of its treatment' (*Cinema Quarterly*).

A scarcely disguised celebration of Sodom, a rare thing, even now, especially now. I don't think it could ever have been mistaken for a Bible epic, for one thing it's only twenty-seven minutes long. Its appeal in 1933 no different from its appeal now. If the Scala survives King's Cross office and Channel Tunnel developments, court and council writs and rulings, and sells enough oranges, I hope they'll show it.*

Lot in Sodom has partly resurfaced, or rather some of the out-takes have, with the director wandering into the shot, to give it that extra avant-garde feel, and incorporated in *Nitrate Kisses. Kisses* is the first feature of 'avant-garde', 'experimental' film-maker Barbara Hammer. I wish there was a new term for this kind of cinema, I'm tired of all these old ones. Hammer intercuts the *Lot in Sodom* out-takes with a black man and a white one making love. A wild film itself, *Nitrate Kisses* has something to suit most deviant tastes, and like the Price it aims to provoke by connecting Aids with burning cities. Aids and Sodom, a cliché of the Moral Majority for ten years, is in danger of becoming one in new queer cinema too.

A Sodom season would be short in length, some of it short on quality too. Some Sodom curiosities might be found, though, like the documentary *Return to Sodom*, its existence briefly reported in a 1975 issue of *Gay News*.

USA: 'As it was in the days of Lot, so shall it also be in the days of the coming Christ.' A film by David Wilkerson, presently being shown in American religious circles, attempts to bring the prophecy to life!

His 50-minute documentary entitled *Return to Sodom* depicts a state of 'moral collapse' in the USA, and he displays as symptoms of this collapse the rise of cult religions, witchcraft and homosexuality.

* They didn't. The Scala closed its doors on 6 June 1993. RIP, but preferably revive.

The film contains footage shot at a mass gay rally in New York's Central Park, and communion being taken at a Metropolitan Community Church service.

This could become a cult, perhaps a born-again Sodomite has hung on to a print?

*

A small room off the main Sodom season should house a video monitor for viewing the 1988 *Sehnsucht nach Sodom* (A Yearning for Sodom), a record of the dying days of the German actor Kurt Raab. This fierce and moving video demands viewing intimacy. Though it is short, the pace is slow, the rhythm dictated by the restrictions of Raab's illness. The actor remembers a melancholic all-night drinking bout in Berlin/Sodom, long before his HIV diagnosis, and smiles as he remarks, 'the sun shining into a gay bar is something terrible.' The dawn was, however, to bring a lover. Later, in a bitter moment, he explains his sister's reluctance to have him home for his last few weeks and her excuses for not wanting him buried in the family plot. The contagion of corpses, not to mention the possible snubs and gossip in her village. His ashes in an urn would be acceptable. Raab explains how well-wishers were eventually to give him an unusual present, his very own graveyard plot. He accepts the gift and chooses burial away from home. Raab leaves a list of almost comic, if essential and heart-felt, exactitude, the specifications for his funeral. Massive, slightly moulded oak coffin, iron mountings, double nailing, interior corner joints, shroud, pillow, quilt and habit of fine silk . . . The video ends with a close shot of his Kaposi's sarcoma, like Christ's stigmata, frail flesh dissolving into a starry night-sky. There's a fuller title for this extraordinary video, it conveys something of the mixed tone:

> A Yearning for Sodom
> or
> Projections in Front of
> an Empty Screen
> on a Dazzling
> Futile Wonderful
> and Wasted Life
> with a Thankless Medium.

*

A Season in Sodom might also contain Marlon verbally fucking the 'holy institution of family', the 'church of good citizens' in *Last Tango In Paris*, whilst smearing the butter. Or it could be a tribute to the stunning Brad Davis. Brad, stripped, humiliated, hung naked and beaten by sodomite Turks (the old stereotype) in *Midnight Express*. Alan Parker's film constantly travels lovingly over Brad's body, yet stirs the audience to rapturous cheers when Brad skewers the head of his Turkish tormentor. A tormentor who means, no ambiguity here, 'to know' him. I saw the film on a Saturday night at the local cinema. There were loud moans of disgust as Brad and his prison friend kissed in the shower. Brad smiling a sweet 'no, no further' when his friend wanted to follow through. An altogether appalling celluloid Sodom, *Midnight Express*, but I can't resist re-running the Brad bits. Brad redeemed himself in Fassbinder's *Querelle*, submitting happily to sodomy, a scene few Hollywood actors would have dared. Bad for the image, Brad. Brad Davis, who died damning Hollywood for its callous treatment of HIV positive actors. Brad, who, like a few boys I've known off-screen, I always wanted, and never did get to sleep with. It stirs in me an eerie, erotic longing.

None of the films I've written (yet) would really qualify for the season, though *Nighthawks*, which I co-wrote and co-produced with Ron Peck, was banned in Greece on the grounds that it might 'dangerously undermine the sane traditions of the Greek people, and the accepted moral disgust for homosexuality, and will have a destructive effect on Greek youth', and it did provoke the *Sun* headline 'CHILDREN TO STAR IN "GAY" FILM'. Well, it was about a schoolteacher who cruised the bars by night and taught geography by day. Difficult to exclude children from the school scenes. The more recent *Caught Looking*, a melancholic comedy on voyeurism and fantasy (written by me, directed by Constantine Giannaris), was shown last year on Channel 4.

> . . . men kissing and caressing other men and apparently indulging in oral sex . . . filth! . . . weakens the moral structure of our country . . . blasphemous, lascivious and obscene and a product of an Anti Christ . . . anti-social, sacrilegious . . . a health hazard . . . normal people don't need it . . . just brought a child into this world and this is absolutely disgusting . . . bestial . . . unadulterated filth and porn . . . the people responsible need a bull-whipping . . . Thank God for the 'Off' Switch.
>
> (A medley of viewer complaint)

The cry was great, even, especially, from squeaky-clean 'gays and' fans. And the Broadcasting Standards Council saw if Giannaris and Hallam had done altogether according to the cry of it. And the judgement upon them was great:

> . . . the scenes in the public lavatory, in the absence of a plot which might justify their inclusion in that form, went beyond acceptable limits.

I was pleased when both *Nighthawks* and *Caught Looking* featured in last year's *Da Sodoma A Hollywood – Festival Internazionale Di Film Con Tematiche Omosessuali*. Made it to a Turin Sodom, so perhaps the Scala Sodom Season could be stretched a little . . .

*

As I leave the foyer, I'll often catch the eye of someone else picking up the papers, I'm not the only addict. Before fitting the papers into a bulging shoulder-bag, I might glance at the *Boyz* centrefold. So many free nudes on offer these days, I've stopped buying the magazines. That's not quite true, I couldn't leave that porn legacy abandoned, slumped in the corner of the bookshop. Charlie Ruff of *Male Only* (Pendulum Publications, 1970) has a new admirer now. This tattooed 'Dixie boy', whose hobbies are 'pool and swimming', is caught, naked, legs spread, in what I take to be the photographer's apartment. Ruff reads a book, I can't make out the title, a minor frustration. The best pose of the sequence is more wholly satisfying. Ruff, still naked, sits with his legs round a desk. Smiling, he tries out the keys on a typewriter. An old Remington, I'd guess. Glorious these Ruff shots, though the fag photographer's taste in furnishings leaves something to be desired.

I walk up the hill from the Scala, head home. *Boyz* doesn't quite fit the bag, *Boyz* protruding. Re-fold and cover, or just leave it? It's a decision I've had to make a thousand times over. Coming home on a bus, do you let people see the gay paper you're carrying, the only thing you picked up at the club? Or do you seal it in your jacket? Leave the title visible, and you never know, a conversation might start with the boy right behind you. Then again, look at the lads at the next stop, they might not take so kindly . . . Depends a bit on how many drinks I've had, this decision. But I know that every single time I've tucked the paper away I've kicked myself. Felt defeated. Sod 'em, show it.

I imagine a braver boy, sunbathing in the park next summer. *The Book of Sodom* sits sweat-marked, settled by his side. A cyclist in lycra weaves towards him. Takes in the boy, takes in the book . . . a slow squeeze of the brakes . . .

*

Last stop on the circuit-walk, the newsagent. I'll call in for the *Independent* or the *Guardian*, and once a month for *Gay Times*. *Gay Times* for its book coverage, fuller than the free ones, and for 'Mediawatch', the latest newsprint nasties. Best of all, the ever-entertaining 'Round Britain', the 'hotspot' photo-spread. Each month a pub or a club, looking pretty much the same as the previous month's. There's usually a shirtless barman, a handsome firm-friend couple, a crowd camping it up for the camera and a shot or two of a drag act or a stripper at the club's horribly cheerful charity do. Perverse, my affection for these hotspots. Partly it's the relief after the pages of 'Worldwatch'. Gay news from China, Iran, Cuba, Nicaragua, Romania . . . the chill spots, sometimes sickeningly chill.

I read, last year, of likely executions in Iran. There'd been a raid on a private gay party, a party behind closed curtains. More than ninety men arrested. Another clean-up, another purge. At the time I was writing about the mollies, pelted in the stocks, carted to Tyburn. I tried to find out what happened to these Iranian men. I didn't catch any news of them in the mainstream press, and an Amnesty print-out of recent human rights abuses in Iran made no mention. They might be dead now, many of these men who met for a party. The story had surfaced in the Iranian opposition newspaper in London, *Kayhan*, and was taken up by *Gay Times* (October 1992). Sodomites hurled from cliffs, stoned, beheaded, suffocated in Iran. In the early 1980s, seventy people were executed for attempting to form a lesbian and gay organisation in Iran (*Gay Times*, May 1991). In the previous year, July 1990, *Gay Times* reported a speech of the Ayatollah Musavi-Ardebili, made at prayers in Tehran University. He explained the role of the 'extermination squads', how they existed to deal with those who 'had committed that vice under the compulsion of physical desire'. The squads should split offenders in two with a sword, 'they should either cut off his neck or they should split him from the head. . . . Or they should dig a hole, make a fire and throw him alive into the fire. We do not have such punishments for other offences. . . . They get what they deserve.'

The late Ayatollah Khomeini, in an interview with Oriana Fallaci published in the *Daily Mail* (reported in *Gay News*, October 1979), answered her question 'Is it right to shoot the poor prostitute, or a woman who is unfaithful to her husband, or a man who loves another man?'

> Khomeini: 'If your finger suffers from gangrene, what do you do? Do you let the whole hand, and then the body, become filled with gangrene, or do you cut the finger off? What brings corruption to an entire country and its people must be pulled up like the weeds that infest a field of wheat. . . . In Islam we want to implement a policy to purify society, and in order to achieve this aim we must punish those who bring evil to our youth.'

Pressed further, asked about a boy shot 'yesterday' for the crime of homosexuality, he lost patience:

> Khomeini: 'Corruption, corruption. We have to eliminate corruption. . . . Stop talking about these things. I am getting tired. These are not important matters.'

That same week, in 1979, Pope John Paul II declared: 'Homosexuality as distinguished from homosexual orientation is morally wrong' to a private lunch and conference of 350 American Bishops held in Chicago.

*

Sodom does make mainstream press and history books more often now. 'Sodom' looks good and a mite risqué in a headline. Before you'd look to the small print, find out in footnotes. Take *The History of England* by Rapin de Thoyras, translated into English and with additional notes by N. Tindal, Rector of Averstocke in Hampshire, for example. You might have been reading the Henry I story for history homework. Henry's son, William, was returning to England from the wars in France, and 'took with him in his Vessel, all the young Nobility, to render his passage more agreeable'. The story goes that William promised his seamen a reward if they were the first ship home. The ship hit the rocks. William was drowned, along with 'several Lords, whose debauched lives, as is pretended, but too justly brought down this Judgment on their heads', adds de Thoryas. King Henry, William's father, was never more seen to laugh. Intriguing this. In my huge folio copy there are copious follow-on footnotes in very small print.

> There perished in this shipwreck a hundred and forty Officers and Soldiers, fifty Sailors, with the Officers belonging to the ship; many of the Nobility of both Sexes, &c. about three hundred in all. Most of them were drunk. See *S. Dunelm*, p. 242. *Ord. Vitalis*. This was looked upon as a just Judgment by our Historians, for their being polluted with the Sin of *Sodomy*. The loss of this young Prince was not very unhappy for the *English* Nation, if that be true which *Brompton* relates from *Malmsbury* (though we can't find it in his History) that he threatened, *if ever he became King, he would make them draw the Plough like Oxen*.

A footnote to seize on. Prince William, aged fifteen in the main text, eighteen in the footnote, hating the English, surrounded by Sodomite friends, drunk then drowned. As good as the Edward II story, this, and far less famous.

Recently the *Independent* reported on the United Nations' decision to investigate the anti-gay laws of the island of Tasmania, where sex between consenting adult males is still illegal. There's a battle going on between Cramp (Concerned Residents Against Moral Pollution) and gay activists: 'We're here, we're queer and we're not going to the mainland'. A campaigner for the gay group quoted the 1847 poem from the *Launceston Examiner* as evidence that anti-gay prejudice was nothing new:

> Shall Tasman's Isle so fam'd
> So lovely and so fair
> From other nations be
> estranged
> The name of Sodom bear?

Early cramped concerns about moral pollution of or by convicts in Australia are admirably and entertainingly discussed in Robert

Hughes's *The Fatal Shore*, a massively popular history of Australia that rehabilitated history book footnotes, put them on top. Sodom in bestsellers at last. Dita in Madonna's *Sex*, on the pleasure/pain of sodomy, saying 'all your nerve endings are in your ass', and saying it in a million homes. But this is the book of Sodom, not of sodomy, though the act will keep surfacing. This is the book of Sodom, not of safe sex. A book, like Madonna's, of fiction.

*

Back to Sodom down-under. Opponents of transportation stressed the moral degradation into which the convicts fell, of 'crimes that, dare I describe them, would make your blood to freeze, and your hair to rise erect in horror upon the pale flesh', according to Bishop Ullathorne, a priest who heard convict confessions, and had therefore, as Hughes remarks, the evidence of his ears. Fears were expressed that the 'contagion' would spread to the mainland. Convict days well over, fears of contagion continued and continue to be expressed. 'New "Sodom" is spared' ran the header for an unsigned article in a 1976 issue of *Gay News*:

> SOUTH AUSTRALIA: For the 800,000 inhabitants of Adelaide it's business as usual this week – which will come as no surprise to anyone, except perhaps housepainter John Nash.
>
> For John Nash predicted that at noon on Monday January 19 God would take a terrible vengeance on the state capital for liberalising South Australia's laws against homosexuality.
>
> As surely as God destroyed Sodom and Gomorrah, said the prophet, so would he send an earthquake and a tidal wave to cleanse Adelaide, round about Monday lunch-time.
>
> Several hundred city-dwellers – Italians and Greeks in particular – began to pack for the hills. Some people even sold their homes.
>
> State Premier Don Dunstan himself intervened as the panic started to run out of control. He promised that Monday lunch-time would find him standing on a city beach to prove that there was nothing to fear.
>
> Local homosexuals told the press that they would join him.
>
> With all the sinners thus conveniently gathered in one place (the state chief and the errant gays), just a little tidal wave would have cleaned up the beach and satisfied the outraged housepainter.
>
> But the sea remained obstinately tranquil, and the refreshment stalls that set up to feed the hundreds of sight-seers did a roaring trade.

In Fiona Cunningham Reid's 1992 documentary on the Mardi-Gras, *Feed Them to the Cannibals*, Sydney Sodomites are shown in full-swing at their Sleaze Ball, a fund-raising event that looks altogether more entertaining and raunchier than the parade itself. Interspersed with the sleaze, the frock and float construction, there's an interview with the Reverend Fred Nile, MP: 'It's not only offensive, but obscene and blasphemous. . . . In the beginning God created Adam and Eve, not Adam and Steve.' An old Fundamentalist joke, this, long past its tell-by date, but delivered as if freshly minted. Nile compares Sydney to Sodom and prays for tornadoes, or at the very least, for rain on the Parade. His wishes were ignored, the local police chief loved the day, and so did big business. Fundamentalists sometimes face a problem here. Sodom sells (I hope). This can create many a moral dilemma for the right-minded Christian whose business might benefit.

Garry Wotherspoon's cautiously titled *City of the Plain* (Hale and Iremonger, 1991) is a history of Sydney's gay subculture. I found it with the Badboy Saul. The cover features Peter Firth's painting *Sodom to Sydney*. A beach boy hunk flees a burning city in the sky, a second naked hunk cloud-climbs to greet him. They might, the painting suggests, descend to the Harbour Bridge, and set up home in Sydney. Wotherspoon refers back to his earlier essay, 'A Sodom in the South Pacific: Male Homosexuality in Sydney 1788–1809'. Sydney seen as Sodom, long before the jibes of the Reverend Niles.

According to Francis King, Robin Maugham used to call Tangier *Sodome-sur-mer* (*Gay Times*, December 1992) but the most notorious Sodom-on-Sea is of course San Francisco. The ideal candidate for destruction, since it is a long-held belief, in some quarters, that sodomy causes earthquakes. The idea stretches right the way back to Justinian. Because of blasphemy and 'disgraceful lusts', Justinian's edict of 538 declared, 'there are famines, earthquakes and pestilences'. He expanded on this theory in his 544 edict. This time his concern was solely with homosexuality.

> . . . we know that God brought a just judgement upon those who lived in Sodom, on account of this very madness of intercourse, so that to this very day that land burns with inextinguishable fire.

Justinian urges those who have been contaminated 'by the filth of this impious conduct' to 'strive for penitence'. There had been, around the time of these edicts, a number of earthquakes, floods and fires, including the fire that destroyed Antioch. In 543, a plague had swept Constantinople. Surely the sins of Sodom were to blame.

In San Francisco Justinian types and the Nileses coalesce. Last year, Todd Wilcox reported in the *Pink Paper*:

> San Francisco's Christian Coalition has complained that the Bay Area is now the 'city of Sodom'. The Coalition's request that a lesbian and gay rainbow flag be removed from the Harvey Milk Library was rejected this week by the city's Library Commissioner.
>
> The flag, presented to the library by a group of gay military veterans, is a 'glorification of the homosexual lifestyle,' says Pastor Bill Holt. Holt believes that homosexuality is a 'pathological illness'.
>
> Josef Yountoub – also of the Christian Coalition – asked the library commission at a public meeting, 'Does this mean we are no longer the city of St. Francis? Are we now the city of Sodom?' He claimed that the flag 'proves once again that gays are given more rights in San Francisco than any other group.'
>
> The library was opened as a tribute to Harvey Milk, the openly-gay city supervisor (councillor) murdered with Mayor George Moscone in 1978. It is home to the Harvey Milk collection, one of the biggest gay and lesbian archives in the United States.
>
> Steven Coulter, for the City of San Francisco, told us: 'I personally can't think of a more appropriate place for this flag to fly than over the Harvey Milk branch of the library.' The City Attorney's office is to issue guidelines on the controversy.
>
> *Pink Paper*, 23 August 1992

The *Pink Paper* also reflected on the meaning of the 1992 Florida hurricane:

> The most expensive hurricane in American history has hit southern Florida. The visitation of God? A portent of divine wrath on a guilty society? What's more, it's called Hurricane Andrew.
>
> Before it is denounced in evangelical sermons as divine vengeance on the Kingdom of Sodom, let's remember history. The Roman Emperor Justinian reacted to unfavourable weather reports by issuing the first main anti-gay laws of the ancient Empire. That was in 538 AD.
>
> Thunder and rainy depressions on his left hand, and Christian 'morals' became Roman law. Homosexuality causes earthquakes, he

announced, with the same certainty that the Pope claims homosexuality is wrong today.

Presumably this bad weather myth began in the Bible and the myth of Sodom. That's Sodom, twinned with Gomorrah. The Lord rained down fire and brimstone around 1400 BC.

Then there was a King of Mercia, in Southern England who confessed in 744 AD, 'the people of England have been living a shameful life, lusting after the fashion of the people of Sodom.'

We've been around a lot and for a long time. However they try to bury our history. The language of condemnation remains illogical.

The Florida hurricane might, of course, have been God's wrath for America's failure to respond to the HIV crisis.

Pink Paper, 30 August 1992

A concise history of the Sodom story, that. I doubt a day passes without some new Sodom scare somewhere in the world, a new tarring with the brimstone brush. I'm unable to resist a last one, closer to home, from 1980 and reported in *Gay News*. The Reverend George Storey, vicar of Christ Church, Accrington, feared the starting up of a gay night at nearby Blackburn's Romeo and Juliet's club might provoke God's judgement. It can't have pleased him that the gay night was to be Sunday. Even basically Romeo and Juliet clubs might try a gay night on a Sunday, when Romeo and Juliet, it seems, prefer to stay home. The Reverend feared 'abomination' in Blackburn and explained: 'This sort of thing happened in Sodom and Gomorrah and it was wiped out. The same thing happened in Babylon, the Roman Empire and Ancient Greece. I fear for our country' (*Gay News*, October 1980). Sodom, Rome, Greece, now Blackburn . . .

These days Sodom even finds a place in newspaper competitions. Invited to write a letter of complaint about an imagined, updated Bible, *Independent* reader Nick MacKinnon won a bottle of champagne for his concern that:

> . . . the most worrying item is in the classified ads at the back. It is surely tampering with the Word of God to suggest that the Number of the Beast is 0898 666 666, and that callers will hear about Saucy Sessions in Sodom, charged at 43p a minute.
>
> (*Independent Magazine* competition, 25 July 1992)

Sodom everywhere, at every time and place. Even in the Classifieds. The Battersea Arts Centre warned any would-be applicant for their

Press Officer vacancy that he or she would have to deal with '120 Days of Sodom to 101 Dalmatians – *sometimes simultaneously!*' (*Guardian*, July 1992).

Some, though, have lost all humour about Sodom. A reader wrote to the *Pink Paper* recently, angrily asserting that 'Genesis Chapter 19 has nothing whatsoever to say about consenting gay sex. It is in fact about an attempt at gang rape on the men who have come to stay with Lot'. Lot's daughter (just one of them), irate reader Derek Rawcliffe insists, was substituted for the men and gang-raped. He goes on to argue the hospitality theory of the story, and suggests the word 'sodomy' should go back to its (unexplained) 'original use' or, better still, be expunged from the English language. Of course anger is justifiable, so many injustices in the name of Sodom, but in his exegesis Mr Rawcliffe slips into some story-telling of his own. There is *no* suggestion in the story that the Sodomites took up Lot's offer of his daughter(s), there is a hint that they might go for Lot. And of course there's no reason to suspect that the entire population of Sodom was gay.

Some scholars more precise than Mr Rawcliffe persist with the, to my mind unlikely, argument that 'to know' (yādha' in the Hebrew being equally ambiguous) might not have meant 'to know' sexually anyway. But I'm doing it myself now, talking about the story, as if the place existed. It's too late, there is no Sodom . . .

It even said as much in the paper.

The Bible can still make front-page news. On 28 March 1993, the *Independent on Sunday* announced, 'Leading archaeologist says Old Testament stories are fiction'. The paper's Archaeology Correspondent, David Keys, reported on the conclusions of a fifteen-year study by leading biblical archaeologist Professor Thomas Thompson. Keys summarises the professor's conclusions: the complete lack of any archaeological or historical evidence for many events portrayed in the Bible suggests that the first ten books of the Old Testament were 'almost certainly fiction, written between 500 and 1,500 years after the events they purport to describe'. The professor himself is more forthright: 'It is out of the question that Saul, David, and Solomon, as described as kings in the Bible, could have existed. I think the biblical accounts are wonderful stories, invented at the time when Jerusalem was part of the Persian Empire in the 5th Century BC.'

Keys reports calm in the face of these revelations, quoting Rabbi Stephen Howard. 'It is the wisdom, not the historicity, of the Bible which is of prime importance.' Rabbi Julian Jacobs is rather more dismissive: 'The Bible, being of divine origin, can stand on its own feet and does not require supportive evidence.'

Each circuit yields a shoulder-bag of books, a newsprint supplement to the Sodom range. Tired and dusty I relax, take a bath. I keep meaning to treat myself to those Dead Sea Bath Salts, noticed at a friend's house. Famous and effective, said the packet, 'since Biblical times'.

* * *

At sixteen, in 1968, had there been *The Book of Sodom*, I would slowly, secretly have saved up for it. Buying it would have taken forethought, planning, courage. Once I had bought it, I would have hidden it. I suspect it would be the same for many a sixteen-year-old now. You have to get over these inhibitions. Not that I ever have, quite. I still hesitate before buying *Gay Times* from the local newsagent, still meet with that paper problem on the bus. At sixteen, in 1968, I would have cautiously approached the bookshop counter, waited for a quiet moment, no one watching, no one waiting to be served. I might have turned the book over, to display the price on the back, a helpful customer, making the ring-up quicker. I would have looked slightly suspicious, I sometimes do. I'm usually stopped at Customs. It's someone else I see sunbathing with my book, not me. Would I dare read this book on the tube? That mix of fear and embarrassment still, and still I resent it. On the 1992 Gay Pride march people wore 'You call it sodomy, We call it fabulous' T-shirts; I smiled, but I wouldn't have dared. Not even with the vast 'we're here, we're queer, and we're not going shopping' crowd to protect me.

Had *The Book of Sodom* been published in the sixties, I would have bought it at Bux, Nottingham's 'alternative' bookshop; '*it* stocked here' the sticker sign said. Trial-triggering *it* and *Oz*, targets of many a raid. I kept the odd copy. In a 1968 issue of '*it*' R.C.A. Records took a full half-page, filled most of it with two words. Big bold letters proclaimed:

SODOMY
HASHISH

An ad for the soundtrack of *Hair*. So I doubt the Bux staff, had I asked for *The Book of Sodom*, would have batted an eyelid. Bux was part of an earlier circuit, by East Midlands bus, from my home town, Mansfield, to the city of Nottingham. Zoar to Sodom, thirteen miles. Not far out of Mansfield, the bus curved off the road, stopped at the smartest bus shelter en route. An old wooden shelter, with seats. Alight here for Newstead Abbey, Byron's ancestral home. I didn't know much about Byron then, I loved the Abbey; like St Bartholomew-the-Great, it too was once a twelfth-century Augustinian priory. I'd wander the ruined cloisters, the grounds, patrolled as they were by alarming peacocks. But I couldn't get to grips with Byron's work at all. I liked my copy of his *Poetical Works*, red, plush, padded and patterned. An old edition, I thought then it must be valuable, it isn't. I was easily impressed. It was given to me by my mother; she, in turn, had been given the book by a vicar in Gainsborough as a war-work reward. During the war his vicarage hall had been turned into a secret munitions factory. Mum worked there, made parts for Lancaster bombers, when not out on bomb rescue work, or pub singing. Perhaps the vicarage address on the inside cover misled me, at sixteen I never associated Byron with sex. The elder son of Mr Laing's 'striving working classes', a *Soviet Weekly* subscribing, pitman father, and a mother who worked at Metal Box, naturally my other deceased literary neighbour, D.H. Lawrence, meant more to me than the poetical lord. Only 'snobs' read Byron. The wooded estates near his home were where the posh boys from Mansfield's ancient grammar schools lived. To get to Lawrence's home you'd have to take a more roundabout route, change buses, leave the main carriage road. I often did, in private pilgrimage.

*

I think I first took to literature when sex became less readily available. From the age of about eight to fourteen, with my gang, I'd haunt the local pit tips, the quarries, the waste land known as 'wrecks'. Our Coal Board estate, the Garibaldi, was carved out of Sherwood Forest. We could go there, or cycle to Derbyshire, to caverns and the Blue John mines. Ideal locations all for playing around with friends. Quantities of sex-play. Tents, caves, dens: I loved them then as now. There was also the back of the bus with the boys from the boxing club, the usual childhood 'show-me' flashes and the wrestling gropes. I say 'usual', but I'm aware that many friends from less privileged and more protected backgrounds lament the lost years of their childhoods. Didn't get up to much till their twenties, had to make up for lost time later.

I played, as a very young boy, a curious variation on the doctors/ nurses game, my invention I think, called 'orphanages'. A kind of 'abuse' game, children taking both adult and child roles. It made a change from the torture by fire ordeals and strip poker.

My 'phase' persisted but friends got more awkward, less willing. You can only pretend to be showing what boys do to girls for so long and retain your straight credibility. Not be a puff, a queer, a pansy, bum-boy or sod.

I was an early reader, but I got more obsessive. 'Paul's allus got his nose in a book,' the oft-repeated observation, or the prouder 'Paul's studying'. As an adolescent I did have a vague sense that Mansfield had a gay past, possibly even a present, rumours of cottages in the grand, green-benched parks. And the pub I underaged drank in had once, long ago, been raided. Local busmen and dignitaries were involved in a scandal. My dad mentioned the pub's murky history, I probably blushed. As for cottaging, I wouldn't have known what to do. Contrary to rumour, and hints in the fiction, I've never done it. I only like the *idea* of it, enjoy listening to the adventures of friends who are regulars. Is there such a such a word as 'aureur'?

Nottingham had a more promising reputation, more than one pub, more than one theatre, a Playhouse and a Royal. I had to go there, I couldn't spend all my life in a bedroom den, with my nose in a book.

What was I looking for, reading avidly, at the age of sixteen, shut off from the family, content or at least happily, adolescently self-pitying in my bedroom? I was searching, then as now, for Sodom. I was looking for gay places, for atmospheres as much as acts, though I treasured any description I found of the latter. I borrowed Genet's thieves and miraculous roses from the locked room in Mansfield Library. There they kept company with books that were fragile, rare and expensive. The Genet books were, mysteriously, brand new, hardbound, and unlimited. Genet was clearly too dangerous for the browsers of Mansfield to know.

My school, Sherwood Hall, was all metal and glass. A 'Technical Grammar for Boys'. A new kind of school intended to turn out engineers and scientists. After French, you took Russian, not Latin. I never did get a grounding in Ganymede. I remember the arts staff with immense affection, I liked them, I could talk to them. I would risk the label 'creep'; there were other ways of keeping friends. Creep or not I was famous for skiving off school, heading for cafés and the cinema. I would 'casually' waylay my favourite teachers, catch them in corridors between lessons, let them know what I'd been reading, what music I'd liked on the radio, what films and plays I ventured to Nottingham to see. I wanted to impress and I wanted 'further reading'. I'd probe on French literature. Gide, Proust, Cocteau were mentioned. Did they realise that my interests weren't entirely cultural? Whether they did or not, they gave me names, a list of books I could look out for in Nottingham.

I never really did find Sodom-on-Trent, except in its bookshops and cinemas. I saw Pasolini's *Theorem* and *Oedipus Rex* at the Co-op art cinema and cried. I thought I'd left Mansfield for ever, moved to Pasolini sandscapes.

I went to the Saturday matinées of almost every play at Nottingham Playhouse for several years. An adventurous place, under the directorship of John Neville and, later, Stuart Burge. The Playhouse had plenty of 'might-be' Sodomite men about, and many a 'difficult' modern play introduced me to a few fictional ones. All this cost money, of course, but Mum and Dad were both generous. I reminded my mum of her adopted dad, a bookish man who, jobless in the thirties, put his head in the gas oven. What he'd missed out on, what she in turn had missed out on, she was determined I would have. Dad, I think, saw me as a future champion of the socialist cause. Dad, knee-deep in water, in the dust. Never able to rest in routine, working shifts. Days, afters, nights. Dad subbed me too, if Mum hadn't already, and if he hadn't, as he sometimes did, chucked his wages away on the horses. Mum and Dad, both keen that I should do well, both encouraged the journeys. In retrospect, I'm surprised that my younger brother and my two older sisters didn't resent it, they must have done at times. But it can't have lasted, any resentment, they've been subbing me since . . .

Before sex, not counting orphanages, there was the comfort of fiction. And it was in Proust, an unlikely choice, given I thought Byron was posh, not in Lawrence, that I found an image to thrill and move me. Proust, so easily dismissed as a 'negative' writer on homosexuality now. But I loved, still love, the monstrous and hilarious and incredibly sad antics of Charlus. I was confirmed in my adolescent misery, M. de Charlus was my Morrissey. Here was a world beyond the Garibaldi mining estate, a million miles from Mansfield, or even Nottingham. A world with its own language and rituals. I became more familiar with

Proust's Sodom than I ever was with the Bible's. I had no hell-fire sermons to contend with at home. My father was set against religion; though in his childhood, he had been a Boy-Bishop. Elected by fellow Anglican choirboys to play a bishop role from St Nicholas's day to Innocents' day. From Boy-Bishop to Bolshevik, later elected as union man. My mother had no doubt that death was The End, wanted no fuss at her funeral, 'Burn me, I like to be warm'. But, hell fire or no, I could never pluck up the courage to say what I was reading. And besides, I rather liked Sodom's secrecy.

I think I first heard of Proust from a history teacher. For a long time I went in search of Proust. The great *Sodome et Gomorrhe* section of *A la recherche* was fortunately translated by C.K. Scott Moncrieff, in the 1920s, as *Cities of the Plain*. The title stuck; only last year, in 1992, did the word 'Sodom' finally appear on the cover of Proust in English translation. On D.J. Enright's revision of Terence Kilmartin's revision of Scott Moncrieff's translation! Nothing embarrassing about buying the Chatto Proust in the sixties. The covers had yellow-tinted scratchy drawings by Philippe Julien, drawings that gave little away. Proust came in a pocket-sized, pricey, multi-volume paperback series. I could gradually buy the entire work, from my spending money, with the odd parental top-up.

Proust had the distinct advantage of being a respected great author, extensive Genet talk with teachers was less likely. I could mention Proust at school, try to impress with my voluntary reading. I wouldn't have to conceal Proust in my bedroom. It was Proust's Sodom I wanted to visit, *Cities of the Plain* was my first 'Sodom Guidebook'. Welcome to the 'cursed race' club. And look at the membership! I was learning that litany of famous artists – Gide, Genet, Michelangelo, Socrates, Shakespeare, Marlowe, Visconti, Pasolini and of course, Proust himself. Compiling my first Sodom list I thought the cursed were surely blessed. I didn't know, or even think, about the existence of gay miners, gay lorry drivers then. The gloomy majesty of Proust thrills me now, at forty, as it did then, at sixteen. I didn't entirely understand it, I was just overwhelmed by the near-biblical sweep of the language, by the sorrow. I still prefer the original translation, for all its imperfections, inaccuracies and infidelities I became a Proust addict. To this day I paste Proust clippings into scrapbooks, any mention of him in any context. From reviews of Proust studies to brochures for Proust country tours on which you might find speakers artfully placed in the trees, blaring Wagner.

On my recent circuit-walks, I found many a religious scrapbook, carefully pasted. Invitations to funerals, notes on sermons, worthy 'thoughts' and prayers, pressed flowers. Mementoes of visits to churches and to shrines. They'd slip from the Bibles, these fragments. Sometimes I'd dismiss these scraps as sickly. But I can't deny the consolations of cheap sentiment. They can move you, these waste-paper supplements. Like my slightly crazed Marcel scrapbooks, book tribute to book. Slightly grubby, littered shores.

*

Sodom was an idea, a place, long before I connected it with specific acts. I don't think I knew what sodomy was at sixteen. And in the end it wasn't Proust, certainly not Lord Byron, but D.H. Lawrence who acted as a catalyst, and moved me closer to the act. I took to a boy in the year above me at school. He was bright, funny, popular and played sports. I plucked up the courage, in time, to show him the passages on friendship in *Women in Love*. The wrestling! The joys of literature, and its embarrassments. When I stayed with him, his parents away, we decided, saying nothing, against going to bed. There were too many empty bedrooms, no excuse to 'lie with mankind, as with womankind: it *is* abomination' (Leviticus 19: 22). We fell asleep by a blazing fire in the front room. We woke in each other's arms, the fire still burning. We went further than Gerald and Birkin in our fireside idyll, developed the literary source.

But Lawrence, I discovered, was down on closet sodomists:

> Ronald you know, is like most Englishmen,
> by instinct he's a sodomist
> but he's frightened to know it
> so he takes it out on women.

'Pansies'

Though in the less sarcastically titled 'Bawdy Can Be Sane' he allows that

> Even sodomy can be sane and wholesome
> granted there is an exchange of genuine feeling.

70

There's a second version of the poem:

> Even, at the right times, sodomy can be sane and wholesome
> granted there is proper give and take.

It concludes: 'In fact, it may be that a little sodomy is necessary to human life.'

Warden John Sparrow of Oxford famously exposed the give-and-take scene in *Lady Chatterley's Lover*, 'Burning out the shames, the deepest, oldest shames, in the most secret places'. The meaning of which, Sparrow chirped, was obvious. The jury, had they read their Lawrence properly, might have returned a guilty verdict on the book, found it obscene. As it was, Penguin were able to release vanloads of Lady C. to an eager, waiting public. A copy even found its way into the kitchen drawers at home, the only novel in the house not in my bedroom bookcase.

Less ambiguously, Lawrence did tell Compton Mackenzie, 'I believe the nearest I've ever come to perfect love was with a young coal-miner when I was about sixteen.' So perhaps he would have approved the literary adaptation, set by the fireside, within walking distance of his Eastwood home. Not that it *was* sodomy, wholesome or otherwise. That happened a couple of years later, with a city boy type, a law student, in a crumbling stone college.

The act was to shock me. Not the initial pain; handled right, you get over that. What hadn't occurred to me was what happened to the semen. It disturbed me, the shitting out, the loss. It took the most outrageous story-telling drag act, in a pub on the Goldhawk Road, to shake me out of what had turned into a strange, near obsessive worry. The drag queen related his previous night's adventures, part of his 'routine'. Told how he'd been feeling a little rough the previous night, and the rough had no objections, that kind of line.

Next day, he awoke. Rough had left. Well, the drag queen drawled, no use lamenting, you can always go shopping. So he 'flushed the babies down the lavatory' and got on with the day. This brief narrative, in an otherwise more obviously crude and funny routine, took the audience aback. Some made mock-vomit sounds, others looked embarrassed. I was deeply shocked, and later hugely grateful. It was as though the whole romantic fantasy of fatherhood had been blasted out of me. Or was it motherhood? There'd been, since the law student, both give and take. Tell the truth, I could take it, or leave it . . . Sodom, for me, always more essential than sodomy.

We might *play* mother and father both, we couldn't be it. Sex is different between men and men. We are a race apart, love, face it, the drag act seemed to tell me. Let it go and get on with it.

I enjoy the role of uncle. I'm a godparent, a great-uncle even. I've worked with children, I miss them if I don't see them for a while. Sometimes, reading the attacks on Sodom, you'd think its inhabitants never went out. But though I might, at times, watch the ball roll across the living-room floor, I've never once really wanted to emigrate. I like dry Sodom. Sodom's barrenness. I've never been a great one for grass. The country makes me claustrophobic. I feel surrounded, stuck in the hold of the Ark, surrounded by creatures, two by two by two. Confronted with a people-less landscape, I'm desperate to leave, to catch a bus back to Sodom. A city on the mainland, in the desert or by the sea. Anywhere but those acres of green.

I was at home in the smoky drag pub in the Goldhawk Road. A temporary home again, like so many a Sodomite settlement. Sooner or later, the warning sign, 'Under New Management'. Sod off, move on. The Goldhawk drag act purged the sentimentality from me, yet played on sentimentality, the edge and essence of the best pub drag. So much a part of the old-style, bawdy Sodoms. They can get to you, the older drag queens, make you laugh, make you cry, and sometimes scare and shock. Some of the best nights in Sodom spent watching them, thrilled.

We *are* a sterile race. This is the book of Sodom, not the book of gay parents, fosterers, adopters (though only the best to them). This is the book of small-town boys leaving, or kicked out of Zoar. The book of orphans. Girls on the run, headed Gomorrah. These days the wildest London clubs seem to be the deviant dyke dives. The Clit Club, ff in overdrive. I've seen a Moral Majority banner, a warning, 'Sodom Today, Tomorrow Gomorrah'. There's a lot in that slogan, more, I suspect, than they think. It's sad that Gomorrah isn't as catchy a word as Sodom. Maybe it doesn't matter, there's always the Lesbos alternative, or new names to be coined. It's a bit more pleasingly confused now, the Sodom scene. In Athens 'Gomorrah' has just opened across the road from 'Sodom'. People cross between clubs. There's no reason to suppose Sodom was a single-sex city anyway, and of course the act has its votaries everywhere. There are signs of altogether new identifications. The photographer Della Grace recently wrote in *Quim* (the magazine 'for dykes of all sexual persuasions') that:

> If the 90s is to be the QUEER DECADE there's a few major behavioural adjustments we have to make. So if you want to call yourself Queer, that's fine. I'm a pussy licking sodomite myself. Because until the white boys are prepared to give it up they can fuck my fat dyke ass. Or I'll fuck theirs. Now *that* would be queer.

I came across a note in Pliny the Elder's *Historia Naturalis*, on some other curious Dead Sea types. To the east of the Dead Sea, he relates:

> . . . dwell the Esseni, a solitary people, the strangest among the inhabitants of the world, for there are no women among them, and they have abjured all sexual pleasure, and possess no money, but abide in palm-groves. Day by day the number of these refugees is renewed, being largely swelled by the accession of those whom the vicissitudes of fortune drive, weary of life, to adopt their usages. In this way, marvellous though it seems, a race exists perpetually in which no one is born, for it is propagated by other men's dissatisfaction with life.

The Dead Sea created some strange and compelling pictures. The melancholic Esseni, like Sodomites, survivors; proof there were ways round this two-by-two pressure. Replenish with dissatisfaction. There must, of course, have been times when a Sodomite longed for Zoar, or thought about joining the Esseni. Where did the women go? I trust they had their own Esseni settlement, and kept it quiet. There are times when I tire of the Sodom round, the gossip, the latest news on who got how much to do what new gay project, the scarcely concealed glee at who didn't. Tired too of the news on the latest gay club, the next knight-graced charity Aids extravaganza. Sometimes I feel like a motherless child, a long ways from home.

Sometimes Sodom just fails me. Or maybe I'm just in the wrong part of town. Some of the more attractive Zoarite features can be found in Sodom. Since HIV, there has been much of that over-the-garden-fence concern about the next-door neighbour. The conversations about symptoms, treatments, illness and death, that seem, whenever I visit, such a feature of Zoar. The running of errands for the neighbour who is sick, the tending of vulnerable flesh. Not that Sodom was ever quite as bad as people made out, there's always been an unobtrusive looking after of friends, it's just easier to see now. Engels and the Countess Waldeck would see only freemasonry here, be blinkered to kindness.

*

What tends to refresh the weary Sodomite is a Christmas visit to Zoar. Sodomite haunts are at their friskiest after traditional Zoarite festivals. You can breathe the relief to be back.

At sixteen, every Saturday, the bus took me out of Zoar, not exactly to Sodom, but to a sense of Sodom. I'd been a member of a Saturday-morning drama group at Nottingham Playhouse. The theatre was turned over to youth drama every Saturday morning. You split into groups, went off and worked on short stage pieces around the chosen theme of the day. 'Death', say, and adolescents often did. You could work with your group in almost any corner of the theatre. Each group would return to the main stage at the end of the morning. Perform their piece. The other groups sat in the stalls, thus providing a guaranteed audience. From an idea to performance, in Nottingham Playhouse, and all in the space of three hours! The thrill for me was not the acting at all, it was the freedom to explore backstage. To wander the scenery store, play with the stage props, to weave through the costume rails, climb ladders, work winches, shift spots, click switches on the lighting board . . . A city in miniature, this backstage world. Compartments, levels, departments, dens.

William Burkitt, Vicar and Lecturer of Dedham in Essex, would not have approved. In the dedicatory grovel to the Right Honourable Charles Lord Fitzwalter, of his *Expository Notes with Practical Observations on the New-Testament of Our Lord and Saviour Jesus Christ*, Burkitt expresses a hope that:

> Whilst *Others* consume their Precious Hours in Plays and Romances, and such-like Corrupting and Effeminating Trash, which the *Superfœtation* of the *Stage* furnishes the Nation with, to the Scandal of Our Holy Religion, and the Grief of all Good Men; Debasing the Minds, and Debauching the Manners of so many amongst us: That Your Lordship (and Others of your *Noble Order* with you) may Taste such Incomparable Delight and Sweetness in, and Experience such Invaluable Benefit and Advantage by, Reading the History of Your Blessed *Redeemer*'s Life and Actions; and may thereby be Transformed into His Holy Likeness here on Earth, and spend an Eternity in the Rapturous Contemplation, and Ravishing Fruition of Him in Heaven . . .

The stage and ungodly songs, outside of church, away from home. In the much-reprinted *The Whole Book of Psalmes* 'Collected into English Meeter' by Thomas Sternhold and 'conferred with the Hebrew and with apt notes to sing them withall' it is explained that the psalms are 'Set forth and allowed to be sung in all Churches . . . & moreover in private houses for their godly solace and comfort, laying apart all ungodly songs and ballades: which tend onely to the nourishing of vice, and corrupting of youth'.

Recommendations for the laying aside of all theatre, all corrupting and effeminating trash, all ungodly songs and ballads. There are countless seventeenth- and eighteenth-century anti-theatrical tracts, you could make a Whole Book of Sodom out of them.

After the morning's backstage explorations I'd head for a setting even more theatrical and imposing. At least it seemed theatrical at the weekend, not theatrical at all, I imagine, if you worked there all week. Nottingham's Lace Market is a maze of massive Victorian red-brick factories, deserted then, on Saturdays. The fire escapes, the rubbish bags bulging with rejected cloth, the machinery, the oil-marked pavements. I'd peer through windows, pick up old stationery discarded by the offices, collect ledgers, order books, indexes, books of carbon. I would read, wander, daydream in the Lace Market, and return there, at the end of the day, after Shakespeare, or Osborne, or Pinter or Arden. A vague, disturbed, excited adolescent, in love with effeminating trash. Half an hour at dusk, in a city that seemed my own, half an hour to absorb the fullest of days, before the journey home, past Byron's place to Mansfield.

> To Carthage I came, where there sang all around me in my ears a caldron of unholy loves. I loved not yet, yet I loved to love, and out of a deep-seated want, I hated myself for wanting not. I sought what I might love, in love with loving, and safety I hated, and a way without snares.
>
> St Augustine, *Confessions*

Augustine found his love.

> . . . my soul was sickly and full of sores, it miserably cast itself forth, desiring to be scraped by the touch of objects of sense. Yet if these had not a soul, they would not be objects of love. To love them, and to be beloved, was sweet to me; but more, when I obtained to enjoy the person

I loved. I defiled, therefore the spring of friendship with the filth of concupiscence and I beclouded its brightness with the hell of lust-fulness . . .

The theatre disturbed him.

Stage-plays also carried me away, full of images of my miseries, and of fuel to my fire. Why is it, that man desires to be made sad, beholding doleful and tragical things, which yet himself would by no means suffer? yet he desires as a spectator to feel sorrow at them, and this very sorrow is his pleasure.

'Filth' again and sure enough, Sodom seeps into his reflections. It's easy to dismiss Augustine, see him as an early Anderton. But his Sodom is no simple cesspit:

Are griefs then to be loved? Verily all desire joy. Or whereas no man likes to be miserable, is he yet pleased to be merciful? which because it cannot be without passion, for this reason alone are passions loved? This also springs from that vein of friendship. But whither goes that vein? whither flows it? wherefore runs it into that torrent of pitch bubbling forth those monstrous tides of foul lustfulness, into which it is wilfully changed and transformed, being of its own will precipitated and corrupted from its heavenly clearness? Shall compassion then be put away? by no means. Be griefs then sometimes loved. But beware of uncleanness.

At least you sense he's been there, Carthage/Sodom. This is no easy pronouncement from a churchman in the country. The Sodomitish Sea washes through Augustine's words and his wanderings. It's a remarkably open confession. Sodom threads through the meditation on the stage, on friendship, on passions real and imagined. At seventeen I read this old, awkward, unattributed translation. I think I'd heard about Augustine, seen him on some pink list.

*

All Sodoms interested me then, whether Purity Pemberton's or Proust's. Augustine's confusions or trashy gay fictions with great tragic endings. Even the Festival of Light diatribes attested to Sodomite existence. The sheer volume of complaint told me there were many of us out there. When, some years later, boy prostitution in Piccadilly was dramatically exposed in the television documentary *Johnny, Go Home*, Johnnys by the dozen sped to London. Warnings can be signals, provide handy route-maps.

I never really suffered that oft-reported teenage gay misery, 'I'm the only one'. There might not have been many immediately visible in Mansfield, but I read the papers. A Sunday sleaze-sheet reported on strange men who stalked the London commons. The parks, not the House, though occasionally you'd hear of one there too. How to spot a homo. The paper advised the reader to watch out for polo-neck pullovers. For weeks, my friends and I would point and laugh at men who proudly sported their smart polo-necks. The men were bewildered at this attack on their sartorial elegance. Probably *Sunday Times* readers. No one had warned them to change their wardrobe. We shouted, 'Polo-neck pullover, polo-neck pullover' across the street. It's the closest I've come to being a queer-basher.

The fireside idyll ended in ashes. Special friendship was fine, but need it be physical? Yes, I had to be honest, for this one, it need. The friend felt guilt, my guilt came later. Not because of the sex, but because I didn't understand the older boy, didn't appreciate his confusion. I stopped speaking to him. The 'let's just be friends' line was the last thing I wanted. It meant I was back to the company of books. From sixteen to eighteen I read great quantities of literature, all of Proust, every play of Shakespeare, and much else besides. All 'great' literature, with a few notably less respectable exceptions, like Genet and the Beats. I still couldn't handle Byron at all, all that Greek and Roman stuff. I've only recently learnt that Ganymede was a Trojan prince in the original story, not a lowly shepherd at all. This still fits the oft-repeated sodomy as an aristo vice theory, and Engels might have read a later variation. Ganymede as the local lad, abducted, seduced, and given a lowly bar job on Olympus. This local boy was waiting for the swoop that never came.

Instead I'd found cheap fiction, schoolboy romances to console me for the failed one of my own, *Special Friendships, Two, Sandel*. I found adolescents meeting older men in *Never the Same Again* and *Finistère*, but unfortunately still never met an older man of my own. The books had embarrassingly, amazingly, explicit covers. The naked back of an adolescent boy, or an older man planting a kiss on a boy's willing head – two examples from a publisher as respectable as Panther. It was still the sixties. But inside the books were a bit rarefied for my taste. Public school hothouses never hot enough. The morals of public schools were compared to those of Sodom and Gomorrah in an 1893 issue of *New Review*, and Sodom's sins suffused Lindsay Anderson's *If . . .* which I saw over and over again; but the schoolboy books struck me as far too sweet and sickly. I should reread them, see if they're better and more varied than I remember them. I only kept them really for the covers.

Real sleaze came from America. Black-and-white covers, photographs of handsome men in string vests, emerging from or disappearing into shadows. *Somewhere Between the Two, Maybe Tomorrow, The Flaming Heart, The Occasional Man, Desire in the Shadows*. There was the occasional home-grown product, the more prosaically entitled *The Pole and Whistle*, but it didn't have quite the same appeal. 'Adult', 'electrifying', 'best-selling', the yellow letters proclaimed. Explorations of unconventional love, abnormal love, a different kind of love, forbidden love or, even better, unbridled desire, suppressed erotic desire, uncontrollable desire, desire in the shadows. Books that were not to be found in Nottingham's respectable second-hand and antiquarian haunts, not even in Bux. You found them in those seedy second-hand paperback shops. The books black-ink stamped on the inside cover: 'This book is exchangeable at half-price'. Took a lot of courage to buy one, no way I'd take it back. The shops that stocked sci-fi (pre-respectability), cowboy books, and books on Hitler's henchmen. Dig through the crates, sift through the racks, and in time you'd find the odd suppressed passion or a lurking unbridled lust. They stood out so in their black and white and yellow.

Not directly Sodom texts? If not in Sodom at least you were well away from school, often in the company of sailors. There was *one* direct reference, a novel by the improbably named Edwin Fey. His *Summer in Sodom* promised a gripping dilemma:

> Ian Raymond wanted Ted Randall more than he had ever desired anyone – and he would use every device of desire and pain to get him!
>
> Set against the strange background of erotic, forbidden acts performed on moonlit beaches, *Summer in Sodom* is the explosive story of the fateful decision virile Ted Randall had to make – to give his lean, hard-muscled body to a woman, or be enslaved by the overpowering masculinity of a hot-blooded male.
>
> NEVER BEFORE HAS A NOVEL LAID BARE WITH SUCH RAW HONESTY THE BORDERLINE WORLD OF NORMAL AND ABNORMAL LOVE!

And moreover it delivered. This lurid tale of rough body juttings, of searing, soaring pleasures, is set in Silver Beach, on the shore-line of Lake Erie. Surely no random choice of Lake name, that. In the explosive heat of day boys bathe, and work on their tan-lines. But at night, boys get together. Hard, driving, ramrod need meets massive manly musculature. *Summer in Sodom* is suffused with strange light. Sex in the shadows, passion at dusk, lust by the light of the moon.

Many Jewish commentators on the Genesis story have remarked on the timing of the fire out of Heaven.

> The destruction of the cities of the plain took place at dawn of the sixteenth day of Nisan, for the reason that there were moon and sun worshippers among the inhabitants. God said: 'If I destroy them by day, the moon worshippers will say, Were the moon here, she would prove herself our saviour; and if I destroy them by night, the sun worshippers will say, Were the sun here, he would prove himself our saviour. I will therefore let their chastisement overtake them on the sixteenth day of Nisan at an hour at which the moon and the sun are both in the skies.'
>
> Louis Ginsberg, *The Legends of the Jews*

The Sodomite revellers were probably just off to bed, looking forward to a lie-in. Abraham was already up and at his morning devotions when the fire struck. I like this note on the story, Sodomites and the hours they keep. There's another possible explanation for the timing. Pre-planned dawn raids are highly effective, you can catch people at their most vulnerable. Ask any Anderton.

*

A couple of these books were buried under layers of Chaucer and Bacon, packed in a trunk, bundled into Dad's friend's Humber, to be joyously unpacked in a room overlooking the Bridge of Sighs. Not the Venetian one, but the bridge over tarmac that links the two parts of Hertford College, Oxford. Mum and Dad went up with me; Mum wrote after:

> It must seem strange to you, and you must have missed home life at first, funny over the past year or two you seem to have grown up and become so self-possessed, but when we left you, you seemed neither – just somebody rather lost. A very small pebble on a very large beach, and I must admit it was rather a wrench . . .

Hertford sought out the bright northern boys, it was a boys-only place in 1970. It took us in a year early, placed less emphasis on the entrance exam. It took me in without Latin O-level, a requirement then to read English. Let me in, Latinless. I was ecstatic. I was also, as Mum said, a little lost at first. The place wasn't full of students talking excitedly about books as I had fantasised. Few admitted to reading at all. When I met a student from Mansfield College who did (the college name had to be an omen), and did so with a skill and assurance that astonished me, and in a voice I could bathe in, I instantly fell. I wanted to listen to him for ever. I've gone off such book-talk since.

I played the 'I happen to have a spare ticket' game, invited him to Bach's *St John Passion* at the Sheldonian Theatre. He slipped a letter under my door: 'Under the circumstances, our friendship *will* have no foundation'. The circumstances weren't really explained. This love story might seem to have no place in a book of Sodom. This is not the book of gay loves, gay lovers, long-lasting relationships. But the secrecy of my adolescent passion made me identify more closely with Proust's Sodomites, his 'cursed race', 'obliged to lie' about this love, as I lied to family, and to many a friend. Though were I an academic investigating the subtext of my mother's funny, warm letters from home, I'd wonder what the problem was.

A television programme on Andy Warhol caused an outcry. Mum wrote:

> The ANDY WARHOL thing – well I found nothing disgusting about it – it just seemed terrible to me that people could get like that – I cannot help wondering what sort of people Mary Whitehouse and party are, they too must have funny minds, surely she must have done something out-rageous (to do with sex) in her life?

Or answering my inquiry:

> About my reading – afraid they are a bit on the rude side – but I am quite enjoying them – they are not teaching me anything as I think my sex life has been as full of incidents as my ordinary life.

I felt fully in *her* world, the letters are packed with family news, Garibaldi estate news, news of strikes. Hugely entertaining gossip and sometimes sad and very personal accounts of troubles with Dad. No angel, Dad, it must be said. Still, he had to put up with a lot, as Mum well knew:

> They had a black day at the pit on Friday – one of the union men (a pal of your dad's for a good many years) collapsed and died in the pit yard, there was trouble with the pit cage and a man had his arm taken off down the pit and your dad says every job was going wrong – he thought it must be Friday the thirteenth but it was only the twelfth.

But still I felt obliged to lie. Writing to her I nevertheless found a way of talking about the men I'd met, men I'd slept with. A way to tell her of their homes, their interests. Simple really, I married the men off, gave them spouses. Mum was pleased I was meeting all these 'interesting' people, hoped I'd find a way of repaying their – little could she know – Sodomite hospitality.

For unrequited love didn't stop my explorations, I'd found the Red Lion, the gay pub. It had an inside door that led, if I remember rightly, directly through to the theatre next door. Theatre again, Sodomite haunt. Perfect.

I still thought of my Mansfield College boy, obsessively. I'd walk past his college, at all times of day and night, sometimes hoping to see him cross the quad, sometimes knowing he was in his room, asleep. I nestled down one night, outside his door.

On a boiling hot summer's day I decided to walk past his college one last time before heading to the University Parks. I knew he wasn't in, he'd be in Schools (the examination hall), taking his first-year exams, 'Mods'. I was meant to have been sitting in the same room.

In a less romantic version of this story I would have to add that I was probably scared to death of failing the exams. I had not worked at all on Old English. Too busy reading Gide and Genet and a host of other writers my tutor disapproved of. The love was in part a romantic excuse for melodramatically skipping exams. Oxford forgave me, and took me back. Put it all down to my nervousness, and my background, I think. I was, after a year off, ecstatic to get back again. In the year off I worked with children in a psychiatric hospital. I also met more men outside of the colleges. Even students could tire of non-stop student company. I generally got more confident. And though the Oxford Campaign for Homosexual Equality, a.k.a. 'the knitting circle', might not sound like Sodom, its parties were regular orgies. I never told the story of that first year to my family. I still felt obliged to lie, but this is not the Book of Coming Out . . .

Sodom was becoming less a dream, a sought-after place. In fact it was where you met friends for a drink, and, on a good night, met someone to go home with. Bad nights (the vast majority) I'd return to college a bit miserable. Sometimes I'd do the walk again, by Mansfield College, imagine the book talks that would never be.

*

I went back home for Christmas. Heading for the pub with Mum and Dad and my brother I must have made a small-town, Mansfield/Zoar-type jibe. I must control this habit. I remember Mum saying she hoped I wasn't laughing at them, I protested. We made up and moved off to the pub. A good night, all of us singing, Dad tackling 'The Man from Laramie' maybe, or 'I'll Take You Home Again Kathleen':

> I will take you back Kathleen
> To where your heart will feel no pain
> And when the fields are fresh and green
> I'll take you to your home Kathleen.

At this point it was usually quite evident that Kathleen would have to take him home. Though I never cared for Christmas much, this year looked to be an exception. I was glad to be back. A sober friend of Dad's arrived for the last half-hour, offered us a lift home. The car skidded on black ice and somersaulted across the road. The driver, my dad, my brother and myself got away with scratches. Mum was dead.

Within weeks of the accident Dad was found to be riddled with cancer, from stomach to skull. He died at Easter, just four months after Mum. The inquest into my mother's death fell on my birthday, Dad was the first witness called. I had to inform the coroner that Dad was dead.

For a year I was rarely sober; friends helped, but I also desperately needed the company of strangers. Sodom as refuge, as comfort, as a reminder too of the pubs I'd known since childhood, of Mum and Dad singing. The comfort of a drop of beer, hot ale and gin, the comfort of strange beds, strange flesh. No harm done, nothing but love. On my own I listened to the most wrenching of music, Beethoven quartets, Purcell's funeral music, Bach *Passions*. I read Yeats's poems over and over. From 'Nineteen Hundred and Nineteen':

> But is there any comfort to be found?
> Man is in love and loves what vanishes
> What more is there to say?

From: 'A Dialogue of Self and Soul':

> A living man is blind and drinks his drop.
> What matter if the ditches are impure?
> What matter if I live it all once more?

And further on the assertion:

> I am content to live it all again
> And yet again, if it be life to pitch
> Into the frog-spawn of a blind man's ditch,
> A blind man battering blind men;

Lines wrenched out of context, read aloud, over and over in my orgy of drunken self-pity. Self-pity, but what matter? I took refuge, too, in Proust's Sodom. Shocked to find myself so soon one of his bereft . . .

> sons without a mother, to whom they are obliged to lie all her life long
> and even in the hour when they close her dying eyes . . .

I was, in short, totally self-indulgent, and wrote what now strike me as very funny, massively pretentious, if understandable diary entries on the consolations of 'great art'. These reflections were interspersed with detailed accounts of pick-ups. For sometimes great art, and even great and loving friends, were not enough. I took more trips to London. I loved the drag pubs, south of the river, distinctly working class. Locals, my parents' age, happy amongst an incredibly mixed and sometimes rough gay crowd. I found pub-singing in smoke again. I loved too the seedier haunts of Earls Court, the cramped and grimy basements. Best of all, The Boltons with its rent-boy crowd, dyke dramas, tranny tantrums. Passionate and sentimental, bawdy and raucous. Sinners exceedingly, and the cry was great, and the police turned up every other night, or so it seemed. A studious, awkward, naïve Sodomite orphan sat in the corner, watching, sometimes crying into his beer. 'You all right?' or 'Worse happens at sea', lines that more than once led to bed.

Sometimes I feel like a motherless child
Sometimes I feel like a motherless child
A long ways from home.

But there were other homes, albeit temporary, and not so far away really. Bedsits round the corner. Some mornings you might wake up in the arms of a Brad or a Ruff.

Lot's daughters lost friends in the fire, and their husbands-to-be. Their mother turned to salt. The first-born got her father drunk with wine and lay with him and the second followed suit. The story's end, avoided by Aldrich, evaded by Huston. An awkward ending, it created many a problem for commentarist clerics. Evasive footnotes, excuse notes, dissertations on old tribal customs, or incest acceptable, under the circumstances. Perhaps, after such death and destruction, the daughters sought a kind of comfort in their father's bed, something beyond the preservation of offspring. Or was it a perverse kind of revenge on their father for his offering them up to the Sodomites? Either of my readings is highly improbable, but no more so than many.

I was worried, writing this. Too much autobiography? But the more I read the commentaries, the more they all seem like autobiographies, albeit disguised. Everyone so certain they've been there, seen Sodom.

Of course even without the deaths, I'd have been in the drag pubs, loving them. There's no trusting these stories.

*

Too autobiographical? Too exclusive? A 1617 *Practice of Piety* directs the Christian 'how to walk' in order to please God. A walk to welcome Death. Death as release from desire. Here *all* flesh is seen as at best displeasing, seen in terms normally reserved for Sodom. Death:

> ... freeth thee from a *corruptible body*, which was conceived in the *weaknesse* of flesh, the *heate* of lust, the *staine* of sinne, and borne in the bloud of filthinesse: a living *prison* of thy soule, a lively *instrument* of sinne, a very *sacke* of stinking dung: the *excrements* of whose nostrils, eares, poares, and other passages (duely considered) will seeme more loathsome than the uncleannest sinke or vault. Insomuch that whereas *trees* and *plants* bring forth leaves, flowers, fruits, and sweet smels, *mans* body brings forth naturally nothing but *lice, wormes, rottennesse*, and *filthy stinch*. His *affections* are altogether *corrupted*; and the *imaginations of his heart are*

onely evill continually. Hence it is that the *ungodly* is not satisfied with *prophannesse,* nor the *voluptuous* with *pleasures,* nor the *ambitious* with *preferment,* nor the *curious* with *precisenesse,* nor the *malicious* with *revenge,* nor the *lecherous* with *uncleannesse,* nor the *covetous* with *gaine,* nor the *drunkard* with *drinking.* New *passions* and *fashions* doe daily grow: new *feares* and *afflictions* doe still arise: here *wrath* lies in wait, there *vaineglory* vexeth; here *pride* lifts up, there *disgrace* casts downe; and every one *waiteth* who shall arise in the *ruine* of another. Now a man is privily *stung* with *bach biters,* like fiery *Serpents*: anon, hee is in danger to be *openly* *devoured* of his *enemies,* like *Daniels Lyons.* And a godly man, where eare hee liveth, shall ever be vexed (like *Lot*) with *Sodomes* uncleannesse.

Death might free us all from all horrors, few worse than the vexatious sight of Sodom.

A 'learned Bishop in Ireland' was equally vexed by the passions and fashions of his day. His 1689 *A Short Treatise on These Heads viz: Of the Sins of Sodom, of Pride in Apparrel and Contempt of God in his Judgments,* etc. was issued anonymously, for names 'beget prejudices'.

What kind of *Pride* is not notorious amongst us? In that of *Luxurious Apparrel* have we not outdone *Sodom* herself? How many expend more in *Clothes* and *Garniture* in one year, than they bestow in Almsdeeds in seven, nay perhaps in their whole Lives? We may daily see some single Persons purchasing a Fantastic sort of Nets or Cobwebs, (for they cannot be called Cloths), through which they may be seen a great part naked, at far greater Sums than would suffice wholesomely to clothe, or cover the nakedness of some Poor, Industrious Families. Thus hath the Vainest sort of *Pride supplanted* the *greatest* of all *Christian Virtues* (thy darling, O Lord, and Image) *Charity.* . . . But O Lord the *Plague* is *Epidemical,* and the several ranks and degrees of People among us are even confounded, and ordinarily not known one from another by this means.

ff boys in their American Retro vests; nets and cobwebs, always a feature of gay fashion. Consider the apparel at Sadie Maisie's, Sin Ministry and Kinky Gerlinky. Visit Club Shame. In the Backstreet leather bar ranks and degrees are surely confounded. How to tell the MP from the miner? If they're both leather-garnished, if they're both talking Callas? There's *something* to be said for the Bishop's observations. But he's wrong about the cobweb queens, the devotees of Regulation. They'll rarely neglect their alms-deeds. Charity has always been a part of the gay scene, many a children's home has benefited, many a kidney machine is born of a charity bash. More recently, as the Countess Waldeck would have noted, we've looked after our own. If the government won't, and it won't, then the strippers must freely show flesh through their nets again, drag acts spruce up their cobwebs and sing.

All this charity cajoling, sometimes I wonder, can it be worth it for a Weekend for Two in Gran Canaria? Can't people simply give cash or sign cheques? But bucket or cheque book, you can't argue the spirit. The spirit of Sodom, in all its gaudy.

The Bishop is by no means finished. He reserves his best vitriol for the gluttons of Sodom.

> We oppress our Tables first, and then our selves: Few meals with us, which are not Feasts: and in those which are professedly Feasts, how seldom do the generality of People, put an End to them, till they have by Drinking raised in themselves a false kind of thirst, and then downright added Drunkenness to their Thirst? . . . That which of old would have made a meal for a Prince, will scarce now go down with a Mechanic; much less with many of us, who ought to be Examples to the World of the greatest Abstinence, Mortification and all virtuous Severities to the Body. Yea, as if bridling the Appetite were one of the most dishonourable qualities; how much the greater number of Persons of liberal Education and Fortunes amongst us, look upon it as one of the bravest and most gentlemanlike Accomplishments to understand Eating, or to be a good Cook? *Alas*! that what is the Necessity, indeed one of the greatest slaveries of Life, to provide for and serve the Belly should now be grown the End, and with too many the Reward both of living and of all their Labors under the Sun. Thus O Lord instead of bringing forth the Christian Fruits of our Plenty; abounding in good Works, we are become Enemies to the Cross of Christ; Our God is our Belly . . .

Now here he's talking. A sandwich in a snack-bar is my favourite food. The rest of the time left for the finer things. Many a friend who might otherwise not expect to appear on the Sodom hit list, some of them of liberal education and of no mean fortunes, are here doomed with the rest of the Sodomite tribe. The good cook and the gourmet as Sodomites. I've often pondered the extraordinary amount of time devoted to the belly. Worse, the talking about food, mouthfuls that stir memories of mouthfuls eaten elsewhere. I can sense the pleasure, but can't share it. And, like the learned bishop, I see no virtue in it. I too find tables oppressed, and favour quickly wiped Formica. Sometimes people go on about food the way, they say, 'gays go on about sex'. They'll ask, 'Why can't you just get on with it?'

Why can't you just sit down and eat quietly? Why the rows of cookbooks, the hours of food-talk? The answer, I take it, is the pleasure of variation, the elaboration. The Perfumed Gardens of food.

I might share the Bishop's frown, he brings out the monastic in me. But unlike the Bishop, I wouldn't wish fire on their tables.

Imagine a world without cobwebs and gaudy, mouthfuls of pleasure, and effeminating trash.

There's another Kitchen of Sodom story, with Ganymede as guest, yet again. The story would confirm the Bishop's worst nightmares, though it does contain a cautionary warning for those who would take their pleasures combined.

> The inhabitants of Sodom, for their part, had women who could have made a painted prick stand, and buggered each other all the more heartily for all that. Do not reply that a rain of burning sulphur consumed them as a punishment for their crime; that is an old fable from the addled brain of some dreamer, which our clerics have been clever enough to establish as truth, in the service of their particular interest. Here are the facts, as they are set down in the glorious annals of buggery. The High Priest [of Sodom], one of the greatest buggers the earth ever brought forth, wanted to celebrate the lupercalia, and ordered his cook, a great expert, to prepare a sumptuous dinner, to which he invited all his favourite boys. A kitchen-boy, a young blond of fifteen, handsome as Cupid, with the bottom of Ganymede, was in a corner of the kitchen washing the dishes. The cook, inflamed with lust, had a monk-sized erection, couldn't take his eyes off his prey, and was hurrying to finish his work, so as to satisfy his burning desires. Finally, the work is done, the spit is turning at speed, in front of a fire, hot as a glass-blower's. The impatient bugger gets his leg over his Ganymede, and makes herculean efforts to get his monstrous prick into the boy's tight arse. Meanwhile, the chimney is ablaze; the bugger, given over completely to pleasure, fails to notice the fire; the fire spreads, and in a few hours the whole city of Sodom is burnt up. The reader will forgive this digression, which was essential to my theme . . .

This unique Sodom commentary surfaces in a French pamphlet, *Les Petits Bougres au manège* (The Little Buggers' Reply) printed in 'Year

Two of the Dream of Liberty' (*L'An second du rêve de la liberté*), that is, in year two of the French Revolution. A reply to a previous pamphlet, *Requête et décret* (Petition and Decree), which was printed in 'the second year of fuckative regeneration' (*L'An second de la régénération foutative*). In the latter the whores of Paris petition the Estates General to put a stop to buggery, since it takes away all their trade. It's a laboriously indecent octosyllabic rant. English poems of the eighteenth century, like Charles Churchill's, similarly accuse Sodomites of punter purloining.

The reply, from which the kitchen theory is taken, is altogether more imaginative. The author's theme was startling enough. It was to state the case for a kind of Sodomite Liberation Front! The two French pamphlets, like so many others, have been unearthed by Patrick Cardon and published in his wonderful *Cahiers GKC* series (gai, kitsch, camp).

The rhetoric of sexual liberation has scarcely changed in two hundred years, though even the Gay Liberation Front, never shy of outrage, might be slightly more circumspect:

> From the moment of creation, going back to Madam Eve, who, if we are to believe historical gossip, let herself be fucked by the serpent, every individual, every creature bearing balls or a cunt, had and still has the right to fuck, to wank or to bugger; only eunuchs, those wretched victims of unbridled asiatic jealousy, are deprived of the pleasure of ejaculating sperm; but never, at any time or in any circumstances, has anyone had the exclusive right to take or to give genital pleasure. Read all the histories; study every historical period; inspect the archives of the brothels established everywhere on the surface of the globe; nowhere will you find a charter giving to any one class of creatures the right to fuck, or to bring another off in any particular way, to the exclusion of other orders of being, to whom a kindly nature has given senses that they might use them in the way best corresponding to their tastes and inclinations. Even if such a charter should exist, which is entirely impossible unless it is signed by the great prick of Priapus himself, and countersigned in sperm on every page; if it does not bear the imprint of the mighty ballocks of lusty Hercules, it is of no more value, and no more merits belief than the paper money of the National Assembly.

The tirade culminates a few pages on:

> Individual liberty, which has been decreed by our most august and most respectable representatives, is clearly no mere fancy. According to this

principle I can dispose of my property, of whatever kind, as I please. Now my prick and my balls belong to me; and whether I put them in a game stew, or fish consommé or, to speak more clearly, whether I put them in a cunt or an arse, no one has the right to complain of the use I make of them; and the whores least of all.

It is unlikely that the author had any serious intent in this argument; but the document remains fascinating. For the argument could, taken out of context, and made less coarse, be read as a serious, sometimes witty dissertation on the right to do what you please with your own body. The pamphleteer is also fond of the famous faggot list argument, there is nothing wrong with sodomy, look at our forebears, Socrates, numerous Roman emperors etc., etc.

The 'use I make of them' (cock and balls) reminded me of the trial of William Brown, a molly in Moorfields, for 'Sodomitical Practices' in July, 1726. A voice from an Old Bailey 'select' trial. Brown was indicted for a misdemeanour in assaulting Thomas Newton, with intent to commit Sodomy with him.

Thomas Szasz, in his *The Manufacture of Madness*, memorably remarked of the strangers in Sodom that they were '. . . in truth not travelers but angels, that is to say, God's plain-clothesmen'. The biblical vice-squad in 'the earliest account in human history of the entrapment of homosexuals'. In Brown's trial for 'Sodomitical Practices' Newton took an angel role, sent, probably under pressure, as *agent provocateur* to Moorfields, which had a reputation as an outdoor molly cruising ground.

Newton spoke first, and then Willis, a constable.

Thomas Newton: Willis and *Stevenson* the Constables, having a warrant to apprehend Sodomites, I went with them to an Alehouse in *Moor-fields*, where we agreed that I should go and pick up one, and that they should wait at a convenient Distance. There's a Walk in the *Upper-Moor-Fields*, by the side of the Wall that parts the Upper-Field from the Middle-Field. I knew that this walk was frequented by Sodomites, and was no Stranger to the Methods they used in picking one another up. So I takes a Turn that Way, and leans over the Wall. In a little time the Prisoner passes by, and looks hard at me, and, at a small Distance from me, stands up against the Wall, as if he was going to make Water. Then, by Degrees he sidles nearer and nearer to where I stood, 'till at last he comes close to me. – *'Tis a very fine Night*, says he; *Aye*, says I, *and so it is*. Then he takes me by the Hand,

and after squeezing and playing with it a little (to which I shewed no dislike) he conveys it to his Breeches, and puts – into it. I took fast hold, and call'd out to *Willis* and *Stephenson*, who coming to my Assistance, we carried him to the Watch-house. – I had seen the Prisoner before, at the house of *Thomas Wright*, who was hang'd for Sodomy.

Willis: We asked the Prisoner, why he took such indecent Liberties with *Newton*, and he was not afraid to answer, *I did it because I thought I knew him, and I think there is no Crime in making what Use I please of my own Body.*

Witnesses spoke on Brown's behalf, said he was long married, honest and sober, and that he 'loved the Conversation of Women better than that of his own sex'. He had women friends, so he could scarcely be a Sodomite. Mollies were popularly believed to be women-haters then. The argument didn't convince the jury. Brown was fined, sentenced to the pillory and to twelve months' imprisonment. Brown's reported remark, on the use of his body, resembles the argument of the pamphlet, but unlike the pamphlet, it sounds like a genuine cry.

Patrick Cardon also unearthed another eighteenth-century Sodom, the remarkable pamphlet *Les Enfans de Sodome* (1790), illustrated with an explicit etching of an all-male threesome in the throes of passion. *Les Enfans* purports to be an account of the setting up of a Society for Sodomite Rights. A petition is addressed to the Assemblée Nationale, Articles of Association are drawn up, there's an account of the formation of committees, the election of deputies, etc. And, appended to the pamphlet, there is a list of prominent Sodomites, with some of their addresses.

'C'est le Gay Power,' Cardon suggests in his introduction. The pamphlet recounts how everyone had been arguing and meeting during the recent upheaval, everyone except the Sodomites, who met only for sex. But even they were coming round to thinking that they had rights too. The freedom to bugger should become one of the articles of the new state. In the future France, the writer predicts, will excel Italy in the new 'science' of buggery.

This must surely be a parody of progressive political rhetoric. There are many cheap puns in the text, and no gay group would have stated so clearly that Jesus was a bugger while printing the names and some addresses of its supporters, Revolution or no. It suggests that their principles should be embodied in law, to be taught and respected throughout France. All members of the Order shall bugger or be buggered as they please. Doctors will be required to treat anal gonorrhoea, and an important manuscript on sodomy will be published, rescued from the conflagration of Sodom! ('un manuscrit sauvé de l'embrasement de Sodome!')

The list includes many famous, powerful and important figures of the time. This *could* be an example of early outing. It is unthinkable that cardinals would willingly and supportively have signed the petition. Sadly, *Les Enfans* is probably just a scurrilous anti-revolutionary tract. There are certain heavy indications in the notes to the original text that sodomy is not approved of, 'cet acte crapuleux de luxure', etc. An early example of 'le Gay Power'? Like so many Sodom texts, there's an ambiguity. The obsessive fascination that revels in the dirt it disapproves.

However, the French Constituent Assembly did abolish the death penalty for the crime of sodomy in 1791 and that paved the way for the legalisation of homosexual acts under the 1810 *Code Napoléon*. Perhaps these bizarre and dirty pamphlets, satiric or not, formed part of a debate that helped clear the air.

Sodom spawns some strange texts, many of them French. Sometimes they mutate, link up with other texts. *Sodome*, Henri d'Argis's 1888 novel, was dedicated to, and had a preface by, Verlaine. It's one of those untranslated French books that has led an underground life in England. Part of the world of untrodden fields, forbidden paths, the crossways of sex, the twilight zones. Verlaine describes the book as 'très chaste' and it was published by a legitimate publisher for open distribution. But the d'Argis is considerably more explicit than, say, Zola.

Soran, the hero, is subjected to innumerable temptations, the reader constantly teased into imagining what *might have* happened, had our hero succumbed. Soran resorts to 'onanisme' for his relief. This is no *Summer in Sodom*. It nevertheless opens promisingly, in a Turkish bath. A classic Sodomite haunt, as my Bomb Division biographies of Cocteau and Proust would attest. That 'Turkish' again. At the baths Soran sees a beautiful, androgynous youth.

His mind drifts back to his childhood. In a busy street, he had put his arm round his much-loved mother, to move her out of the way of the traffic. But an omnibus approaches unseen. His mother is hit, her legs have to be amputated, but nothing can save her! She dies. Difficult for me to make cheap stabs here, for obvious reasons, but this is atrocious story-telling and Sodom Made Simple psychology, I shouldn't get precious.

At school Soran resists the advances of an older boy who tries to excite him with the dirty word *brothel*. The exotic and heterosexual fantasies conjured up for Soran by this shocking word are of 'women as beautiful as the Holy Virgin in the Chapel'. This works against the proposed seduction, and Soran is for the time being saved.

The adolescent Soran falls for a country girl who turns out to be, upon closer inspection, a boy. But all is not lost. Soran eventually meets, and indeed marries, a nice Catholic girl. But temptation returns in the form of a male prostitute who works the Champs Elysées. From the street Soran is persuaded back to the prostitute's home, an awful example of seedy Sodomite décor, from which Soran unsurprisingly flees.

This section of the book found its way into English, appearing under the title 'Solicitation by a little Jesus' in the 'Masculine Prostitution' section of *Crossways of Sex: A Study in Eroto-Pathology* by 'Dr Jacobus X . . .'. Earlier in the chapter there's a helpful definition: 'The *little Jesuses* are originally children of a vicious turn of mind, who, impelled by their evil instincts, have begun to prowl about in solitary places of an evening, unaware themselves what evil spirit is prompting them. Just like female prostitutes, they commence with chance lapses from the path of virtue . . .' Soon, having 'learnt to put on an affected manner and to feminize his whole person', the little Jesus will be out on the game. Seeking Sorans.

Crossways, which contains this fragment from a French *Sodome*, was purportedly published in Paris by the British Bibliophiles' Society and 'Privately Issued for the Subscribers' in 1904. My copy was pencil-marked 'Eso/Eroticism' (esoteric?) by the bookseller I bought it from. Gold-stamped on the cover, 'U.V.T.'. The initials, I discovered, of Lady Una Troubridge, Radclyffe Hall's lover! I imagine them laughing at the adventures of Dr Jacobus X . . . in the land of 'Lesbians, Tribades, Fricarelles and Saphists (sic)', *Crossways*, Volume Two, Chapter One, a few turns before *Sodome*.

To return to our hero. Not surprisingly Soran can't stomach the prostitute's room. Lifted from Jacobus, the description appears later in this *Book of Sodom*. Soran flees, but yet more temptations assail him. Henri, a boy from the baths (we're back to the beginning of the story), is the image of his lost androgyne. Soran continues to live with his wife, but Henri increasingly haunts his imaginings. Soran breaks up the boy's relationship with a girl. In despair, Henri takes a laudanum overdose. Soran takes him away to recuperate. They take a symbolic trip down a coal-mine. This touches a personal fantasy of mine, D.H. Lawrence might have shared it. After the visit Henri is naturally in need of a bath. Soran washes him ... lovingly ... and ... nothing happens! And *yet* Soran still manages to fall victim to a degenerative disease, whose symptoms are those of tertiary syphilis. Soran goes mad, tries to murder Henri, masturbates volcanically and is carried away in a straitjacket. The last scene shows him near to death, attended by heartbroken friends, and in something of a state:

> Jacques Soran is there, besieged by the most terrifying halluci-nations. . . . Sometimes, he roars with fury, or rolls on the ground groaning, fighting off imaginary enemies. . . . Get away! Get away! he screams. Can't you see the rain of sulphur and flames! Can't you smell the horrible smell of the lakes of burning pitch that are swallowing me up and devouring me? Escape while you can! I must die alone, it's God's will. Sodom! Sodom! The earth is opening and the flames are springing out and already my body is burning. Listen! everything is cracking and the abyss is swallowing me up! Escape! Escape! It's written in the Bible in letters of fire: Flee, and do not look behind you, and do not stop until you have left the country. Flee onto the mountain-top if you do not want to die. Sodom! Sodom! Mercy! Mercy! Oh, I am burning!

Sometimes he turns on his friends and cries:

> 'Traitors, you have destroyed me, but you will burn with me. There are the flames: can you see them? How beautiful they are!' (and he looks at them with satisfaction). They are red and blue. Cowards! You are afraid. But it is the hand of God; but I don't want to die alone. – And he lunges at them again.
>
> 'It's five o'clock, gentlemen', says the doctor, 'If you would like to leave'.

D'Argis also wrote the less interesting *Gomorrhe*, a follow-up (1889). Perfunctory stuff, I'm told, and without the strange and obsessional quality of *Sodome*. I was certainly startled to come across a famous-last-words 'Sodom! Sodom!'

*

Neil Bartlett suggests, in his city-wandering homage to Wilde, *Who Was That Man?*, that Wilde had read this portrait of a self-loathing, divided Sodomite. In 1896 Wilde wrote to the Home Secretary from Reading gaol, begging compassion and release. He wrote of the 'horrible form of erotomania' that had possessed him, that drove him, like Soran, from his wife. Wilde said he feared a relapse, feared madness. In solitary confinement his mind inevitably strayed to the 'sexual perversity', the very loathsome erotomania that had brought him there. The symptoms of his 'mania' and the possible outcome are indeed close to the language of *Sodome*, though the book, not surprisingly, is never referred to.

Wilde's plea is in one of his saddest, if entirely understandable, letters. It draws on the language of grim pseudo-scientists who saw homosexuality as a mania, in need of cure. Wilde refers approvingly to Max Nordau's hideous book *Degeneration*, an influential attack on almost everything of any interest in the art, music and literature of the late nineteenth century, including Wilde himself.

Wilde even flatters Nordau, calls him an 'eminent man of science'. Nordau had seen madness as the inevitable outcome of degenerate erotomania. He had scoured contemporary literature for signs of physical and mental degeneracy, for insanity, emotionalism, hysteria, morbid eroticism and mysticism. He attacked the 'filthy' realists just as much as the decadents. Not surprisingly, there's hardly an author, major or minor, who didn't fall foul of Nordau's standards. Nordau proposed a 'Society of Ethical Culture' for Berlin, its board to consist of those with sufficient taste to distinguish between the 'morally healthy artist' and 'the vile speculation of a scribbling ruffian'. Such a scribbling ruffian once found, both 'work and man would be annihilated'. Psychiatrists, Nordau thunders, should back his campaign to characterise 'leading degenerates as mentally diseased' and in the 'unmasking and stigmatizing of their imitators as enemies to society'. Verlaine, Tolstoy, Ibsen, Zola, decadents, aesthetics, pre-Raphaelites, Wilde, one and all on that blacklist.

If Neil Bartlett is right, then it's surely one of the sadder stories of Sodom that Wilde should have to use d'Argis and *Degeneration* against himself. Not exactly a quality text, *Sodome*, but one of the very few that dealt with something like Wilde's own situation. *Degeneration* employed to try to free himself, not from Sodom at all, but from Reading Gaol, where his eyesight was weakening, his hearing worsening. Or is it sad at all? It was a shrewd move, claiming erotomane status, a Sodomite strategy. It's difficult to believe a word Wilde says in the letter, difficult to believe he could have taken either book seriously. But pleading insanity, he should have sounded less articulate. Perhaps the Home Secretary thought as much. At any event, Wilde's plea didn't work. That was more than sad. Oscar Wilde, posing 'Somdomite', continued to suffer in prison. Not long after his release he was, of course, done for.

*

Often when I've spoken of this book I've retold the story of Sodom. Most people remember Lot's wife, though a friend of a friend said she thought the idea of the pillar of salt was brilliant. I was credited with its invention! Most people know Sodom was destroyed, beyond that knowledge appears patchy. Nearly everyone had forgotten the daughters. Many resolved to look at Genesis again. This book might lead to a modest increase in Bible sales. Before the book I, too, had not looked at the Bible for some time. From aged sixteen I used to read St John at Easter. I think someone told me the rumour about Jesus and John, his beloved disciple. Marlowe reportedly said not only that 'all they that love not Tobacco and Boies were fooles', but more scandalously still, 'that St. John the Evangelist was bedfellow to Christ and leaned alwaies in his bosome, that he used him as the sinners of Sodoma'. Even I though that was going a bit far, stretching the evidence. Marlowe was only said to have said it.

In my early twenties, just moved to London from Oxford, I kept a kind of Easter ritual. I would read my pocket copy of St John, bought years before from a Derbyshire church. I played records of Bach's *St John Passion*, or attended a performance in St Bartholomew-the-Great. I'd look to see if Pasolini's *Gospel According to St Matthew* was showing anywhere. Hating Christmas, orphan time, I could nevertheless join in at Easter. I would think of Christ, no denying the power of that story. But my ritual was mostly concerned with the boy that I'd fallen for. The empty seat beside me in the Sheldonian Theatre as I wept at the Bach. The boy partly. Mostly my parents. I never told them about him. I regretted that for years.

I suspect the Bible's consolations have always been a muddled thing. I read Job at college, almost as often as I read *King Lear*, and for much the same reasons. When my parents died, though neither of them was religious, I was hugely disappointed with the brusque speeches at the cremations. I wanted ashes to ashes, dust to dust in a graveyard. They wanted no fuss.

You can devise your own rituals, structure your grief around the Bible. It has the appeal of the definitive, no need to bother with the rest. All other books, 'but waste paper'. It is the ultimate book for obsessives and I'm an obsessive. I came to enjoy the lists, the tables, genealogies, variant readings, all illustrated with 'proper maps'. Researching this one short story in Genesis, I got hooked. In a way, for a while, I'd joined the legions of commentators, sofers and scribes.

I remember my grandmother, dying, reciting over and over, 'The Lord is my Shepherd'. I was very young and it moved me immensely. Dad later took me through to the front room, to see her on her death-bed. One of those 'you're an adult' moments that made me proud, but scared. Grateful to Dad, but confused. 'The Lord is my Shepherd, I shall not want.' Over and over. The Reverend Troy Perry adapted the title for his autobiography, *The Lord Is My Shepherd and He Knows I'm Gay*. I admit that Perry's title made me squirm. It felt like an invasion. But it's no more so than the countless uses and adaptations before it.

I soon felt trapped by the commentaries, turned back to waste paper, picked up the flyers. I remembered that for me the Sodom story was never really the Bible's at all. It was all of these stories, *Summer in Sodom* included, *Summer in Sodom* especially. But mostly Sodom was living in that sentence hijacked by the Countess Waldeck to justify State Department expulsions. For years, I would wrap myself in its convolutions, its grand melancholy. Climb in. It seemed to demand a special way of breathing, it offered a refuge.

I've always relished being a part of that

> Race upon which a curse weighs and which must live amid falsehood and perjury, because it knows the world to regard as a punishable and a scandalous, as an inadmissible thing, its desire . . .

A Sodom Anthology

Sodome et Gomorre

Race upon which a curse weighs and which must live amid falsehood and perjury, because it knows the world to regard as a punishable and a scandalous, as an inadmissible thing, its desire, that which constitutes for every human creature the greatest happiness in life; which must deny its God, since even Christians, when at the bar of justice they appear and are arraigned, must before Christ and in His Name defend themselves, as from a calumny, from the charge of what to them is life itself; sons without a mother, to whom they are obliged to lie all her life long and even in the hour when they close her dying eyes; friends without friendships, despite all those which their charm, frequently recognised, inspires and their hearts, often generous, would gladly feel; but can we describe as friendship those relations which flourish only by virtue of a lie and from which the first outburst of confidence and sincerity in which they might be tempted to indulge would make them be expelled with disgust, unless they are dealing with an impartial, that is to say a sympathetic mind, which however in that case, misled with regard to them by a conventional psychology, will suppose to spring from the vice confessed the very affection that is most alien to it, just as certain judges assume and are more inclined to pardon murder in inverts and treason in Jews for reasons derived from original sin and racial destination. And lastly – according at least to the first theory which I sketched in outline at the time and which we shall see subjected to some modification in the sequel, a theory by which this would have angered them above all things, had not the paradox been hidden from their eyes by the very illusion that made them see and live – lovers from whom is always precluded the possibility of that love the hope of which gives them the strength to endure so many risks and so much loneliness, since they fall in love with precisely that type of man who has nothing feminine about him, who is not an invert and consequently cannot love them in return; with the result that their desire would be for ever insatiable did not their money procure for them real men, and their imagination end by making them take for real men the inverts to whom they had prostituted themselves. Their honor precarious, their liberty provisional, lasting only until the discovery of their crime; their position unstable like that of the poet who one day was feasted at every table, applauded in every theatre in London, and on the next was driven from every lodging, unable to find a pillow upon which to lay his head, turning the mill like Samson and saying like him: 'The two sexes shall die, each in a place apart!'; excluded even, save on the days of general disaster when the majority rally round the victim as the Jews rallied round Dreyfus, from the sympathy – at times from the society – of their fellows, in whom they inspire only disgust at seeing themselves as they are, portrayed in a mirror which, ceasing to flatter them, accentuates every blemish that they have refused to observe in themselves, and makes them understand that what they have been calling their love (a thing to which, playing upon the word, they have by association annexed all that poetry, painting, music, chivalry, asceticism have contrived to add to love) springs not from an ideal of beauty which they have chosen but from an incurable malady; like the Jews again (save some who will associate only with others of their race and have always on their lips ritual words and consecrated pleasantries), shunning one another, seeking out those who are most directly their opposite, who do not desire their company, pardoning their rebuffs, moved to ecstasy by their condescension; but also brought into the company of their own kind by the ostracism that strikes them, the opprobrium under which they have fallen, having finally been invested, by a persecution similar to that of Israel, with the physical and moral characteristics of a race, sometimes beautiful, often hideous, finding (in spite of all the mockery with which he who, more closely blended with, better assimilated to the opposing race, is relatively, in appearance, the least inverted, heaps upon him who has remained more so) a relief in frequenting the society of their kind, and even some corroboration of their own life, so much so that, while steadfastly denying that they are a race (the name of which is the vilest of insults), those who succeed in concealing the fact that they belong to it they readily unmask, with a view less to injuring them, though they have no scruple about that, than to excusing themselves; and, going in search (as a doctor seeks cases of appendicitis) of cases of inversion in history, taking pleasure in recalling that Socrates was one of themselves, as the Israelites claim that Jesus was one of them, without reflecting that there were no abnormals when homosexuality was the norm, no anti-Christians before Christ, that the disgrace alone makes the crime because it has allowed to survive only those who remained obdurate to every warning, to every example, to every punishment, by virtue of an innate disposition so peculiar that it is more repugnant to other men (even though it may be accompanied by exalted moral qualities) than certain other vices which exclude those qualities, such as theft, cruelty, breach of faith, vices better understood and so more readily excused by the generality of men; forming a freemasonry far more extensive, more powerful and less suspected than that of the Lodges, for it rests upon an identity of tastes, needs, habits, dangers, apprenticeships, knowledge, traffic, glossary, and one in which the members themselves, who intend not to know one another, recognise one another immediately by natural or conventional, involuntary or deliberate signs which indicate one of his congeners to the beggar in the street, in the great nobleman whose carriage door he is shutting, to the father in the suitor for his daughter's hand, to him who has sought healing, absolution, defence, in the doctor, the priest, the barrister to whom he has had recourse; all of them obliged to protect their own secret but having their part in a secret shared with the others, which the rest of humanity does not suspect and which means that to them the most wildly improbable tales of adventure seem true, for in this romantic, anachronistic life the ambassador is a bosom friend of the felon, the prince, with a certain independence of action with which his aristocratic breeding has furnished him, and which the trembling little cit would lack, on leaving the duchess's party goes off to confer in private with the hooligan; a reprobate part of the human whole, but an important part, suspected where it does not exist, flaunting itself, insolent and unpunished, where its existence is never guessed; numbering its adherents everywhere, among the people, in the army, in the church, in the prison, on the throne; living, in short, at least to a great extent, in a playful and perilous intimacy with the men of the other race, provoking them, playing with them by speaking of its vice as of something alien to it; a game that is rendered easy by the blindness or the duplicity of the others, a game that may be kept up for years until the day of the scandal, on which these lion-tamers are devoured; until then, obliged to make a secret of their lives, to turn away their eyes from the things on which they would naturally fasten them, to fasten them upon those from which they would naturally turn away, to change the gender of many of the words in their vocabulary, a social constraint, slight in comparison with the inward constraint which their vice, or what is improperly so called, imposes upon them with regard not so much now to others as to themselves, and in such a way that to themselves it does not appear a vice. But certain among them, more practical, busier men who have not the time to go and drive their own bargains, or to dispense with the simplification of life and that saving of time which may result from co-operation, have formed two societies of which the second is composed exclusively of persons similar to themselves.

This is noticeable in those who are poor and have come up from the country, without friends, with nothing but their ambition to be some day a celebrated doctor or barrister, with a mind still barren of opinions, a person unadorned with manners, which they intend, as soon as possible, to decorate, just as they would buy furniture for their little attic in the Latin quarter, copying whatever they had observed in those who had already 'arrived' in the useful and serious profession in which they also intend to establish themselves and to become famous; in these their special taste, unconsciously inherited like a weakness for drawing, for music, a weakness of vision, is perhaps the only living and despotic originality – which on certain evenings compels them to miss some meeting, advantageous to their career, with people whose ways, in other respects, of speaking, thinking, dressing, parting their hair, they have adopted. In their quarter, where otherwise they mix only with their brother students, their teachers or some fellow provincial who has succeeded and can help them on, they have speedily discovered other young men whom the same peculiar taste attracts to them, as in a small town one sees an intimacy grow up between the assistant master and the lawyer, who are both interested in chamber music or mediaeval ivories; applying to the object of their distraction, the same utilitarian instinct, the same professional spirit which guides them in their career, they meet these young men at gatherings to which no profane outsider is admitted any more than to those that bring together collectors of old snuff-boxes, Japanese prints or rare flowers, and at which, what with the pleasure of gaining information, the practical value of making exchanges and the fear of competition, there prevail simultaneously, as in a sale-room of postage stamps, the close co-operation of the specialists and the fierce rivalries of the collectors. No one moreover in the café where they have their table knows what the gathering is, whether it is that of an angling club, of an editorial staff, or of the 'Sons of the Indre,' so correct is their attire, so cold and reserved their manner, so modestly do they refrain from anything more than the most covert glances at the young men of fashion, the young 'lions' who, a few feet away, are making a great clamour about their mistresses, and among whom those who are admiring them without venturing to raise their eyes will learn only twenty years later, when they themselves are on the eve of admission to the Academy, and the others are middle-aged gentlemen in club windows, that the most seductive among them, now a stout and grizzled Charlus, was in reality akin to themselves, but differently, in another world, beneath other external symbols, with foreign labels, the strangeness of which led them into error. But these groups are at varying stages of evolution; and, just as the 'Union of the Left' differs from the 'Socialist Federation' or some Mendelssohnian musical club from the Schola Cantorum, on certain evenings, at another table, there are extremists who allow a bracelet to slip down from beneath a cuff, sometimes a necklace to gleam in the gap of a collar, who by their persistent stares, their cooings, their laughter, with mutual caresses, oblige a band of students to depart in hot haste, and are served with a civility beneath which indignation boils by a waiter who, as on the evenings when he has to serve Dreyfusards, would find pleasure in summoning the police did he not find profit in pocketing their gratuities . . .

Admittedly, every man of the kind of M. de Charlus is an extraordinary creature since, if he does not make concessions to the possibilities of life, he seeks out essentially the love of a man of the other race, that is to say a man who is a lover of women (and incapable consequently of loving him); in contradiction of what I had imagined in the courtyard, where I had seen Jupien turning towards M. de Charlus like the orchid making overtures to the bee, these exceptional creatures whom we commiserate are a vast crowd, as we shall see in the course of this work, for a reason which will be disclosed only at the end of it, and commiserate themselves for being too many rather than too few. For the two angels who were posted at the gate of Sodom to learn whether its inhabitants (according to Genesis) had indeed done all the things the report of which had ascended to the Eternal Throne must have been, and of this one can only be glad, exceedingly ill chosen by the Lord, Who ought not to have entrusted the task to any but a Sodomite. Such an one the excuses 'Father of six children — I keep two mistresses,' and so forth could never have persuaded benevolently to lower his flaming sword and to mitigate the punishment; he would have answered: 'Yes, and your wife lives in a torment of jealousy. But even when these women have not been chosen by you from Gomorrah, you spend your nights with a watcher of flocks upon Hebron.' And he would at once have made him retrace his steps to the city which the rain of fire and brimstone was to destroy. On the contrary, they allowed to escape all the shame-faced Sodomites, even if these, on catching sight of a boy, turned their heads, like Lot's wife, though without being on that account changed like her into pillars of salt. With the result that they engendered a numerous posterity with whom this gesture has continued to be habitual, like that of the dissolute women who, while apparently studying a row of shoes displayed in a shop window, turn their heads to keep track of a passing student. These descendants of the Sodomites, so numerous that we may apply to them that other verse of Genesis: 'If a man can number the dust of the earth, then shall thy seed also be numbered,' have established themselves throughout the entire world; they have had access to every profession and pass so easily into the most exclusive clubs that, whenever a Sodomite fails to secure election, the black balls are, for the most part, cast by other Sodomites, who are anxious to penalise sodomy, having inherited the falsehood that enabled their ancestors to escape from the accursed city. It is possible that they may return there one day. Certainly they form in every land an Oriental colony, cultured, musical, malicious, which has certain charming qualities and intolerable defects. We shall study them with greater thoroughness in the following pages; but I have thought it as well to utter here a provisional warning against the lamentable error of proposing (just as people have encouraged a Zionist movement) to create a Sodomist movement and to rebuild Sodom. For, no sooner had they arrived there than the Sodomites would leave the town so as not to have the appearance of belonging to it, would take wives, keep mistresses in other cities where they would find, incidentally, every diversion that appealed to them. They would repair to Sodom only on days of supreme necessity, when their own town was empty, at those seasons when hunger drives the wolf from the woods; in other words, everything would go on very much as it does to-day in London, Berlin, Rome, Petrograd or Paris.

Marcel Proust, 'Sodome et Gomorrhe', in *A la recherche du temps perdu*, 1921–22. Translated as 'Cities of the Plain' by C.K. Scott Moncrieff. London, Alfred Knopf, 1929.

The Talmud

Now, in these days Sodom and four other cities were inhabited by men of evil actions, who provoked the anger and indignation of the Most High. They planted in the valley a beautiful garden many miles in extent, a place adorned with fruits and flowers, and objects pleasing to the sight and intoxicating to the senses. Thither the people flocked four times a year with music and with dancing, indulging in all sorts of excesses and acts of idolatrous worship, with none to utter a word of warning or rebuke.

In their daily life they were both cruel and treacherous, oppressing the stranger and taking advantage of all persons thrown in contact with them. If a trader entered their city they would seize his goods either with violence or through trickery, and if he remonstrated they but mocked him and drove him from the place.

It happened once that a man from Elam, journeying to a place beyond Sodom, reached this latter city even as the sun was setting. He had with him an ass bearing a valuable saddle to which some rare and precious merchandise was attached. Unable to find a lodging for himself and stabling for the animal, he resolved to pass the night in the streets of Sodom, and journey on in the morning. A certain citizen of Sodom, named Hidud, chanced to observe this stranger, and being cunning and treacherous, he accosted him, saying,

'Whence comest thou, and whither art thou travelling?'

'I am journeying from Hebron,' replied the stranger; 'my destination is beyond this place; but lo, the sun has set; I can obtain no lodging, and so I remain here in the streets. I have bread and water for myself and straw and provender for my beast, so I need not be under any obligation to anybody.'

'Nay, this is wrong,' returned Hidud, 'come pass the night with me, thy lodging shall cost thee naught, and I will attend also to the wants of thy animal.'

Hidud led the stranger to his house. He removed the valuable saddle from the ass, and the merchandise which was attached to it he also removed, placing them in the closet in his house, then he gave the ass provender and set meat and drink before the stranger, who partook of the meal, and lodged that night with him.

In the morning the stranger rose up early intending to pursue his journey, but Hidud said to him, 'Take first thy morning meal, then go thy way.'

After the man had eaten he rose to go on his way, but Hidud stopped him, saying, 'It is late in the day, remain I pray thee, bide with me yet this day and then depart.'

The stranger remained in Hidud's house until the following morning and then, declining another pressing invitation to remain one day more, he prepared for his depature.

Then said Hidud's wife,

'This man has lived with us two days and paid us naught.' But Hidud answered,

'Keep thy peace.'

He then brought forth the stranger's ass, and bade him 'fare thee well.'

'Hold,' said the stranger, 'my saddle, the spread of many colors, and the strings attached to it, together with my merchandise, where are they?'

'What!' exclaimed Hidud.

'I gave thee,' returned the stranger, 'a beautiful spread with strings attached; thou hast hidden it in thy house.' 'Ah!' said Hidud pleasantly, 'I will interpret thy dream. That thou hast dreamed of strings, signifies that thy days will be prolonged even as strings may be stretched from end to end; that thou hast dreamed of a spread of many colors signifieth that thou wilt one day possess a garden rich in flowers and luscious fruits.'

The stranger answered,

'No, my lord, I dreamed not; I gave to thee a spread of many colors with strings attached, and thou hast hidden it in thy house.'

And Hidud said,

'And I have interpreted thy dream; I have told thee its meaning, 'tis useless to repeat it. For the interpretation of a dream people generally pay me four pieces of silver, but as for thee, behold I will ask of thee only three.'

The stranger was very angry at this outrageous conduct, and he accused Hidud in the court of Sodom of stealing his goods. Then when each man told his story, the judge said,

'Hidud speaks the truth; he is an interpreter of dreams; he is well known as such.'

And Hidud said to the stranger,

'And as thou art such a liar, thou must even pay me the full price, four pieces of silver, as well as for the four meals eaten in my house.'

'Willingly will I pay thee for thy meals,' replied the other, 'if thou wilt but return my saddle and my goods.'

Then the two men wrangled with angry words, and they were driven forth from the court-house, and the men in the streets joined on Hidud's side, and they fought the stranger and thrust him forth from the city, robbed of all his possessions.

When a poor man entered the city of Sodom the people would give him money in order to save a reputation for charity, but they made an agreement among themselves that no one should either give or sell him food, or allow him to depart from the city. The man would consequently die of starvation, and the people would then regain the money they had given him. They would even rob the body of the rags which covered it, and bury it naked in the wilderness.

Upon one occasion Sarai sent her servant Eleazer to Sodom to inquire concerning the welfare of Lot and his family. As he entered the city, Eleazer observed a Sodomite fighting with a stranger whom he had defrauded, and who, running to Eleazer, implored him for assistance. 'What art thou doing to this poor man?' said Eleazer to the Sodomite; 'shame upon thee to act in this manner towards a stranger in your midst!'

And the Sodomite replied,

'Is he thy brother? What is our quarrel to thee?' and picking up a stone, he struck Eleazer with it on the forehead causing his blood to flow freely in the street. When the Sodomite saw the blood, he caught hold of Eleazer, crying,

'Pay me my fee as a leech; see, I have freed thee of this impure blood; pay me quickly, for such is our law.'

'What!' exclaimed Eleazer, 'thou has wounded me and I am to pay thee for it!'

This Eleazer refused to do, and the Sodomite had him brought into the court, and there before the judge reiterated his demand for a fee.

'Thou must pay the man his fee,' said the judge, addressing Eleazer, 'he has let thy blood, and such is our law.'

Eleazer paid the money, and then lifting up the stone he struck the judge heavily with it, and the blood spurted out in a long stream. 'There!' exclaimed Eleazer, 'follow thy law and pay my fee to this man; I want not the money,' and he left the court-house.

At another time a certain poor man entered Sodom, and as everybody refused to give him food, he was very nearly starved to death when Lot's daughter chanced to meet him. For many days she supported him, carrying him bread whenever she went to draw water for her father. The people of the city, seeing the poor man still living, wondered greatly as to how he managed to support life without food, and three men constituted themselves a committee to watch his goings and his doings. They saw Lot's daughter giving him bread, and seizing her they carried her before the judges, who condemned her to death by burning, and this punishment was inflicted on her.

Another maiden, who assisted a poor stranger, was smeared with honey, and left to be stung to death by bees.

For such acts were Sodom and her sister cities destroyed by fire from Heaven, and only Lot and his family spared through God's love for his servant Abram.

From *Selections from The Talmud: Being Specimens of the Contents of that Ancient Book, Its Commentaries, Teachings, Poetry and Legends.* Translated from the original by H. Polano. Philadelphia, published by Claxton, Remsen & Haffelfinger, 1876.

TWELFTH CENTURY, ANON.

A perverse custom it is . . .

A perverse custom it is to prefer boys to girls,
Since this type of love rebels against nature.
The wildness of beasts despises and flees this passion.
No male animal submits to another.
Animals curse and avoid evil caresses,
While man, more bestial than they, approves and pursues such things.
The irrational obeys reason's law;
The rational strays far from reason.
When the Lord blessed the first parents on earth,
He ordered them to be fruitful, to farm and fill the earth.
They were not both created men but a man and a woman,
And thus multiplied, filling the earth.
If both had been men and had favored this passion,
They would have died out without posterity.
Although he hates all vices, God despises this one particularly:
Of which – if you are doubtful – the destruction of Sodom is proof,
Where we read that sulfur and fire annihilated
The residents of Sodom and that an evil people perished with fit
    penalties.
Those who follow this heresy had better reconsider now
Or face condemnation to flames and sulfur.
Let them perish and go to hell, never to return,
Who wish to have tender youths as spouses.

Translated by John Boswell in *Christianity, Social Tolerance and Homosexuality: Gay People in Western Europe from the Beginning of the Christian Era to the Fourteenth Century.* Chicago and London, University of Chicago Press, 1980.

DI' BIL IBN 'ALI

The Sodomites of Baghdad

[I]

Sometimes he uses the arrow of Ali,
Sometimes he uses the quiver of 'Amr.

[II]

Abu Sad, the notorious:
A cock up his ass. How snug!
He sucks it. How sweet!
He smells it. How fragrant!
His ass is a perch for the falcon,
a saddle for the horseman.

[III]

Abu Sad, with weakness of soul,
allows snakes up his asshole.
Farmers plant their cucumbers
up his ass in large numbers.

[IV]

All men dip their pens in the inkwell
of Huwayy ibn Amr As-Siksiki.

[V]

Others boast of their glorious deeds.
Khuzaah boasts about having used his
needle to mend certain holes.

Di' Bil Ibn 'Ali (AD 765–860), 'The Sodomites of Baghdad'. Translated by
Stephen W. Foster.

NED WARD

The Mollies

THERE are a particular Gang of *Sodomitical* Wretches in this Town, who call themselves the *Mollies*, and are so far degenerated from all masculine Deportment, or manly Exercises, that they rather fancy themselves Women, imitating all the little Vanities that custom has reconcir'd to the female Sex, affecting to speak, walk, tattle, courtesy, cry, scold, and to mimick all manner of Effeminacy, that ever has fallen within their several Observations; not omitting the Indecencies of lewd Women, that they may tempt one another, by such immodest Freedoms, to commit those odious Bestialities, that ought for ever to be without a Name. At a certain Tavern in the City, whose sign I shall not mention, because I am unwilling to fix an Odium upon the House, where they have settled a constant Meeting every evening in the Week, that they may have the better Opportunity of drawing unwary Youth into the like Corruption. When they are met together, it is their usual Practice to mimick a female Gossiping, and fall into all the impertinent Tittle-Tattle, that a merry Society of good Wives can be subject to, when they have laid aside their Modesty for the delights of the Bottle. Not long since, upon one of their Festival Nights, they had cushion'd up the Belly of one of their *Sodomitical* brethren, or rather Sisters, as they commonly called themselves, disguising him in a Woman's Night-Gown, Sarsnet-Hood, and Nightrale, who, when the Company were met, was to mimick the wry Faces of a groaning Woman, to be deliver'd of a joynted Baby they had provided for that Purpose, and to undergo all the formalities of a Lying-in. The wooden Off-Spring to be afterwards christen'd, and the holy Sacrament of Baptism to be impudently profan'd, for the Diversion of the Profligates, who, when their infamous Society were assembled in a Body, put their wicked Contrivance accordingly into practice.

One in a high crown'd Hat, and an old Bedlams Pinner representing a Country Midwife, another busy Ape, dizen'd up in a Hussife's Colf, taking upon himself the Duty of a very officious Nurse, and the rest as Gossips, apply'd themselves to the travelling woman, according to the Midwife's direction, all being as intent upon the Business in Hand, as if they had been Women, the Occasion real, and their Attendance necessary. After Abundance of Bustle and that they had ridiculously counterfeited all the Difficulties that they fancy'd were customary in such Cases, their Buffoonary Maukin was at length disburthen'd of her little jointed Bastard, and then putting their shotten Impostor to bed upon a double Row of Chairs; the Baby was drest by the Midwife; the Father brought to compliment his New-born Son, the Parson sent for; the Gossips appointed; the Child christen'd, and then the Cloth was spread; the Table furnished with cold Tongues and Chickens; the Guests invited to sit down, and much Joy expressed that my Gammar *Molly* had brought her honest Gaffer a Son and Heir to Town, so very like him, that as soon as born, had the Eyes, Nose, and Mouth of its own credulous Daddy. Now for the further Promotion of their unbecoming Mirth, everyone was to tattle about their Husbands and Children: And to use no other Dialect but what Gossips are wont to do upon such loquacious Occasions. One would up with a story of her little *Tommy*, to show the promising Genius of so witty a Child, that if he let but a Fizzle, would perfectly cry out, *Mammy how I tink*. Another would be extolling the Vertues of her Husband, and declare he was a Man of that affable, kind, and easy Temper, and so avers'd to Jealousy, that she believed, were he to see another Man in Bed with her he would be so far from thinking her an ill Woman, that no-body should perswade him they had been naught together. A third would be telling what a forward Baggage her Daughter *Nancy* was; for though she was but just turn'd of her seventh Year, yet the young Jade had the Confidence to ask her Father 'Where Girls carry'd their Maidenheads that they were so apt to loose them?' A fourth would be wishing no Woman to marry a drunken Husband, for her Sake; for all the Satisfaction that she found in Bed with him, was to creep as close to the Wall as she could to avoid his Tobacco breath and unsavory Belches, swearing that his son *Roger* was just like him, for that the guzling Rogue would drink a Pint of Strong Ale at a Draught before he was three Years old, and would cry *Mam, more Ale*. A fifth would sit sighing at her ill Fortune, and wishing her Husband would follow the steps of his Journeyman; for that was as careful a young Fellow as ever came into a Family. A sixth would express himself sorrowfully under the Character of a Widow; saying, 'Alas, you have all Husbands, and ought to pray heartily that you never know the Miss of them; for though I had but a sorry one, when I was in your Condition, yet, God help me, I have cause enough to repent my Loss; for I am sure, both Day and Night, I find the Want of him.' Thus every one in his turn, would make a Scoff and Banter of the little effeminate Weaknesses which Women are subject to when gossiping o'er their Cups, on purpose to extinguish that natural Affection which is due to the fair Sex, and to turn their juvenile Desires towards preternatural Pollutions. No sooner had they ended their Feast, and run through all the Ceremonies of their theatrical Way of Gossiping, but having wash'd away with Wine, all fear of Shame, as well as the checks of Modesty, then they began to enter upon their beastly Obscenities, and to take those infamous Liberties with one another, that no Man who is not sunk into a state of Devilism, can think on without Blushing, or mention without a Christian Abhorrence of all such heathenish Brutalities. Thus, without Detection, they continu'd in their odious Society for some Years, till their sodomitical Practices were happily discover'd by the cunning Management of some of the under Agents to the reforming Society; so that several were brought to open Shame and Punishment; others flying from Justice to escape the Ignominy, that by this Means the Diabolical Society were forc'd to put a Period to their filthy scandalous Revels.

> Tis strange, that in a Country, where
> Our Ladies are so kind and fair,
> So gay and lovely to the sight,
> So full of Beauty and Delight;
> That men should on each other doat,
> And quit the charming Petticoat:
> Sure the curs'd Father of this Race,
> That does both Sexes thus disgrace,
> Must be a Master, mad or drunk,
> Who bedding some prepost'rous Punk,
> Mistook the downy Seat of Love,
> And got them in the Sink above;
> So that at first a T--d and They
> Were born the very self-same Way;
> From whence they drew this cursed Itch,
> Not to the Belly, but the Breech;
> Else who could Woman's Charms refuse,
> To such a beastly Practice use?
> 'Tis true that Swine on Dunghills bred,
> Nurs'd up in Filth, with Offel fed,

Have oft the flow'ry Meads forsook,
To wallow Belly-deep in Muck;
But Men who chuse this backward Way,
Are fifty times worse Swine than they;
For the less Savage four-leg'd Creature,
Lives but according to his Nature;
But the *Bug'ranto* two-leg'd Brute,
Pursues his Lust contrary to't;
The brawny Boar will love his Sow;
The Horse his Mare; the Bull his Cow;
But *Sodomites* their Wives forsake,
Unmanly Liberties to take;
And fall in Love with one another,
As if no Woman was their Mother:
For he that is of Woman born,
Will to her Arms again return;
And surely never chuse to play
His lustful Game the backward Way:
But since it has appear'd too plain,
There are such Brutes that pass for Men;
May he that on the Rump so doats,
Be damn'd as deep as Doctor *Oates*,
That Scandal unto all black Coats.

From Ned Ward, *A Compleat and Humorous Account of all the Remarkable Clubs and Societies In The Cities of London and Westminster From the R---l-S---y down to the Lumber-Troop, &c.* Their Original with Characters of the most noted Members, containing great Variety of entertaining Discourses, Frolicks, and Adventures of the principal Managers and Members, a Work of great Use and Curiosity. Compil'd from the original Papers of a Gentleman who frequented those Places upwards of Twenty Years. The Seventh Edition (2nd. Edition – 1710) London Printed for WREN, at the *Bible and Crown*, in the Salisbury-Court, Fleet Street, 1756. (Price Sew'd Two Shillings, Bound 2s. 6d.)

The Phoenix of Sodom

The Phoenix of Sodom, or *The Vere Street Coterie* . . . is written by a lawyer, who signs himself HOLLOWAY . . . it is in defence of, and for the benefit of James Cook, landlord of the White Swan Public House in Vere Street, Clare Market, where the Sodomitical Club assembled. Cook had been fleeced whilst in Newgate by an attorney named WOOLEY, under pretence of 'bringing him through,' and had, as Holloway opined, been in many other ways oppressed . . . It appears that Cook had not been guilty of the capital offence, his crime being limited to his keeping a house for the purpose. He offered, in the hope of mitigating his punishment, to divulge the names of the noble and wealthy frequenters of his house, but this only incensed the ministers the more, and he was ordered to the pillory forthwith. That Cook's revelation, had it been permitted, would have compromised many men of position, there can be no doubt, 'for there is scarcely any description of men, but some individual is comprehended in the associates of this vice; even men in the sacerdotal garb have descended from the pulpit to the gulley-hole of breathing infamy in Vere-street, and other places for similar vice:' &c . . .

The fatal house in question was furnished in a style most appropriate for the purposes it was intended. Four beds were provided in one room: − another was fitted up for the ladies' dressing room, with a toilette, and every appendage of rouge, &c. &c.; − a third room was called the Chaple, (sic) where marriages took place, sometimes between a *female grenadier*, six feet high, and a petite maître not more than half the altitude of his beloved wife! These marriages were solemnised with all the mockery of *bride maids* and *bride men*; and the nuptials were frequently consummated by two, three, or four couple, in the same room, and in the sight of each other!

Incredible as this circumstance may appear, the reader may depend it is all provable: − the upper part of the house was appropriated to wretches who were constantly in waiting for casual customers; who practised all the allurements that are found in a brothel, by the more

115

natural description of prostitutes; and the only difference consisting in that want of decency that subsists between the most profligate men and depraved women. – Men of rank, and respectable situations in life, might be seen wallowing either in or on the beds with wretches of the lowest description: but the perpetration of the abominable act, however offensive, was infinitely more tolerable than the shocking conversation that accompanied the perpetration; some of which, Cook has solemnly declared to me, was so odious, that he could not either write, or verbally relate. It seems many of these wretches are married; and frequently, when they are together, make their wives, who (sic) they call *Tommies*, topics of ridicule; and boast of having compelled them to act parts too shocking to think of . . .

It seems the greater part of these reptiles assume feigned names, though not very appropriate to their calling in life: for instance Kitty Cambric is a Coal Merchant; Miss Selina a Runner at a Police office; Black-eyed Leonora, a Drummer; Pretty Harriet, a Butcher; Lady Godina, (sic) a Waiter; the Duchess of Gloucester, a gentleman's servant; Duchess of Devonshire, a Blacksmith; and Miss Sweet Lips, a Country Grocer. It is a generally received opinion, and a very natural one, that the prevalency of this passion has for its object effeminate delicate beings only: but this seems to be, by Cook's account, a mistaken notion; and the reverse is so palpable in many instances, that Fanny Murray, Lucy Cooper, and Kitty Fisher, are now personified by an athletic Bargeman, an Herculean Coal-heaver, and a deaf tyre Smith: the latter of these monsters has two sons, both very handsome young men, whom he boasts are full as depraved as himself. These are merely part of the common stock belonging to the house; but the visitors were more numerous, and, if possible, more infamous, because more exalted in life: and *these ladies*, like the ladies of the petticoat order, have their favourite men; one of whom was White, a drummer of the guards, who, some short time since, was executed for a crime of the most detestable description with Hebden an ensign. White, being an universal favourite, was very deep in the secrets of the fashionable part of the coterie; of which he made a most ample confession in writing, immediately previous to his execution; the truth of which he averred, even to his last moments; but it is impossible to give it literally, for the person who took it, in the presence of a magistrate, said that the recital made him so sick he could not proceed . . .

That the reader may form some idea of the uncontrollable rage of this dreadful passion, Cook states, that a person in a respectable house in the city, frequently came to this sink of filth and iniquity, and stayed several days and nights together; during which time he generally amused himself with eight, ten and sometimes a dozen different boys and men! . . .

Sunday was the general, and grand day of rendezvous! and to render their excuse the more entangled and doubtful, some of the parties came a great distance, even so much as thirty miles, to join the festivity and elegant amusements of grenadiers, footmen, waiters, drummers, and all the Catamite brood, kneaded into human shape, *from the sweepings of Sodom, with the spawn of Gomorrah* . . .

The existence of such a club could not be kept entirely secret, the Bow-street magistrates had their suspicions some time before its actual dissolution in July 1810. In a journal of the time we read: 'About 11 o'clock last Sunday evening, three separate parties of the patrole, attended by constables, were detached from Bow-street upon this service; and such was the secrecy observed, that the object of their pursuit was unknown, even at that moment, to all but the confidential agents of Mr. Read, who headed the respective parties. The enterprize was completely successful.'

Twenty three individuals were captured, and taken to the watch-house of St. Clement's Danes; whence they were 'conveyed in hackney-coaches, between ten and eleven on Monday, to Bow-street for examination,' amidst an 'enraged multitude, the majority of whom were females,' and who were so violent that 'it was with the utmost difficulty the prisoners could be saved from destruction.'

At the Middlesex Sessions, Clerkenwell, on Saturday 22nd September following, seven of these men, viz., William Amos, alias Sally Fox; James Cooke, the landlord; Phillip Kett, William Thomson, Richard Francis, James Done, and Robert Aspinal were tried, and all found guilty. Amos, having been twice before convicted of similar offences, was sentenced to three years' imprisonment, and to stand once in the pillory in the Haymarket, opposite Panton Street; Aspinal, as not having appeared so active as the others, to one year's imprisonment; and the rest were each sentenced to two years' imprisonment, and the pillory in the same place.

The treatment they experienced at the hands of the mob whilst they were in the pillory was most brutal; the following account of it I extract from a newspaper of the time:

'The disgust felt by all ranks in Society at the detestable conduct of these wretches occasioned many thousands to become spectators of their punishment. At an early hour the Old Bailey was completely blockaded, and the increase of the mob about 12 o'clock, put a stop to the business of the Sessions. The shops from Ludgate-Hill to the Haymarket were shut up, and the streets lined with people, waiting to see the offenders pass . . .

Shortly after twelve, the *ammunition waggons* from the neighbouring markets appeared in motion. These consisted of a number of carts which were driven by butchers' boys, who had previously taken care to fill them with the offal, dung &c. appertaining to their several slaughter-houses. A number of hucksters were also put in requisition, who carried on their heads baskets of apples, potatoes, turnips, cabbage-stalks and other vegetables, together with the remains of divers dogs and cats. The whole of these were sold to the populace at a high price, who spared no expence to provide themselves with the necessary articles of assault.

A number of fishwomen attended with stinking flounders and the entrails of other fish which had been in preparation for several days. These articles, however, were not to be sold, as their proprietors, hearty in the cause, declared they wanted them "for their own use."

About half-past 12 the Sheriffs and the City Marshals arrived with more than 100 Constables mounted and armed with pistols, and 100 on foot. This force was ordered to rendezvous in the Old Bailey Yard, where a caravan, used occasionally for conveying prisoners from the gaols of London to the Hulks, waited to receive the culprits. The caravan was drawn by two shaft horses, led by two men, armed with a brace of pistols. The gates of the Old Bailey Yard were shut, and all strangers turned out. The miscreants were then brought out, and all placed in the caravan. Amos began a laugh, which induced his vile companions to reprove him, and they all sat upright, apparently in a composed state, but having cast their eyes upwards, the sight of the spectators on the tops of the houses operated strongly on their fears, and they soon appeared to feel terror and dismay. At the instant the church clock went half-past twelve, the gates were thrown open. The mob at the same time attempted to force their way in, but they were repulsed. A grand sortie of the police was then made. About 60 officers, armed and mounted as before described, went forward with the City Marshals. The caravan went next, followed by about 40 officers and the Sheriffs. The first salute received by the offenders was a volley of mud, and a serenade of hisses, hooting and execration, which compelled them to fall flat on their faces in the caravan. The mob, and particularly the women, had piled up balls of mud to afford the objects of their indignation a warm reception. The depots in many places appeared like pyramids of shot in a gun wharf. These were soon exhausted, and when the caravan passed the old house which once belonged to the notorious Jonathan Wild, the prisoners resembled bears dipped in a stagnant pool. The shower of mud continued during their passage to the Haymarket. Before they reached half way to the scene of their exposure, they were not discernible as human beings. If they had had much further to go, the cart would have been absolutely filled over them. The one who sat rather aloof from the rest, was the landlord of the house, a fellow of a stout bulky figure, who could not stow himself away as easily as the others, who were slighter; he was therefore, as well on account of his being known, attacked with double fury. Dead cats and dogs, offal, potatoes, turnips &c. rebounded from him on every side; while his apparently manly appearance drew down peculiar execrations on him, and nothing but the motion of the cart prevented his being killed on the spot. At one o'clock four of them were exalted on a new pillory, made purposely for their accommodation. The remaining two, Cooke and Amos, were honoured by being allowed to enjoy a triumph in the pillory alone. They were accordingly taken back in the caravan to St. Martin's watch-house. Before any of them reached the place of punishment, their faces were completely disfigured by blows and mud; and before they mounted, their whole persons appeared one heap of filth. Upwards of 50 women were permitted to stand in the ring, who assailed them incessantly with mud, dead cats, rotten eggs, potatoes, and buckets filled with blood, offal, and dung, which were brought by a number of butchers' men from St. James's Market. These criminals were very roughly handled; but as there were four of them, they did not suffer so much as a less number might. When the hour was expired, they were again put in the cart, and conveyed to Cold Bath Fields Prison, through St. Martin's-lane, Compton-street, and Holborn, and in their journey received similar salutes to what they met with in their way from Newgate. When they were taken from the stand, the butchers' men, and the women, who had been so active, were plentifully regaled with gin and beer, procured from a subscription made upon the spot. In a few minutes, the remaining two, Cook, (who had been the landlord) and Amos, alias Fox, were desired to mount. Cook held his hand to his head, and complained of the blows he had already received; and Amos made the same complaint, and shewed a large brick-bat, which had struck him in the face. The Under Sheriff told them that the sentence must be executed, and they reluctantly mounted. Cook said nothing; but Amos seeing the preparations that were making, declared in the most solemn manner that he was innocent; but it was vociferated from all quarters that he had been convicted before, and in one minute they appeared a complete heap of mud, and their faces were much more battered than those of the former four. Cook received several hits in his face, and he had a lump raised upon his eye-brow as large as an egg. Amos's two eyes were completely closed up; and when they were untied, Cook appeared almost insensible, and it was necessary to help them both down and into the cart, when they were conveyed to Newgate by the same road they had come, and in their passage they continued to receive the same salutations the spectators had given them in going out. Cook continued to lie upon the seat in the cart, but Amos lay down among the filth, till their entrance into Newgate sheltered the wretches from the further indignation of the most enraged populace we ever saw. As they passed the end of Catherine-street, Strand, on their return, a coachman stood upon his box, and gave Cook five or six cuts with his whip.

'It is impossible for language to convey an adequate idea of the universal expressions of execration which accompanied these monsters on their journey; it was fortunate for them that the weather was dry, had it been otherwise they would have been smothered. From the moment the cart was in motion, the fury of the mob began to display itself in showers of mud and filth of every kind. Before the cart reached Temple-bar, the wretches were so thickly covered with filth, that a vestige of the human figure was scarcely discernible. They were chained, and placed in such a manner that they could not lie down in the cart, and could only hide and shelter their heads from the storm by stooping. This, however, could afford but little protection. Some of them were cut in the head with brickbats, and bled profusely. The streets, as they passed, resounded with the universal shouts and execrations of the populace.'

The practice of sodomy in England was not confined to London, or to the votaries in the Vere Street Coterie; very numerous were the convictions about the same time for that and similar offences. The crime seems to have taken root in England already a century earlier. In *Satan's Harvest Home* printed in 1749, we read: 'Till of late Years, Sodomy was a Sin, in a manner unheard of in these Nations; and indeed, one would think where there are such Angelic Women, so foul a sin should should never enter into Imagination: On the contrary, our Sessions-Papers are frequently stain'd with the Crimes of these beastly Wretches; and tho' many have been made Examples of, yet we have but too much Reason to fear, that there are Numbers yet undiscover'd, and that this abominable Practice gets Ground ev'ry Day.' The author of *The Phoenix of Sodom* further informs us that: 'About five and twenty years ago, there existed a society of the same order with the Vere-street gang, in the City of Exeter, most of whom were men of rank and local situation; they were apprehended, and about fifteen of them tried; and though they were acquitted by the letter of the law, the enraged multitude was so convinced of their guilt, that, without any respect to their rank, they burnt them in effigy.

'About the same period, another disgraceful scene was exhibited in London, at Clement's-lane, near the new Church in the Strand; this scene was, if possible, more ridiculously wicked; for though it embraced all the turpitude of the Vere street Coterie, yet the public indignation was in some measure for the moment allayed, by the grotesque appearance of the actors: – they were seized in the very act of giving caudle to their *lying-in women*, and the new-born infants personated by large dolls! and so well did they perform the characters they assumed, that one miscreant escaped the vigilance of the officers and the examining magistrates, and was discharged as a woman!'

From the extensive bibliographical entry on *The Phoenix of Sodom, or the Vere Street Coterie*: Being an Exhibition of the Gambols Practised by the Ancient Lechers of Sodom and Gomorrah, embellished and improved with Modern Refinements in Sodomitical Practices, by members of the Vere Street Coterie, of detestable memory. Sold by J. COOK . . . and to be had at all the booksellers. 1813. HOLLOWAY, Printer, Artillery Lane, Tooley Street. Quoted in Pisanus Fraxi (Henry Spencer Ashbee), *Index Librorum Prohibitorum* (Bibliography of Prohibited Books), vol. 1, London, 1877.

Ashbee notes that Ensign John Newball Hepburn (not Hebden) and Thomas

White were convicted at the Old Bailey, in December 1810, for an unnatural crime committed on the 27th of the previous May, at the White Swan in Vere Street, found guilty, and both sentenced to death.

The Four Wise Men

With passionate interest, Taor observed the men, women and children about him – all Sodomites, secret inhabitants, – unless their neighbors merely disregarded them by virtue of a tacit agreement – of the accursed city, survivors of a population which the fire of heaven had exterminated a thousand years before. 'This race,' he thought, 'must be indestructible, if God himself was unable to destroy them.' He searched their faces and forms for the distinguishing marks of the Sodomite race. Their leanness and air of strength made them seem tall, though they were hardly above middle height. Even in the women and children neither bloom nor tenderness was discernible; their bodies seemed hard and weightless, and their facial expression, suggesting instant readiness to utter sarcasms, had a certain charm but also inspired fear. 'The Devil's beauty,' Taor thought, for he did not forget that this was a minority, condemned and hated for their customs. But their whole mien and bearing made it clear that they were resolutely committed to their way of life. Their attitude was free from provocation, but not without pride . . .

Indeed, the former Prince of Sweets found nothing more invigorating than the spectacle of these men and women, who were not the salt of the earth because, as they themselves said, there was no earth in Sodom, but the salt of the salt. Not that he felt unreserved sympathy for these damned souls with their abrasive spirit of negation and derision, their inveterate skepticism and deliberate arrogance. They were too patently prisoners of their age-old attitude of disparagement and denigration, which they respected scrupulously as their only tribal law.

For a time Taor was attached to the service of a couple who lived on a grand scale and whose dinners were attended by the most brilliant and caustic personalities of Sodom. Their names were Semazar and Amraphelle. Though husband and wife, they looked as much alike as brother and sister, with their lashless eyes and unblinking lids, their insolent upturned noses, thin, sinuous, sneering lips, and the two bitter wrinkles that scarred their cheeks. Faces, aspark with intelligence, which always smiled and did not know how to laugh. A harmonious couple, no doubt, but after the manner of Sodom, and an uninformed observer would have been surprised at the atmosphere of vigilant malice they maintained between them. With the instinct of an unerring marksman each was constantly on the lookout for the other's weak spot, which once detected became the target for a cloud of poisoned darts. Relations among Sodomites were governed by the unwritten law that the greater their love the more cruelly they tormented one another. Indulgence meant indifference, benevolence contempt.

Taor moved like a shadow through these enormous, hermetically sealed rooms, where the Sodomites banqueted all night. Toxic-colored liquors distilled in the Asphalt Lake laboratories fired imaginations, swelled voices, encouraged cynical gestures. Abominable things were said and done; Taor couldn't help witnessing them, but he did not take part. He understood that Sodomite civilization was rooted in three closely related factors: salt, the telluric depression, and a certain erotic practice. As for the salt mines and their bassitude, Taor had experienced them in his body and soul for so many years that the day would soon be at hand – if it were not already – when he would have lived longer in this hell than anywhere else. That sufficed no doubt to give him a certain abstract, intellectual understanding of the Sodomite spirit. He remembered how, when taking his first steps into the city, he had observed that the usual relief, the elevations usually seen in a city, were replaced by projected shadows. Thrown into the subterranean life of this city, he had later come to realize that the elevations profiled by these shadows had not only been flattened beneath Yahweh's foot, but had also been turned about, converted into negative values. Thus every elevation was inverted into a similar but diametrically opposite depression. And this inversion had its equivalent in the Sodomitic spirit, which saw all things as black angular, trenchant shadows, plunging to vertiginous depths. In the Sodomitic view all elevated vision was converted into fundamental analysis, all ascendance into penetration, all theology into ontology, and the joy of acceding to the light of intelligence was frozen by the angst of the nocturnal re-searcher, who excavates the foundations of being.

But Taor's understanding went no further, and he was well aware that the two elements of Sodomitic civilization known to him – salt and telluric depression – would have been no more than unrelated accidents, had Eros not enveloped them in its carnal warmth and density. There could be no doubt that, for want of being born in Sodom and of Sodomite parents, that sort of love would always inspire him with instinctive horror, and that the admiration he could not deny these people would always be mingled with pity and revulsion.

And so he listened attentively as they glorified their loves, but he lacked the sympathy without which such things cannot be fully understood. They rejoiced at having escaped the horrible mutilation of the eyes, sex, and heart – symbolized by circumcision – which the law of Yahweh inflicts on his people to make them unfit for all sexual activity apart from procreation. They had nothing but irony for the fanatical procreationism of other Jews, which leads inevitably to all manner of crime, ranging from abortion to the abandonment of children. They recalled the infamy of Lot, the Sodomite who had repudiated his native place and opted for Yahweh, only to be made drunk and raped by his own daughters later on. They rejoiced in the sterile desert where they lived, in its crystalline substance with its geometrical forms, and in the pure, fully assimilated food they ate, thanks to which their intestines, instead of functioning like sewers clogged with filth, were hollow columns, the props and centers of their bodies. According to them, the two 'o's of Sodom, like those of Gomorrah, but in a different sense, signified the two opposing sphincters – oral and anal – of the human body, the alpha and omega of life, which communicate with each other, echo and call out of each other from end to end of man, and the sexual act of the Sodomites is the only fit response to this great and somber tropism. They also said that in sodomy the sexual act, instead of being confined to a cul-de-sac, is hooked up to the intestinal labyrinth, irrigates every gland, stimulates every nerve, stirs every entrail, and finally discharges full in the face, so transforming the whole body into an organic trumpet, a visceral tuba, a mucous ophicleide, with infinitely ramified coils and volutes. All this was not quite clear to Taor, but he understood the Sodomites better when he heard them say that sodomy, instead of subordinating sex to the propagation of the species, exalts it by directing it into the royal road of the digestive system.

Because sodomy respects the virginity of young girls and does not threaten wives with the dangers of childbearing, it enjoyed special favor with the women and formed the basis of a veritable matriarchy. Indeed, the entire population worshipped a woman – Lot's wife – as their tutelary deity.

Tipped off by two angels that the fire of heaven was about to descend on the city, Lot betrayed his fellow citizens and fled in time with his wife and two daughters. They were forbidden to look behind them. Lot and his daughters obeyed. But his wife could not restrain herself from looking back to bid a last good-bye to her beloved city, which was perishing in the flames. Her tender gesture was not forgiven – Yahweh turned the poor woman into a pillar of salt.

On their national holiday, the Sodomites celebrated her martyrdom by gathering around the statue, which for the last thousand years had been fleeing from Sodom, but so reluctantly that a torsion of her whole body made her face the city – a magnificent symbol of courage and fidelity. The people sang hymns, danced, copulated 'in the good old-fashioned way' around the Salt Mother, as she was affectionately termed – and covered this impetuous yet motionless woman, enveloped in the hard spiral of her petrified veils, with all the flowers the country had to offer: desert roses, fossil anemones, quartz violets, and sprays of gypsum.

From Michel Tournier, *The Four Wise Men*, translated by Ralph Manheim. London, Collins, 1982.

Satan's Harvest Home, 1749

I am confident no Age can produce any Thing so preposterous as the present Dress of those Gentlemen who call themselves pretty Fellows: their Head-Dress especially, which wants nothing but a Suit of Pinners to make them down right Women. But this may be easily accounted for, as they would appear as soft as possible to each other, any Thing of *Manliness* being diametrically opposite to such unnatural Practices, so they cannot too much invade the Dress of the Sex they would represent. And yet with all this, the present Garb of our young Gentlemen is most mean and unbecoming. 'Tis a difficulty to know a Gentleman from a Footman, by their present Habits: The low-heel'd Pump is an Emblem of their low Spirits; the great Harness Buckle is the Height of Affectation; the Silk Waistcoat all belac'd, with a scurvey blue Coat like a Livery Frock, has something so poorly preposterous, it quite enrages me; I blush to see 'em aping the Running Footman, and poising a great Oaken Plant, fitter for a Bailiff's Follower than a Gentleman. But what renders all more intolerable, is the Hair strok'd over before and cock'd up behind, with a *Comb* sticking in it, as if it were just ready to receive a Head Dress: Nay, I am told, some of our Tip top Beaus dress their Heads on quilted *Hair Caps*, to make 'em look more *Womanish*; so that Master *Molly* has nothing to do but slip on his *Head Cloaths* and he is an errant Woman, his rueful Face excepted; but even that can be amended with Paint, which is as much in Vogue among our Gentlemen, as with the Ladies in *France*.

But of all the customs *Effeminacy* has produc'd, none more hateful, predominant, and pernicious, than that of the Mens *Kissing* each other. This *Fashion* was brought over from *Italy*, (the *Mother* and *Nurse* of *Sodomy*); where the *Master* is oftner *Intriguing* with his *Page*, than a *fair Lady*. And not only in that *Country*, but in *France*, which copies from them, the *Contagion* is diversify'd, and the Ladies (in the *Nunneries*) are criminally *amorous* of each other, in a *Method* too gross for Expression. I must be so partial to my own *Country-Women*, to affirm, or, at least, hope they claim no Share of this *Charge*; but must confess, when I see two Ladies *Kissing* and *Slopping* each other in a *lascivious Manner*, and *frequently* repeating it, I am shock'd to the last Degree; but not so much, as when I see two *fulsome* Fellows, *Slavering* every Time they meet, *Squeezing* each other's Hand, and other like *indecent Symptoms*. And tho' many Gentlemen of Worth, are oftentimes, out of pure good *Manners*, obliged to give into it; yet the Land will never be purged of its *Abominations*, till this *Unmanly, Unnatural Usage* be totally abolish'd: For it is the first *Inlet* to the detestable Sin of *Sodomy*.

Under this Pretext vile *Catamites* make their preposterous *Addresses*, even in the very *Streets*; nor can any thing be more shocking, than to see a couple of *Creatures*, who wear the Shapes of *Men, Kiss* and *Slaver* each other, to that Degree, as is daily practised even in our most publick Places; and (generally speaking) without Reproof; because they plead in Excuse, *That it is the Fashion*. Damn'd *Fashion*! Imported from *Italy* amidst a Train of other *unnatural Vices*. Have we not *Sins* enough of our own, but we must eke 'em out with those of *Foreign Nations*, to fill up the Cup of our *Abominations*, and make us yet more ripe for *Divine* Vengeance.

From the 'Reasons for the Growth of Sodomy' section in: *Satan's Harvest Home*: or the Present State of Whorecraft, Adultery, Fornication, Procuring, Pimping, Sodomy, And the Game of Flatts, (Illustrated by an Authentick and Entertaining Story) And other Satanic Works, daily propagated in this good Protestant Kingdom. Collected from the Memoirs of an intimate Comrade of the Hon. Jack S * * n * *r; and concern'd with him in many of his Adventures. To which is added, 'The Petite Maître', a Poem, by a LADY OF DISTINCTION. London: Printed for the Editor, and sold at the Change, St. Paul's, Fleet Street, by DOD against St. Clement's Church; LEWIS, Covent Garden; Exeter Change, at Charing Cross, and in the Court of Requests; JACKSON, JOLLIFFE, DODSLEY, BRINDLEY, STEIDEL, SHROPSHIRE, CHAPPEL, HILDYARD at York; LEAK, at Bath; and the Snuff Shop in Cecil Court, St. Martin's Lane, 1749.

Quoted in the extensive entry on *Satan's Harvest Home*, in Pisanus Fraxi (Henry Spencer Ashbee), *Index Librorum Prohibitorum* (Bibliography of Prohibited Books), vol. 1, 1877.

Ashbee notes: 'The "Game of Flats," an appellation which may be new to many of my readers, indicates a criminal love between women. Our author tells us that it was a "new sort of Sin" which had "got footing among W-n of Q-y," and was practised at *Twickenham* as well as in Turkey.'

[I take 'W-n of Q-y' to be Women of Quality, Twickenham types.]

Yokel's Preceptor: or,
More Sprees in London!

The increase of these monsters in the shape of men, commonly designated *Margeries, Pooffs,* &c., of late years, in the great Metropolis, renders it necessary for the safety of the public, that they should be made known. The punishment generally awarded to such miscreants is not half severe enough, and till the law is more frequently carried to the fullest extent against them, there can be no hopes of crushing the bestiality. The wretches are too well paid – they being principally, it is well known, supported by their rich companions – to care a jot about a few months' imprisonment. Why has the pillory been abolished? Would it not be found very salutary for such beasts as these? for can they be too much held up to public degradation and public punishment? Will the reader credit it, but such is nevertheless the fact, that these monsters actually walk the streets the same as the whores, looking out for a chance!

Yes, the Quadrant, Fleet-steet, Holborn, the Strand, &c., are actually thronged with them! Nay, it is not long since, in the neighbourhood of Charing Cross, they posted bills in the windows of several respectable public houses, cautioning the public to 'Beware of Sods!'

They generally congregate around the picture shops, and are to be known by their effeminate air, their fashionable dress &c. When they see what they imagine to be a chance, they place their fingers in a peculiar manner underneath the tails of their coats, and wag them about – the method of giving the office.

A great many of them flock the saloons and boxes of the theatres, coffee-houses &c.

We could relate many instances of the gross bestiality of the practices of these wretches, but think it would be occupying too much of the reader's time on so disgusting a subject . . .

Yokel's Preceptor: or, More Sprees in London! being a regular and Curious Show-Up of all the Rigs and Doings of the Flash Cribs in this Great Metropolis;

Particularly Goodered's Famous Saloon – Gambling Houses – Female Hells
and Introducing Houses! The most Famous, Flash, and Cock-and-Hen Clubs,
&c. – A full Description of the Most Famous Stone-Thumpers, particularly
Elephant Bet, Finnikin Fan, the Yarmouth Bloater, Flabby Poll, Fair Eliza, the
Black Mott, &c.: And it may be fairly styled Every Swankey's Book, or the
Greenhorn's Guide Thro' Little Lunnon. Intended as a Warning to the
Inexperienced – Teaching them how to Secure their Lives and Property
during an Excursion through London, and calculated to put the Gulpin always
upon his guard. – Here will be found A Capital Show-Up of the most infamous
Pegging Kens. Bellowsing Rooms. Dossing Hotels. Sharking Fakes. Fencing
Cribs. Fleecing Holes. Gulping Holes. MollyClubs. &c., &c., &c. . . . etc. Price
One Shilling. London: Printed and Published by H. SMITH, 37, Holywell
street, Strand. Where may be had a Catalogue of a Most Extensive Variety of
every choice and Curious Facetious Work.

Quoted in Pisanus Fraxi (Henry Spencer Ashbee), *Index Librorum Prohibitorum* (Bibliography of Prohibited Books), vol. 1, 1877.

The Times, 1764

With our own island vices not content
We rob our neighbours on the Continent;
Dance Europe round, and visit every court,
To ape their follies and their crimes import:
To different lands for different sins we roam,
And, richly freighted, bring our cargo home,
Nobly industrious to make Vice appear
In her full state, and perfect only here . . .

Nor stop we here – the soft luxurious East,
Where man, his soul degraded, from the beast
In nothing different but in shape we view,
They walk on four legs, and he walks on two.
Attracts our eye; and flowing from that source
Sins of the blackest character, sins worse
Than all her plagues, which truly to unfold,
Would make the best blood in my veins run cold,
And strike all manhood dead; which but to name,
Would call up in my cheeks the marks of shame;
Sins, if such sins can be, which shut out grace;
Which for the guilty leave no hope, no place,
E'en in God's mercy; sins 'gainst Nature's plan
Possess the land at large; and man for man
Burns in those fires which Hell alone could raise
To make him more than damned; which, in the days
Of punishment, when guilt becomes her prey,
With all her tortures she can scarce repay . . .

Go where we will, at every time and place,
Sodom confronts, and stares us in the face;
They ply in public at our very doors
And take the bread from much more honest Whores.
Those who are mean high Paramours secure,

And the rich guilty screen the guilty poor;
The Sin too proud to feel from Reason awe,
And Those, who practise it, too great for Law.
Woman, the pride and happiness of Man,
Without whose soft endearments Nature's plan
Had been a blank, and Life not worth a thought;
Woman, by all the loves and Graces taught,
With softest arts, and sure, tho' hidden skill
To humanize, and mould us to her will;
Woman, with more than common grace formed here,
With the persuasive language of a tear
To melt the rugged temper of our Isle,
Or win us to her purpose with a smile;
Woman, by Fate the quickest spur decreed,
The fairest, best reward of every deed
Which bears the stamp of honour, at whose name
Our ancient Heroes caught a quicker flame,
And dared beyond belief, whilst o'er the plain,
Spurning the carcases of Princes slain,
Confusion proudly strode, whilst Horror blew
The fatal trump, and Death stalked full in view;
Woman is out of date, a thing thrown by
As having lost its use; No more the eye
With female beauty caught, in wild amaze,
Gazes entranced, and could for ever gaze;
No more the heart, that seat where Love resides,
Each breath drawn quick and short, in fuller tides
Life posting through the veins, each pulse on fire,
And the whole body tingling with desire,
Pants for those charms, which Virtue might engage
To break his vow, and thaw the frost of Age,
Bidding each trembling nerve, each muscle strain,
And giving pleasure which is almost pain.
Women are kept for nothing but the breed;
For pleasure we must have a Ganymede,
A fine, fresh Hylas, a delicious boy,
To serve our purposes of beastly joy . . .

Is a son born into the world of woe?
In never-ceasing streams let sorrow flow;
Be from that hour the house with sables hung,
Let lamentations dwell upon thy tongue,
E'en from that moment that he first began
To wail and whine, let him not see a man;
Lock, lock him up, far from the public eye;
Give him no opportunity to buy,
Or to be bought; B--, though rich, was sold,
And gave his body up to shame for gold.
  Let it be bruited all about the town,
That he is coarse, indelicate, and brown,
An antidote to lust; his face deep scarred
With the small-pox, his body maimed and marred;
Ate up with the king's evil, and his blood
Tainted throughout, a thick and putrid flood,
Where dwells Corruption, making him all o'er,
From head to foot, a rank and running sore.
Shouldst thou report him, as by Nature made,
He is undone, and by thy praise betrayed:
Give him out fair, lechers, in number more,
More brutal, and more fierce, than thronged the door
Of Lot in Sodom, shall to thine repair,
And force a passage, though a god is there.
  Let him not have one servant that is male;
Where Lords are baffled, servants oft prevail.
Some vices they propose, to all agree;
H-- was guilty, but was M-- free?
  Give him no tutor – throw him to a punk,
Rather than trust his morals to a monk;
Monks we all know – we, who have lived at home,
From fair report, and travellers who roam,
More feelingly; nor trust him to the gown,
'Tis oft a covering in this vile town
For base designs: ourselves have lived to see
More than one parson in the pillory.
Should he have brothers, (image to thy view
A scene, which, though not public made, is true)
Let not one brother be to t'other known,

Nor let his father sit with him alone . . .

But if, too eager in my bold career,
Haply I wound the nice, and chaster ear;
If, all unguarded, all too rude, I speak,
And call up blushes in the maiden's cheek,
Forgive, ye fair – my real motives view,
And to forgiveness add your praises too.
For you I write – nor wish a better plan,
The cause of woman is most worthy man;
For you I still will write, nor hold my hand
Whilst there's one slave of Sodom in the land.
    Let them fly far, and skulk from place to place,
Not daring to meet manhood face to face;
Their steps I'll track, nor yield them one retreat
Where they may hide their heads, or rest their feet,
Till God, in wrath, shall let his vengeance fall,
And make a great example of them all,
Bidding in one grand pile this town expire,
Her towers in dust, her Thames a lake of fire;
Or they (most worth our wish) convinced though late
Of their past crimes and dangerous estate,
Pardon of women with repentance buy,
And learn to honour them as much as I.

DANTE

Purgatory

While singly thus along the rim we walked,
Oft the good master warned me: 'Look thou well.
Avail it that I caution thee.' The sun
Now all the western clime irradiate changed
From azure tinct to white; and, as I passed,
My passing shadow made the umbered flame
Burn ruddier. At so strange a sight I marked
That many a spirit marvelled on his way.

    This bred occasion first to speak of me.
'He seems,' said they, 'no insubstantial frame:'
Then, to obtain what certainty they might,
Stretched towards me, careful not to overpass
The burning pale. 'O thou! who followest
The others, haply not more slow than they,
But moved by reverence; answer me, who burn
In thirst and fire: nor I alone, but these
All for thine answer do more thirst, than doth
Indian or Aethiop for the cooling stream.
Tell us, how is that thou makest thyself
A wall against the sun, as thou not yet
Into the inextricable toils of death
Hadst entered?' Thus spake one: and I had straight
Declared me, if attention had not turned
To new appearance. Meeting these, there came,
Midway the burning path, a crowd, on whom
Earnestly gazing, from each part I view
The shadows all press forward, severally
Each snatch a hasty kiss, and then away.
E'en so the emmets, 'mid their dusky troops,
Peer closely one at other, to spy out
Their mutual road perchance, and how they thrive.
    That friendly greeting parted, ere dispatch

Of the first onward step, from either tribe
Loud clamour rises: those, who newly come,
Shout 'Sodom and Gomorrah!' these, 'The cow
Pasiphae entered, that the beast she wooed
Might rush unto her luxury.' Then as cranes,
That part towards the Riphaean mountains fly,
Part towards the Lybic sands, these to avoid
The ice, and those the sun; so hasteth off
One crowd, advances the other; and resume
Their first song, weeping, and their several shout.
   Again drew near my side the very same,
Who had erewhile besought me; and their looks
Marked eagerness to listen. I, who twice
Their will had noted, spake: 'O spirits! secure,
Whene'er the time may be, of peaceful end;
My limbs, nor crude nor in mature old age,
Have I left yonder: here they bear me, fed
With blood, and sinew-strung. That I no more
May live in blindness, hence I tend aloft.
There is a dame on high, who wins for us
This grace, by which my mortal through your realm
I bear. But may your utmost wish soon meet
Such full fruition, that the orb of heaven,
Fullest of love, and of most ample space,
Receive you; as ye tell (upon my page
Henceforth to stand recorded) who ye are;
And what this multitude, that at your backs
Have passed behind us. 'As one, mountain-bred,
Rugged and clownish, if some city's walls
He chance to enter, round him stares agape,
Confounded and dumb-struck; e'en such appeared
Each spirit. But when rid of that amaze
(Not long the inmate of a noble heart),
He, who before had questioned, thus resumed:
'O blessed! who, for death preparing, takest
Experience of our limits, in thy bark;
Their crime, who not with us proceed, was that
For which, as he did triumph, Caesar heard
The shout of "queen", to taunt him. Hence their cry

Of "Sodom", as they parted; to rebuke
Themselves, and aid the burning by their shame.
Our sinning was hermaphrodite: but we,
Because the law of human kind we broke,
Followed like beasts our vile concupiscence,
Hence parting from them, to our own disgrace
Record the name of her, by whom the beast
In bestial tire was acted. Now our deeds
Thou know'st, and how we sinned. If thou by name
Wouldst haply know us, time permits not now
To tell so much, nor can I. Of myself
Learn what thou wishest. Guinicelli I;
Who having truly sorrowed ere my last,
Already cleanse me.' With such pious joy,
As the two sons upon their mother gazed
From sad Lycurgus rescued; such my joy
(Save that I more repressed it) when I heard
From his own lips the name of him pronounced,
Who was a father to me, and to those
My betters, who have ever used the sweet
And pleasant rhymes of love. So naught I heard,
Nor spake; but long time thoughtfully I went
Gazing on him; and, only for the fire,
Approached not nearer. When my eyes were fed
By looking on him; with such solemn pledge,
As forces credence, I devoted me
Unto his service wholly. In reply
He thus bespake me: 'What from thee I hear
Is graved so deeply on my mind, the waves
Of Lethe shall not wash it off, nor make
A whit less lively. But as now thy oath
Has sealed the truth, declare what cause impels
That love, which both thy looks and speech bewray.'

   'Those dulcet lays,' I answered; 'which, as long
As of our tongue the beauty does not fade,
Shall make us love the very ink that traced them.'

   'Brother!' he cried, and pointed at the shade
Before him, 'there is one, whose mother speech
Doth owe to him a fairer ornament.

He in love ditties, and the tales of prose,
Without a rival stands; and lets the fools
Talk on, who think the songster of Limoges
O'ertops him. Rumour and the popular voice
They look to, more than truth; and so confirm
Opinion, ere by art or reason taught.
Thus many of the elder time cried up
Guittone, giving him the prize, till truth
By strength of numbers vanquished. If thou own
So ample privilege, as to have gained
Free entrance to the cloister, whereof Christ
Is Abbot of the college; say to him
One paternoster for me, far as needs
For dwellers in this world, where power to sin
No longer tempts us.' Haply to make way
For one that followed next, when that was said,
He vanished through the fire, as through the wave
A fish, that glances diving to the deep.
    I, to the spirit he had shown me, drew
A little onward, and besought his name,
For which my heart, I said, kept gracious room.
He frankly thus began: 'Thy courtesy
So wins on me, I have nor power nor will
To hide me. I am Arnaut; and with songs,
Sorely waymenting for my folly past,
Through this ford of fire I wade, and see
The day, I hope for, smiling in my view.
I pray ye by the worth that guides ye up
Unto the summit of the scale, in time
Remember ye my sufferings.' With such words
He disappeared in the refining flame.

Dante Alighieri, *The Divine Comedy*, 'Purgatory', Canto XXVI. Translated by
Henry Francis Cary.

A Great Sodomy Company Ltd

The Emperor Napoleon III experienced mortification when he learned that some of the most eminent men of his reign were compromised in a great Sodomy Company limited business. The originator, or at least the director of this affair, in which very important sums of money were invested on mutual account, was, it was said, Mr C-n, the syndic (president) of the Parisian Association of Stockbrokers. This gentleman, one of the richest members of this association, was perhaps no more than the not over scrupulous and obliging friend of these personages of the Court, of the Senate and of Financial circles, with whom banking operations had brought him into intimate contact. However that might be, an association, or rather club, of sodomists had already been four or five years in existence without the fact being noted, when mere chance made it known.

The Colonel of the *Dragons de l'Impératrice* was advised that the soldiers of this crack regiment were making extravagant expenses of all kinds and that they had most of them gold in their pockets. It was not easy to explain how these men could possibly have so suddenly become rich, it being known that neither they nor their families possessed the least amount of income. They were chosen among the most handsome and pretty-faced men in the army, and their coquettish uniform appeared to be their sole appanage. Several of them were searched; they were found possessed of well-lined purses; one had 25 louis (£20) on him. They pretended that this money was gained at play, but they did not or would not say at what game they had made it. They were temporarily put for a few days under arrest. At the same time it transpired that the *Cent-Gardes* of the Emperor had made their fortune, at all events a great number of them, and particularly those who were specially remarkable for effeminate beauty of face, bodily beauty or elegant appearance. These latter possessed, besides splendid jewels, watches, chains, rings, and a little stock of ready cash, which could not be the result of avowable economies. There were new questionings, new researches, but always with the same uncertainties. At last a witness declared that one of the dragoons, still under arrest, had told him, after a copious dinner largely moistened with wine, that he would one day become a millionaire, because no one could do the Empress better than he. The question suggested itself what was the meaning of: *to do the Empress*. This was soon made clear, when the police, which had been put on the scent, discovered the headquarters of the *Ebugors*, in a mansion in the *Allée des Veuves*, the property of the Society and which served for the cult of Sodom. This mansion, purchased at the expense of the members, had been furnished and arranged specially for its purpose; there were to be seen there splendid apartments, that were never but transitorily occupied, by unknown persons who were received only on presentation of a medal or sort of *abraxas* showing mysterious signs and monograms. The door-keeper and the servants of this house were taken into custody, after a visit to the premises had left no doubt of their usual destination. In the interior two wardrobes were discovered filled with all kinds of costumes, feminine of course, and among them, the costumes worn by the Empress Eugénie in ceremonies and official receptions. This strange discovery led to another still more significant. A quantity of correspondence was seized, letters in all sorts of hand-writings, anonymous or pseudonymous, interchanged between the associates and their adherents, who were none other than *Cent-Gardes* and *Dragons de l'Impératrice*. A judicial enquiry was instituted, and the porter-manager of the establishment was forced to speak. The recognized head of the affair, Mr. C....n, was summoned before the Procureur-Général who, after a simply confidential examination, thought it necessary to refer the matter to the Emperor in person, communicating to him at the same time the reports of the police, in which were mentioned the names of several eminent personages, who were on the point of being involved in the most scandalous prosecution. The Emperor had no sooner listened to the Procureur-Général and perused the documents he had brought, than he judged it prudent to suspend proceedings and to hush up the affair, keeping at the same time in his possession all the documents connected with it, and among them the famous correspondences, in which the acts and doings of the interested parties were exposed without any veil and in the most figurative and burning language . . .

Translation from the French text in Pisanus Fraxi, *Centuria Librorum Absconditorum*, London (privately printed), 1879. Found in *Untrodden Fields of Anthropology* by a French Army-Surgeon, vol. 1, Paris, Librairie de Médecine, Folklore et Anthropologie, 1898.

GEORGE LESTEY

Lament of the Sodomites, 1675

Oh Heav'ns! I'm choack'd with Smoak, I'm burn'd with fire,
Brimston, Brimston! Where shall we retire?
We dye, we dye, O may this be the last
Of Heav'ns dreadful Sentence on us past!
We're burn'd and damn'd, there is no remedy;
We would not hear *Lot*, when he bid us fly
From wrath to come. O how our Limbs crack
With fire! Our Conscience is upon the rack
For by-past Crimes; our beastly Lusts Torment
Us, as the pretious time that we have spent.
O wretched Nature, whither hast thou brought
Us fools, and made us sell our Souls for nought?
Luxurious Eyes, why wer ye so unkind
To dote on objects, who have made you blind?
And you Tenacious hands, why did you grasp
The Poyson of the Spider? Why from Wasp
Did you seek Honey? did not Heav'n bestow,
As upon *Lot*, so also upon you,
The Lawful helps, and remedies for lust?
Was not all this enough? but that you must
In spite of Heav'n, lay hold on all that came,
Although they man his members had or name.
Could not a lawful Wedlock satisfie
Thy burning flame, proud flesh? No, thou must cry
Bring out thy handsome Guests, them we must know,
Not knowing they were not from below:
Whose Just revenge doth make us miserable,
To bear these scorching flames we were not able.
And yet alas! our wo doth but begin,
The vengeance is Eternal that's for sin.
O that *Lot's* God would grant us a reprieve
But for one hour, that wretched we might live,

To wail our by-past sins; and beg his aid,
Who never yet to humble sinners said,
I scorn your plaints, but always graciously
Prepar'd a bottle for a melting Eye,
And piece-meal Pray'rs made whole with his own merit,
Sa'ing be comforted, 'tis you must inherit
My endless Joy; which sentence now doth pierce
Our Souls so much, that we cannot rehearse
Our woes, though Oh! alas! it is too late,
We must expect nought but Almightie's hate.
See how the Devils laugh, whom we have serv'd:
O cursed Spirits is't this we have deserv'd
From you, for all those things that we have done
At your Command?

George Lestey (or Lesley or Leslie), 'Lament of the Sodomites', in *Fire and Brimstone; or the Destruction of Sodom*, London, 1675.

GUILLAUME APOLLINAIRE

The Sodomite's Minion

A boy called Louis Gian, son of a modest oil merchant in Nice, never showed the least picty; unlike the rest of his schoolfellows, who, at least at the time of their first communion, gave proofs of a touching devotion to the church.

The limping vicar of Saint-Réparate had said to him one day during catechism class, as he wiped his glasses on his dirty cassock:

'Louis! You will come to no good, because you are a hypocrite. To look at you, one would take you for an angel. But what's the truth? You're as low as a kneeling bedbug. You make fun of me. I know all about it, and you may go on doing it. But God is not mocked. You may find this out sooner than you wish.'

Louis Gian listened to the vicar's admonition standing before him humbly, his eyes lowered. But the moment the priest's back was turned, the graceless boy mimicked his halting gait, and sang ironically:

'Five and three make eight. Five and three make eight.'

The young man from Nice did not improve with the years. Until the age of fourteen he hardly went to school at all, but spent his time under the bridges of the Paillon and at the castle, debauching at first boys of his own age, then little girls.

At the age of fourteen, he was apprenticed to a shirtmaker, and left the old quarter of Nice, with its perfumes of fruit and spices, mingled with the rankness of raw meat, sour dough, dried codfish and latrines, for a shop in the new town. From the first days the owner and his wife, who, like all good people of Nice, did not let their apprentice go short of work, either by night or by day, kept a close eye on him.

The owner's wife had hair as red as an orange, but the owner smelt of pissaladière. Louis Gian was enticed away from them at carnival time by a meticulous Russian, whom he had to call General, and who in return called him Ganymede.

When he discovered that the Russian was both exacting in his requirements and miserly, Louis first robbed and then left him.

He next bestowed himself on a brutal and lasciviously greedy Turk.

The Turk, however, ruined himself at Monte Carlo, and was duly replaced by an American. Louis Gian had understood that to maintain himself fruitfully, he must devote himself, like a rounded map of the world, to all nationalities.

Yet, in his good fortune, he failed to keep that serenity which is the privilege of the virtuous. He despised his former companions, and would walk by them pretending not to see them. First, they returned insult for insult. They did not fail, when they met him, to make a certain gesture which consists of placing the left hand at the elbow of the bent right arm, and shaking the right clenched fist. Or again, as he walked by, they mouthed the obscene letter z of the silent alphabet of insult used by the people of Nice, the Monégasques and the people from La Turbie and Menton.

Finally, Louis Gian's misconduct became as abhorrent to the Heavens as to his friends. He who pisses against the wind wets his shirt; and it pleased God to punish the sins of the sodomite's minion in a manner fitting the offence.

Louis Gian one day insulted a former friend who had apostrophized him, telling him to mend his ways. There was a quarrel which led to blows and threats of revenge.

Four young men, who were really not that much better than Louis Gian himself, lay in wait for him one night when he had gone alone to the theatre. They got drunk on Corsican wine, the reputation of which has fallen so greatly since the sixteenth century, then lay in wait for him in front of the villa where he lived with an unsavoury Austrian.

When Louis Gian arrived after midnight, they fell upon him, gagged him, and then hauled him to the town gate, where they impaled him on one of its spikes, and ran off nudging one another obscenely.

The impaled one died, voluptuously perhaps. He was as beautiful as Atys. The fireflies glowed round him . . .

Guillaume Apollinaire, 'The Sodomite's Minion', in *The Wandering Jew and Other Stories*. Translated by Rémy Inglis Hall. London, Rupert Hart-Davis, 1967.

Lot; or,

The Unhappy Choice, 1876

Lot was the son of Haran, Abraham's brother. We first read of him in Gen. xi. We are there told of his being one of that little band of emigrants who set out with Abraham, at God's command, to settle in the land of Canaan.

Lot appears to have lost his father at an early age, and to have been taken under Abraham's special care. It must have been no small blessing to have been trained under the eye of so holy a man; for you will remember that it was said of Abraham, 'I know him, that he will command his children and his household after him, and they shall keep the way of the Lord.'

One cannot but doubt that Lot must have learnt from Abraham many a holy lesson, which proved a blessing to him in after life. He could not have been a member of such a household without seeing daily before his very eyes the beautiful pattern of a believer's life.

Happy for us, if we have passed our early days with those who fear and love God, if we have breathed from our childhood the atmosphere of religion, and have taken sweet counsel with those who are God's people. A good man, who was often thrown into the company of Archbishop Leighton, used to say, that he felt that his acquaintance with that man of God was a talent, for which he must give an account hereafter. Truly there is much to be learnt from our intercourse with godly persons; and great indeed will be our condemnation if we do not profit by it.

Lot grew up to be a man of piety; and he doubtless passed many a happy year under his uncle's roof. Abraham had become 'very rich in cattle, in silver, and in gold;' and Lot also had 'flocks and herds, and tents.' The consequence was that there arose a 'strife between the herdsmen of Abraham's cattle and the herdsmen of Lot's cattle.' A jealousy spang up, which grieved Abraham to the heart; so much so that he felt a separation to be necessary for the sake of peace.

145

And now observe the generous and unselfish conduct of Abraham. Being the elder, he might well have made his own choice; and then have desired his nephew to leave him. But instead of that, he proposed to Lot that he should take for himself the spot which he preferred; 'If thou wilt take the left hand, then I will go to the right; or if thou depart to the right hand, then I will go to the left.'

Here we see how little Abraham was influenced by worldly motives. He was rich; but he cared little for his riches. He lived as a stranger upon earth, looking for 'a better and more enduring substance.'

Well would it have been for Lot, if he had shown the same unworldly spirit. But, alas, the bad part of his character now came out. He made just the very choice which we should expect a worldly man to make. He 'lifted up his eyes, and beheld all the plain of Jordan, that it was watered everywhere, even as the garden of the Lord. Then Lot chose him all the plain of Jordan.'

How wrong he was to fix upon that district, merely because it was a fruitful country, and pleasing to the eye! Would the beauty of the spot, or the richness of the land, bring him happiness? It needed something else to ensure this. Was it a land where the inhabitants were a God-fearing people? No, on the contrary, these men of Sodom were notorious for their ungodliness; and yet Lot, who was himself a servant of God, went deliberately and plunged himself among them.

This was indeed a false step, the consequences of which he felt for years to come. It is true, he had this pleasant plain for his residence. He had there rich and fruitful pasture for his flocks and herds. His wealth no doubt increased. But was he happy? Oh, no; the sin which he daily witnessed around him was enough to make his eyes run down with tears. How could he, who was a good man, live in the very midst of sinners, and be happy? We are told that 'in seeing and hearing he vexed his righteous soul from day to day with their ungodly deeds.' When he heard their wicked language, it grated upon his ears. Their unholy deeds made him shudder. Sodom was a hell upon earth to one who had tasted of the peace and blessedness of true religion.

My dear reader, beware lest *you* fall into the snares which proved so ruinous to Lot. Oftentimes we are called to make an important choice. Let us be guided in making it, not by what delights the eye, or by the prospect of worldly advantage, but by an earnest desire to do what is pleasing to God, and what will be likely to help us on the way to heaven. Above all, let us in such cases seek counsel of God and ask Him to guide and direct our steps. Had Lot done this, he would have been spared many an hour of after sorrow, and many a feeling of remorse and self-reproach.

It happened one day, whilst Lot was living thus miserably in Sodom, two strangers suddenly made their appearance. They were no common visitors. In form they were like ordinary men; but they were bearers of a message from God Himself. They had no sooner entered the city than they found Lot; and seeing that they were strangers he invited them to take shelter in his own house. They then made known to him their errand. They were come on a message of mercy to him. The Lord had determined to destroy the city; and He had sent His angels to hasten Lot from the guilty place, before His wrath was poured out upon it.

What awful tidings were these to hear! What must he have felt, when he pondered over the many precious souls that were in a moment to be hurried to destruction! His heart bled especially for the members of his own family; and without a moment's delay he speeds off to warn his sons-in-law of the approaching danger. But, like Noah before the flood, he met only with scorn. They gave no heed of his message. 'He seemed as one that mocked' unto them.

The night passed. It was to Lot a night of much anxiety, and doubtless of much prayer. And at daybreak the Angels urged the favoured family to depart, assuring them that not a moment was to be lost, but that God's hand was lifted up to strike the coming blow.

But how hard to give up all at God's bidding! What a wrench it is, when we are called upon to snap asunder some earthly cord which has bound itself round our hearts! How trying to part with those things that are dear to us, for our Lord's sake.

'Look not behind thee, neither stay thou in all the plain,' was the command in the present case. And Lot, and his two daughters, strictly obeyed it. His wife, though she went out with them, afterwards wavered. Ah, her heart was in Sodom! She turned to take one lingering look at the doomed city; and she was in a moment struck to the ground, an awful monument of God's righteous anger!

Two thousand years after this, when God sent another, and a still greater, Messenger from heaven, even His own beloved Son, that heavenly Messenger raised His warning voice to a world of sinners, saying; 'Remember Lot's wife.'

We hear but little more of Lot. The last days of his pilgrimage were clouded over; they were dark and melancholy. This man of God fell into sin. For a time he gave place to the devil – thus showing us that whilst 'we *think* we stand,' we have great cause to 'take heed lest we fall.' We believe that Lot found pardon for his sin; and that he is now sitting down with Abraham, Isaac, and Jacob, in the kingdom of God. Still, there are some painful features in his history, which we cannot but mourn over.

Reader, know for your comfort that the blood of Jesus Christ is able to blot out *all your sins*. But know also, that unless your sins *are* blotted out, and unless your heart is made holy and pure within, it is utterly impossible for you to enjoy the light of God's countenance here, or to dwell with Him in heaven hereafter.

The Right Reverend Ashton Oxenden, D.D., Bishop of Montreal, and Metropolitan of Canada, 'Lot; or, The Unhappy Choice', in *Portraits from The Bible* (Old Testament Series), Hatchard's, Piccadilly 1876.

Lot in Sodom, 1878

The more the reader thinks of Lot, the more difficult his case seems to us. From all that appears in the history, there was nothing very lovely in his character; for even his being eventually saved, was more for Abraham's sake than his own. He appears, from the history, to have been a weak and selfish character. On the return from Egypt, he seems to have taken part with his herdsmen in their quarrels with those of Abraham; and when at length the latter proposes a separation for the sake of peace, and leaves him the choice of situation, he has not the grace to decline the generous offer of his elder and uncle, but grasps it eagerly, and adopts for his home the fat pastures of Sodom, although he well knows that the men in that quarter are the most wicked in the land. At first he did not intend, however, to mix with the citizens, but to live in his tent. But it is dangerous to palter with duty, or to venture too near the strongholds of sin. Even as the moth careers merrily and thoughtlessly around the flame, and at last is overcome by the fascination, and plunges therein to its ruin, so Lot, ere long, has left his tent, and has got a house in Sodom. There he forms family ties; there his daughters marry; and he gradually gets more and more entangled. So strong is that entanglement, that even his capture and rescue by Abraham do not suffice to break the chains which the world has cast around him. He goes back to Sodom, and tarries there; and it would appear that this was under circumstances which inflicted much pain upon Abraham, and probably offended him greatly. It is else difficult to see how, in looking to the possibility of dying childless, he refused to regard Lot as his heir.

One of Lot's measures, or suggestions, when the angels who went to destroy Sodom were with him, seems to show that although still a good man, his moral sense had been somewhat weakened by daily intercourse with the ungodly people with whom he had fixed his home; and his reluctance to leave Sodom, and the enormities into which his too easy nature was led, after his escape to the mountains, are facts of the same purport, and speak with trumpet-tongue of the danger of this intercourse with sinners. No good can ever come from such intercourse – in his day or in ours; and let none of us, as he perhaps did, rely too much on his own strength; for who can daily touch pitch without being defiled? If Lot had been altogether right-minded, not the finest pastures of the world, not all the conveniences and apparent advantages for the settlement of his daughters which a residence in the town presented, would have induced him to go or stay there. Rather would he have fled the place. Rather would he have plunged at once into the desert. There was nothing to prevent him; for he was not, like his uncle, under any command to remain in the land of Canaan.

For all that appears in the history, we might have strong fears of this man's state. But St. Peter calls him 'just Lot,' and says, that while in Sodom, 'that righteous man, dwelling among them, in seeing and hearing, vexed his righteous soul from day to day, with the unlawful deeds and filthy conversation of the wicked.' This relieves us, by showing that his character was still *substantially* true. But it does not altogether clear him from these imputations. It shows that he had good feelings and perceptions; but was a feeble-spirited man, lacking the strength to act on his own convictions. He was content to mourn over the guilt he saw; and would rather passively sit down amid the certainties of danger, and the probabilities of judgement, than rouse himself to one great and energetic effort to be free, and, at whatever sacrifice, to depart from the tainted and abominable place.

Let us profit from the example, which is less different than it may seem from the experience of many of us. Still there are Sodoms; and still there are Lots who think that, with a religious profession they may live in the world, and pursue its profits and its pleasures without danger. Let them beware. They are in great peril. If we be indeed God's people, let us come out of the world, and touch not the unclean thing – remembering that the Church of God is not mixed up in the world, and to be left undistinguishable from it; but is, indeed,

> 'A people walled around,
> Chosen, and made peculiar ground;
> A little spot enclosed by grace
> Out of the world's wide wilderness.'

John Kitto, D.D., F.S.A., 'Lot in Sodom', in *Daily Bible Illustrations*: Morning Series: Genesis to Esther. New Edition, Revised and Enlarged, by J.L. Porter, D.D., L.L.D., and John Stoughton, D.D. William Collins, Sons, & Company, 1878.

JOHN KITTO

The Pillar of Salt, 1878

One of the most remarkable incidents in the history of the destruction of the Cities of the Plain is, that the wife of Lot, looking and probably lingering behind, 'became a pillar of salt.'

The explanation of this which is now usually current is that of Bishop Patrick. The reader has, no doubt, seen it in many varied forms of phraseology, and we may therefore present it in the words of the author. The Bishop thinks, then, 'that some of that storm which overwhelmed her country, overtook her; and falling upon her, as she stood staring about, and minded not her way or guide, suddenly wrapt her body in a sheet of nitro-sulphurous matter; which congealing into a crust as hard as stone, made her appear, they say, a pillar of salt, her body being, as it were, candied in it.' This explanation is, however, older than Patrick, though he may be regarded as having made it current in this country; for this view of the subject had been before entertained by many Jewish and Christian writers.

We have no explanation to offer that seems to us better suited to meet the recorded circumstances. From the nature of the case, and from the peculiarly bituminous and saline character of the locality, through which this phenomenon was produced, we must not expect to discover many parallel instances which might be quoted in illustration. Accordingly we find that the illustrative parallels which have been diligently sought by old commentators, have rarely any real bearing on the subject, being for the most part accounts of persons frozen to death, and long preserved in that condition uncorrupted, in the boreal regions; or else of persons first suffocated and then petrified by the mineral vapours of the caves in which they were hid; or otherwise of persons 'turned to stone,' and found, generations after, standing in the postures wherein they found their death. The only instance which we have met with that seems appropriate, and which rests on the authority of a contemporary of fair credit, is related by Aventinus, who states that in his time, about fifty country people, with their cows and calves, were, in Carinthia, destroyed by strong and suffocating saline exhalations which arose out of the earth immediately upon the earthquake of 1348. They were by this reduced to saline statues or pillars, like Lot's wife, and the historian tells us that they had been seen by himself and the chancellor of Austria. (*Annal. Bavar.*, lib. 7).

It would scarcely seem that such a saline body was likely to be of long duration in a very humid climate, subject in winter to heavy rains and the action of water-courses. If God designed that it should be preserved as a monument of the transaction, there is no difficulty in supposing that it was so. But this does not appear to have been the case. There is no allusion to any such monument as still subsisting in the whole Scripture; and the usual formula 'unto this day,' by which the sacred writers in the history of great transactions usually indicate the continuance, to their own times, of ancient monuments and names, is in this instance omitted. Besides, the whole appearance of the district, and of the lake which now covers the vale of Siddim, is, to this day, a most grand and standing monument of the whole of the dreadful judgment of which the death of Lot's wife was one incident; and of the woman herself, the record in the book of Genesis is itself the most striking and ineffaceable memorial . . .

The first notice of its supposed existence is in the apocryphal Book of Wisdom, written in the first or second century before Christ. Speaking of the destruction of the Cities of the Plain, the writer says: 'Of whose wickedness even to this day the waste land that smoketh is a testimony, and plants bearing fruit that never come to ripeness: *and a standing pillar of salt is a monument of an unbelieving soul.*' Wisd. x. 7. This shows clearly enough the opinion prevailing among the Jews in the time of the writer of the Book of Wisdom.

Josephus declares that it was standing in his time, and that he had seen it with his own eyes. This must be taken to show that he had seen a pillar of salt by the Dead Sea, and that he believed it to be the one into which Lot's wife was changed; but we have no evidence which can satisfy us that his evidence was correct. Any actual transmitted *knowledge* of such a monument must have been broken during the sojourn in Egypt for some generations; and ever afterwards, and indeed always, the monument, if it still existed, lay in a quarter away from all travelled routes, and but rarely visited by Jews, even when Palestine was fully peopled. Clement of Rome, a Christian contemporary of Josephus, also states in one of his epistles, that the pillar of Lot's wife was still in existence; and Irenæus, in the next century, repeats the statement, with the addition of a hypothesis as to how it came to last so long with all its parts entire.

The statement of Jewish rabbis and Christian fathers is to the same effect; but as they merely repeat these earlier statements, little is really added to the weight of testimony. At length travellers began to enquire after this remarkable monument. The success of their enquiries may enlighten us as to the origin of the earlier accounts; and may well suggest that the natives of the region and the neighbouring shepherds have in all instances imposed upon the credulity of travellers, by following their usual practice of answering leading questions in accordance with the supposed wish of the inquirer, and even by pointing out any object that could be made to pass for what the traveller sought. We have been at some pains to make, for our own satisfaction, a collection of instances; and we find that hardly any two of them agree as to the locality in which the mysterious pillar was shown to them, or in which they were assured that it existed . . .

The researches of the recent American expedition to the Dead Sea, have thrown new and interesting light upon the matter. The course of their survey could hardly fail to bring under notice every marked object upon either shore; and one they did find, an obviously natural formation, which – or others in former times like which – might readily be taken by persons unaccustomed to weigh circumstances with the precision we are now accustomed to exact, for the pillar of Lot's wife.

Among the salt mountains of Usdum, on the *west* side of the kind of bay which forms the southern extremity of the Dead Sea, the party beheld, to their great astonishment, while boating along the shore, a lofty round pillar, standing apparently detached from the general mass, at the head of a deep, narrow and abrupt chasm. They landed, and proceeded towards this object. . . . The pillar was found to be of solid salt, capped with carbonate of lime, *cylindrical in front and pyramidal behind*. The upper or rounded part is about forty feet high, resting upon a kind of oval pedestal or mound, from forty to sixty feet above the level of the sea. It slightly decreases in size upwards, crumbles at the top, and is one entire mass of crystallization . . .

It had previously been heard from the Arabs that such a pillar was to be found somewhere upon the shores of the sea; but their reports in all other matters had proved so unsatisfactory that little attention had been paid to them in this instance. Lieut. Lynch, the officer in command of the expedition, and who has written the account of its discoveries, does not suppose he here found the pillar of Lot's wife, nor does it appear that even the Arabs supposed it to be such; but it is very properly pointed out that it was probably a pillar of this sort, produced by the action of water upon one of the masses of rock salt, which abound toward the southern end of the Dead Sea, that the ancient writers had in view, and which they supposed to be that into which Lot's wife was turned. We are by this instance enabled to see the natural process by which such pillars are formed. It seems to us that the real pillar of Lot's wife must have been on the opposite side of the lake, for the fugitives were proceeding to Zoar, which lay in that direction. And it must not escape our notice, that the unhappy woman appears to have been overtaken by her death in the plain; whereas this pillar stands upon a hill from forty to sixty feet above the beach, with loftier mountains immediately behind. The pillar itself also is forty feet high, which we should suppose to be considerably taller than either Lot or his wife. Yet all these circumstances would, in ages of less exact observation, have had no weight, and this very pillar would assuredly have been pronounced as beyond all doubt or question, the 'monument of an unbelieving soul.'

John Kitto, D.D., F.S.A., 'The Pillar of Salt', in *Daily Bible Illustrations*: Morning Series: Genesis to Esther. New Edition, Revised and Enlarged, by J.L. Porter, D.D., L.L.D., and John Stoughton, D.D. William Collins, Sons, & Company, 1878.

The Pilgrim's Progress

Now I saw that just on the other side of this Plain, the pilgrims came to a place where stood an old monument, hard by the highway-side, at the sight of which they were both concerned because of the form thereof; for it seemed to them as if it had been a woman transformed into the shape of a pillar: here therefore they stood looking and looking upon it, but could not for a time tell what they should make thereof. At last Hopeful espied written above upon the head thereof a writing in an unusual hand; but he being no scholar called to Christian (for he was learned) to see if he could pick out the meaning: so he came, and after a little laying of letters together he found the same to be this, *Remember Lot's wife*. So he read it to his fellow, after which they both concluded that that was the Pillar of Salt into which Lot's wife was turned for her looking back with a covetous heart when she was going from Sodom for safety. Which sudden and amazing sight gave them the occasion for this discourse.

Christian. Ah, my brother, this is a seasonable sight, it came opportunely to us after the invitation which Demas gave us to come over to view the Hill Lucre: and had we gone over as he desired us, and as thou wast inclining to do (my brother) we had, for aught I know, been made ourselves a spectacle for those that shall come after to behold.

Hopeful. I am sorry that I was so foolish, and am made to wonder that I am not now as Lot's wife; for wherein was the difference 'twixt her sin and mine? She only looked back, and I had a desire to go see; let grace be adored, and let me be ashamed, that ever such a thing be in mine heart.

Christian. Let us take notice of what we see here for our help for time to come: this woman escaped one judgement; for she fell not by the destruction of Sodom, yet she was destroyed by another; as we see, she is turned into a Pillar of Salt.

Hopeful. True, and she may be to us both caution and example; caution that we should shun her sin, or a sign of what judgement will overtake such as shall not be prevented by this caution. So Korah, Dathan, and Abiram, with the two hundred and fifty men that perished in their sin, did also become a sign, or example to others to beware: but above all, I muse at one thing, to wit, how Demas and his fellows can stand so confidently yonder to look for that treasure, which this woman, but for looking behind her (for we read not that she stepped one foot out of the way), after was turned into a Pillar of Salt; especially since the judgement which overtook her did make her an example within sight of where they are; for they cannot choose but see her, did they but lift up their eyes.

Christian. It is a thing to be wondered at, and it argueth that their heart is grown desperate in the case; and I cannot tell who to compare them to so fitly, as to them that pick pockets in the presence of the judge, or that will cut purses under the gallows. It is said of the men of Sodom, that they were sinners exceedingly, because they were sinners before the Lord, that is, in his eyesight; and notwithstanding the kindness that he had showed them, for the land of Sodom was now like the Garden of Eden heretofore. This therefore provoked him the more to jealousy, and made their plague as hot as the fire of the Lord out of Heaven could make it. And it is most rationally to be concluded that such, even such as these are, that shall sin in the sight, yea, and that too in despite of such examples that are set continually before them to caution them to the contrary, must be partakers of severest judgements.

Hopeful. Doubtless thou hast said the truth, but what a mercy it is, that neither thou, but especially I, am not made myself, this example: this ministreth occasion to us to thank God, to fear before him, and always to remember Lot's wife.

From John Bunyan, *The Pilgrim's Progress* (from This World To That Which Is To Come: Delivered Under the Similitude of a Dream), London, 1678.

Remember Lot's Wife

Sometimes in later years
  dining with bosom pals
Lot felt a nervous wreck
  passing the salt,
But on the evidence
  (Genesis 19 *et seq.*)
Mrs Lot's tragic end
  wasn't his fault.

Poor sod was queer of course,
  shouldn't have married her,
Sex-starved and sore-eyed
  she looked back in tears,
Nothing but ashes and
  sodium chloride,
Thank God I'm hetero;
  whiskey please; cheers.

Stanley J. Sharpless, 'Remember Lot's Wife' (a parody of Kingsley Amis) in
Imitations of Immortality: A Book of Literary Parodies. Compiled and edited by E.O.
Parrott. New York, Viking, 1986.

A Sermon Preached before Queene
Elizabeth

LUKE Chap. XVII. Vers. XXXII
Memores estote Uxoris Lot
Remember Lots *Wife*.

The words are few, and the sentence short; no one in Scripture so short. But it fareth with *Sentences* as with *Coines*: In coines, they that in smallest compasse containe greatest value, are best esteemed: and, in sentences, those that in fewest words comprise most matter, are most praised. Which, as of all sentences is it true; so specially of those that are marked with *Memento*. In them the shorter, the better; the better, and the better carried away, and the better kept; and the better called for when we need it. And such is this here; of rich contents, and withall exceeding compendious: So that, wee must needs be without all excuse, it being but three words, and but five syllables, if we do not remember it.

The Sentence is our SAVIOURS, uttered by Him upon this occasion. Before, (in Vers. 18) He had said: that the daies of the *Son of man should be as the daies of* LOT, in two respects: [1] In respect of the suddenness of the destruction that should come: [2] and in respect of the securitie of the people, on whom it should come. For, the *Sodomites* laughed at it, and *Lot's Wife* (it should seeme) but slightly regarded it. Being then in *Lots* storie; very fitly, and by good consequence, out of that storie, He leaveth us a *Memento*, before he leaveth it.

There are in *Lots* story, two very notable monuments of GODS *judgement*, [1] The *Lake of Sodom,* [2] *and Lots Wives Pillar*. The one, the punishment of *resolute sinne*, the other of *faint vertue*. For, the *Sodomites* are an example of impenitent wilfull Sinners; and *Lots wife* of imperseverant and relapsing righteous persons.

Both these are in it: but CHRIST, of both these, taketh the latter onely. For, two sorts of men there are, for which these two *Items* are to bee fitted: [1] To those in state of Sinne that are wrong, the *Lake of*

Sodome: [2] To those in state of Grace, that are well (if so they can keepe them) *Lots wives Pillar*. To the first in state of Sinn, *Moses* propoundeth the Vine of *Sodome and grapes of Gomorra* . . . that if yee but touch them, turne to *ashes*. To the other in state of grace, CHRIST here, *Lots wives pillar* . . . if we lay it to our selves, we shall lay it right; that *Lot's Wife* be our example, and that we sprinkle our selves with the Salt of her *Pillar, ne putrescamus*, that we turn not again to folly, or fall away from our own stedfastnesse . . .

Wherein, as there is a tender part not able to endure the crosse, for which we need the vertue of *Patience*: So is there also a *flitting humour*, not able to endure the *tediousnesse* of any thing long; for which we no lesse need the vertue of *Perseverance*.

. . . The wavering and *amaze* of others that stand in the Plain (with LOTS wife) looking about, and can not tell, whether to go forward to little *Zoar*, or back again to the ease of *Sodome*; shew plainly that *Lots wife* is forgotten, and this is a needfull *Memento, Remember Lots wife* . . .

The Division

1. First, CHRIST sending our memory to a story past; of the use of *remembring stories* in generall.
2. Secondly, Of this particular of *Lots wife*, and the points to be remembred in it.
3. Thirdly, How to apply those points, that (as S. *Augustine* saith) the *Salt* of this *Pillar* may be the *Season* of our lives . . .

The Prophet *Esay* doth call us, that stand in this place, the LORDS *Remembrancers*: As to GOD, *for the people*, by the office of *Prayers*; so from GOD, *to the People*, by the office of *Preaching*, we are imployed as much about *recognosce*, as about *cognosce*; as much in calling to their minds the things they know and have forgot, as in teaching the things they know not, or never learnt. The things are many, we have commission to put men in mind of. Some touching themselves: For, it is many times, too true, which the Philosopher saith: Nothing is so farre from our mindes, as we our selves. For, naturally (as saith the *Apostle*) we do *leake*, and *runne out*; and when we have looked in the *glasse*, we straight *forget our fashion againe*. Therefore we have in charge to put men in minde of many things, and to call upon them with divers

Mementos, Remember the basenesse of our mould what it is: Remember the frailnesse of our life how short it is. Remember, the *daies of darknesse* are coming, and *they be many*. All which we know well enough, and yet need to be put in mind of them.

But, the *storehouse*, and the very *life of memory*, is the *History* of time; and a speciall charge have we, all along the Scriptures, to call upon men to looke to that. For, all our wisdome consisting either in *Experience* or *Memory*; Experience *of our own*, or Memory of *others*; our daies are so short, that our *Experience* can be but slender, and our own time cannot afford us observations enough for so many cases, as we need direction in. Needs must we then (as he here adviseth) ask the former age, what they did in like case: search the *Records* of former times; wherein, our cases we shall be able to match, and to pattern them all . . . there is nothing new under the Sun of which it may be said, *it is new*, but it hath been already in former generations . . .

So read stories past, as we make not our selves matter for stories to come.

Now, of and among them all, our Saviour CHRIST after a speciall manner commendeth unto us, this of *Lots wife*. Of which thus much we say, That it is the only one storie, which of all the stories of the Old Testament, He maketh His choice of, to put in his *Memento*; which he would have them, which have forgotten, to *remember*, and those that remember, never to forget. Oft to repaire to this *story*, and to fetch *salt* from this *Pillar*: that they lose not that they have done, and so perish in the *recidivation* of *Lots wife*.

Then to descend into the particulars: I find in *stories*, two sorts of *Memento*: 1. Remember to *follow*: 2. Remember to *flie* the like. *Mary Magdalens ointment*, an example of one; *Lots wives salt-stone*, an example of the other. Or (to keep us, to this story) *Lot looked not back*, till he came safe to *Zoar*. *Lots Wife* did, and dyed for it: *memento & fuge*.

The verse before sheweth, why CHRIST laid the *memento* upon her, that we should not turne or returne back, as she did: that we should not follow her, but, when wee come at this *Pillar*, turne at it and take another way. That is, we should *remember Lots wife*, but *follow Lot*; remember her, but follow him.

Now in either of both *memento's*, to follow, or to *flie*, we always enquire of two points (and so, here) *what they did*: whose storie we read; and, *how they sped*: The *Fact* and the *Effect*. The *Fact*, *Vice* or *Vertue*: the *Effect*, *Reward* or *Punishment*.

Both which, concerning this unfortunate woman, we set downe in one verse (in the XIX. of *Genesis*) what she *did*; that *Shee drew backe, or looked backe*: this was her *Sinne*. The *effect*, that *She was turned into a Salt stone*: this was her *punishment*. And these two, are the two *Memorandum's* concerning her, to be *remembred*. First of her *fault*.

The *Angell* had given charge to *Lot* and his companie (in the seventeenth of that Chapter) *Scape for thy life: Stay not in the plaine: Looke not once behind thee lest thou perish. Scape for thy life*: She trifled for all that, as if no perill were. *Stay not in the Plaine*, yet stayed shee behind. *Looke not back lest thou die*; she would, and did looke back, to die for it. So that, she did all that she was forbid, and regarded none of the *Angels* words, but *despised the counsell of God against her owne soule*. This was her sinne, the sin of disobedience; but consisteth of sundry *degrees* by which she fell: needfull, all, to be remembred.

1. The first was: That she did not strictly keepe her to the Angels charge, but, dallied with it, and regarded it by halves; that is, say what he would, she might use the matter as she would; goe, or stay and looke about as she list. Such light regard is like enough to have growne of a wandring *distrust*; lest happily, she had left *Sodome* in vaine, and the *Angell* feared them with that which never should be. The *Sun rose* so *cleare*, and it was so goodly a morning, she repented, she came away. Reckoning her *Sons in law* more wise in staying still, than *Lot* and her selfe, in so unwisely departing. Which is the sin of *unbeliefe*, the bane both of *Constancie* and *Perseverance*. Constancie, in the *purpose of our minde*; and Perseverance in the *tenour of our life*.

2. From this grew the second, That she began to tire, and draw behinde, and kept not pace with LOT and the *Angels*. An evill signe. For (ever) *fainting* is next step to *forsaking*. . . . He that hath no list to *follow*, will picke some quarrell or other *to be cast behinde*.

3. This *tiring*, had it grown to weakenesse, or wearinesse, or want of breath, might have been borne with; but it came of another cause, which is the third degree. It was (saith the Text) at least to *looke backe*, and to cast her eye to the place, her soule longed after. Which sheweth, that the love of SODOME sticketh in her still: that though her feet were come from thence, her heart stayed there behinde: and that, in looke and thought shee returned thither, whither in body shee might not; but (possibly) would in body too, if, as NINIVE did, so SODOME had still remained.

4. *Looking backe* might proceede of divers causes; So might this of

hers, but that CHRIST'S application directs us. The verse before saith, *somewhat in the house*, something left behinde affected her: Of which he gives us warning. She grew weary of trouble, and of shifting so oft: From *Ur* to *Haran*; thence to *Canaan*; thence to *Egypt*; thence to *Canaan* againe; then to *Sodome*; and now to *Zoar*; and that, in her old daies, when she would fainest have beene at reste. Therefore, in this wearisome conceit of new trouble now to begin; and withall remembring the convenient seat she had in *Sodome*, she even desired to *dye by her flesh-pots*, and to be buried in the *graves of lust*: wished them at *Zoar*, that would, and her selfe at *Sodome* againe: desiring rather to end her life with ease in that *Stately City*, than to remove, and be safe, perhaps not, in the *desolate mountaines*. And this was the sin of restinesse of soule, which affected her eyes and knees, and was the cause of all the former. When men weary of a good course, which long they have holden, for a little ease or wealth, or (I wote not what) other secular respect, fall away in the end: so losing the praise and fruite of their former perseverance, and relapsing into the danger and destruction, from which they had so neere escaped.

Behold, these were the sinnes of LOT'S *Wife*; A wavering of minde: Slow steps: the convulsion of her necke: all these caused her wearinesse and feare of new trouble, she preferred SODOM'S *ease* before ZOAR'S safety. *Remember Lots Wife.*

This was her sinne: and this her sinne, was in her, made much more heynous by a double circumstance, well worth the remembring: as (ever) weighty circumstances are matter of speciall regard, in a *story* specially. 1. One, that she *fell* after she had *stood long*. 2. The other, that she fell, even then, when GOD, by all meanes offered her safety, and so *forsooke* her own mercy . . .

Saul that for *two* yeeres; *Judas*, that for *three*; *Nero*, that for *five* kept well, and then fell away, though it be much, yet may it be borne. But this woman had continued now *thirty* yeere (for, so they reckon from ABRAHAM'S going out of *Ur*, to the destruction of *Sodome*): This, this is the griefe, that she should *persist* all this time, and after all this time fall away. The rather, if wee consider yet further, that not only shee *continued* many yeeres, but *sustained many things* in her continuance, as being companion of *Abraham* and *Lot*, in their exile, their travell, and all their affliction. This is the griefe, that after all these stormes in the broad *sea* well past, shee should in this pitifull manner, be wracked in the *haven*. And when she had been in *Egypt*, and not poisoned with the *superstitions* of *Egypt*; when lived in *Sodome*, and not defiled with the *sinnes* of *Sodome*; not fallen away from the *famine* of *Canaan*, nor taken harme by the *fulnesse* of the *City of the Plaine*; after all this shee should loose the fruit of all this, and doe and suffer so many things all in vaine: This is the first: *Remember* it.

The second is no whit inferiour: That, at that instant shee wofully perished, when GODS speciall favour was profer'd to preserve her: and that, when, of all other times she had meanes and cause to stand; then of all other times, she fell away. Many were the mercies she found and felt at GODS hand, by this very title, that shee was *Lots Wife*. For, by it, shee was incorporated into the House and Family, and made partaker of the blessings of the *faithfull Abraham*. It was a mercy, to be delivered from the errors of *Ur*; a mercy to be kept safe in *Egypt*; a mercy, to be preserved from the *sinne of Sodome*; a mercy, to be delivered from the *Captivity of the five Kings*; and this the last and greatest mercy, that shee was sought to be delivered from the *perishing of the five Cities*. This (no doubt) doth mightily aggravate the offence, that, so many waies before remembred by God in trouble, she so coldly remembred Him: and that now presently being offered grace, she *knoweth not* the *day of her visitation*: but being brought out of *Sodome*, and warned of the danger that might ensue; having the *Angells* to goe before her, *Lot* to beare her company, her daughters to attend her, and being now at the entrance of *Zoar*, the haven of her rest; this very time, place and presence, shee maketh choyce of, to perish in, and to cast away that, which God would have saved; in respect of her selfe, *desperately*; of the Angels *contemptuously*; of her husband and daughters, *Scandalously*; of God and His favours, *unthankfully*; forsaking her owne mercy, and perishing in the sinne of wilfull defection . . .

And remember this withall, That she *looked backe* onely, and *went not* backe: Would, it may be, but that it was all on fire. But, whether she would or no, or whether we doe or no, this fore-thinking our selves, we be gone out, this faint proceeding, this staying in the plaine, this convulsion of the necke, and writhing the eyes backe; this irresolute wavering whether we should choose, either bodily *plesures* in perishing *Sodome*, or the *safety of our soules* in little *Zoar*, was her sinne; And this is the sinne of so many as *stand* as shee stood, and *looke* as shee looked, though they goe not backe: but, if they goe back too, they shall justifie her, and heape upon themselves a more heavy condemnation. So much for the sinne, which we should *remember to avoid*.

Now for her punishment, which we must *remember*, to *escape*. This relapse in this manner, that the world might know it to be a sinne highly displeasing his Majesty, God hath not onely marked it for a *sinne*, but *salted* it too, that it might never be forgotten.

The wages and punishment of this sinne of hers, was it, which is *the wages of all sinne*, that is, *Death*. *Death*, in her (sure) worthily, that refused life with so easie conditions, as the holding of her head still, and would needs *looke backe* and dye.

The sound of *Death* is fearefull, what death soever: yet it is made more fearefull foure waies; which all be in this of hers.

1. Wee desire to die with respite; and *sudden death*, wee feare and pray against. Her death was sudden, backe shee looked, and never looked forward more. It was her last looke.

2. Wee desire to have *remorse of sinne* ere we bee taken away; and death in the very act of sinne is most dangerous. Her death was so. She died in the very *convulsion*; She died with her *face* to *Sodome*.

3. Wee would die the *common* death of mankinde, and be visited *after the visitation of other men*: and an unusuall strange death is full of terrour. Hers was so, Gods owne hand from Heaven, by a strange and fearfull visitation.

4. Our wish is, to die, and to be *buried*, and not to remaine a spectacle above ground which Nature abhorreth: She so died, as she remained a spectacle of Gods wrath and a by-word to posterity, and as many as passed by. For untill CHRISTS time, and after, this monument was still extant, and remained undefaced so many hundred yeares, *Josephus* (a Writer of good account, which lived after this) saith, I my self have seen and beholden it, for it stands to be seen to this day. A *reed* she was, a *Pillar* she is; which she seemed to be, but was not. She was *melting water*: She is congealed to *salt*. Thus have we both her *fault* and *punishment*: Let us *remember* both: To shun the fault, that the penalty light not on us.

And, an high benefit it is for us, that He not only embalmeth the memory of the *lust* for our *Imitation*; but also powdreth and maketh brine of the *Evill, for our admonition*; that as a *Sent* from *Mary Magdalens ointment*; So, a *relish* from *Lots wives Pillar*, should remaine to all posterity.

Prophane persons, in their perishing, GOD could dash to peeces, and root out their remembrance from off the earth. He doth not, but suffereth their *Quarters* (as it were) to be set up in stories . . . that their punishment may be our advertisement. Powreth not out their blood, nor casts it away, but saves it, for a Bath . . . that the *Righteous* may *wash their footsteps in the blood of the ungodly*: that *all* (even the *ruine of the wicked*) may *cooperate to the good of them that feare* GOD). This woman, in her inconstancy, could He have sunk into the earth, or blowen-up as *salt-petre*, that no remembrance should have remained of her: He doth not; but, for us, and for our sakes, He erecteth a *Pillar*: And not a *Pillar* only, to point and gaze at; but a *Pillar* or *rocke of salt*, whence we may and must fetch, wherewith to season whatsoever is unsavoury in our lives. And this, this, is the life and soule of memorie: this is wisdome, The art of *extracting salt*, out of the *wicked; Triacle*, out of *vipers* . . . For (sure) though *Lots wife* were evill, her *salt* is good. Let us see then, how to make her evill, our good; see, if we can draw any savoury thing from this example.

. . . as she perisheth; So, at the same time, that *Sodome*: Shee, by it, and it, by her. That, one end commeth to the sinner without *repentance*, and to the just without *perseverance*. One end to the abomination of *Sodome*, and to the recidivation of *Lots wife*: They that *goe not out* of her, perish; and they that go out of her, perish too, if they look *back*.

. . . we need stir up our care of *continuing*, seeing we see it is nothing to begin, except we continue; nor to continue, except we do it to the end.

Remember, wee be not weary to goe whither GOD would have us . . . and never buy the ease of our body, with the hazard of our soule, or a few days of vanity with the losse of eternity.

Remember, we slack not our pace, nor *stand still* on the Plaine. For, if we stand still, by still standing, we are meet to be made a *Pillar*, even to stand still, and never to remove.

But specially *remember* we *leave not our heart behind* us, but that we take that with us, when we go out of *Sodome*: for if that stay, it will stay the feet, and writh the eye, and neither the one nor the other will do their duty. *Remember*, that our *heart* wander not, that our heart long not. This *Care*, if it be fervent, will bring us *Perseverance* . . .

Let us *remember* also, that as to her, so to us, God may send some *unusuall visitation*, and take us suddenly away, and in the act of sin too.

Remember the danger and damage: It is no lesse matter we are about, than *perdet animam* . . .

Remember the folly: that *beginning in the spirit* we *end in the flesh*: turning our backs to *Zoar*, we turne our face to *Sodome*: joyning to a *head* of fine *gold, feet* of clay, and to a precious foundation, a covering of thatch.

Remember the *Scandall*: That, falling our selves, we shall be a block for to make others fall: a sin no lighter; nor lesse, nor lighter than a *mil-stone*.

Remember the *Infamy*: That we shall leave our memory remaining in stories, among *Lots Wife* and *Jobs Wife, Demas* and *Ecebolius* and the number of *Relapsed*, there to stand to be pointed at, no less than this heap of *Salt*.

And lastly, *Remember* that we shall justifie *Sodome* by so doing, and her *frozen sin* shall condemn our *melting vertue*. For, they in the wilfulnesse of their wickednesse persisted till fire from heaven consumed them: And, they being thus obdurate in sin, ought not she (and we much more) to be constant in vertue? And, if the drunkard hold out, till he have lost his *eyes*; the unclean person, till he have wasted his *loynes*; the contentious, till he have consumed his *wealth*, What shame is it, that *God*'s unhappy people should not be as constant in vertue, as these miscreants *have beene*, and be in vice!

Each of these by it selfe; all these put together, will make a full *Memento*: which if she had *remembred*, she had been a *Pillar* of light in heaven, not of *salt* in earth. It is too late, for her: we, in due time yet, may remember it . . .

And *Blessed be God and the Father of our* LORD JESUS CHRIST, that we stand in the presence of such a *Prince*: who hath ever accounted of *Perseverance*, not only as of *Regina virtutum*, the Queene of vertues; but, as of *virtus Reginarum*, the vertue of a *Queene*. Who (like *Zorobabel*) first, by *Princely magnanimity*, laid the *Corner-stone*, in a troublesome time: and since, by *Heroicall constancy*, through many both alluring proffers and threatning dangers, hath brought forth the *Head-stone* also, with the Prophets acclamation, *Grace, grace, unto it: Grace*, for so happy a *beginning*; and *Grace*, for so thrice happy an ending. No terrours, no enticement; no care of her safety hath removed her from her stedfastnesse: but, with a fixed eye, with straight steps, with a resolute mind, hath entred her selfe, and brought us unto *Zoar. It is a little one*, but therin *our soules shall live*; and we are in safety, all the Cities of the *Plaine* being in *combustion* round about us . . .

A SODOM ANTHOLOGY

A Sermon Preached Before Queene Elizabeth, at *Hampton Court*, on *Wednesday*, being the VI. of March, A.D. MDXCIIII. LUKE Chap. XVII. Vers. XXXII., Memores estote Uxoris Lot. *Remember* Lots *Wife*.

SUE GOLDING
The Address Book

I will be quite frank with you: I've always preferred black leather bindings fitted smooth across hand-sized address books. Nothing else written on or near the cover; discreet and rather disciplined, though not without its smells, its textures and its raunch. That's black leather for you; and that's how I've always preferred it. Address books, case in point.

Like most people in our condition, I have, over the years, improved on the necessary ritual involved in choosing the perfect address book. Of course it requires one to be in the right frame of mind, utterly focused and with sturdy step (though not to the extent that you might draw attention to yourself). Personally, it has always included a long slow dip into water – hot baths or springs, if you're lucky – a long slow dip to exaggerate last night's debauched pleasures or its succulent pains. Lately, I've taken to wearing, on that special day, the finest starched white shirt buttoned exact and to the top. And more recent still, I've included some small new trophy, like the extravagant dildo from last year's indiscretions, or the silk scarf from the time before . . . I'll just quietly tuck it away against my body so as to call up the tongue of S– or maybe the hands of J–, sweeping gently but urgently against my skin as if to coax me forward and remind me of that special kind of something, that special kind of nakedness, so required of each and every one of us (I mean, the people in our condition) who try madly and sometimes in vain not to falter at the exact moment when the reality of the Address Book is nigh.

For as we all know, it is a very delicate task – this choosing of the Book – and the smallest slip, the tiniest crack in style or in mood will disturb the momentum, might even tarnish the memory and in any case will propel you stupidly and without grace toward that stoically menacing ever-present arena, blandly called: the checkout-counter. Without ritual, without a well-selected, polished little routine honed to fine art, how many times can you muster that special kind of courage before another year slides by and the moroseness settles in? For the passage from the land of un-deadness to some other shore, is tricky indeed.

And I've often thought to myself, eyes half-closed, lips half-opened: how many indiscriminate baths would I have to take if the ritual had not yet firmly been set; how many haircuts would I have to afford; how many pairs of shoes must I buy in order to prepare body and soul, permanently, for the rawness of that moment; for the endurance required, year after year *to pick up that new replacement and hold it and smell it and write in their names*? Page after page, life after life.

One time, after several consecutive deaths (every week, another, more dreadful than the previous; and the headlines were as usual, gleefully shouting 'Sodom and Gomorrah Gets Gays At Last!!'); well, that particular time (it was after David died to be exact), I bought myself an especially useful gift for our purpose: a tight pair of tit clamps, exquisitely engraved at the top and along its sterling silver edges, with tiny (removable) rubber pads neatly tucked under each tongue. The pair had a nice weight and you could moderate the pressure, should you or your various partners require such moderation. They were versatile, too, with enough chain-link to be used in almost any position, and on almost any part of the body.

You know precisely what I mean.

During the night, before the next day's Event, I wandered across the Cross, a seedy little space rife with curb crawlers and police. All the rest – those without the money – huddled against the pavement or munched on some trash or drank bootleg or just laughed out loud. My intentions were obvious to anyone with half a brain cell and some enthusiasm for the more playful sides of life, anuses included. I began to imagine whole initiation scenes with those body temples, now hoisted well atop stilettoes and, for the most part, scattered over here or, to a much lesser extent, over there. Oh how I hungered for that special sacred grease of the someone else and the something other! Oh for the fluids that might scatter wildly about, spraying, spraying, and shooting so alive! This obsession, our obsession, for the laughter, for the joke, for the orifice wrapped up in a sweaty surprise, red lipstick included; wrapped up and delivered through some minor rite of passage! A craving directed only and always toward transforming forever (or at least for a few hours) a world without cunning or the pleasure of its dare.

(This obsession, our obsession for the dark, for the moist, for the scented and the risk; this obsession, pulsates lewd and slow within me and mingles with that strange hospitality so conspicuous to anyone on the prowl.)

But the sour smell of patrol-dog-fur changed from its background hover to an ugly flash: it is almost like a dream, I tell you . . . With open howls crashing dead against the tarmac of the street, they leapt upon the not-so-innocent dirty, moist citizens of this night. And those who could, raced about, frantic for cover, coughing and spitting and diving into waiting cars (if lucky). And when, after fifteen minutes – count them: fifteen lousy minutes – I stood there, feeling terribly alone (though an old whore stood nearby), I was trembling with anger and mesmerized with fear. For there was nothing left! neither hide nor hair of what stood – only minutes before, fifteen lousy minutes earlier – as nasty irritants, stoic reminders for all those who need reminding, that this was our house! the dwelling of our past, the figment of our future! But now, now it were as if a seamless mouth with no body nor mind nor wing nor song, impaled itself, bloodlusting against the fray. And it swallowed deep and hard, leaving not the smallest trace of our madness or the slightest scent of our play.

Stabbed in mid-run, my eyes could not close: watching, watching, watching. An interminable pierce! And as the blood oozed out, I can still smell the very surface of my skin, the smell of individual rotting, the putrid terror in each and every second of that fifteen minute span; 900 moments of the Law galvanizing and swirling more relentless with every screaming footstep. HOW COULD YOU *NOT* WATCH IT? Well, as for me, I stood there; I watched, all right; I watched even though the bile spilled up into my throat and over onto my tongue, coating the backsides of my teeth; burning me, burning all of me. And it burned and burned and burned, until the I of me was reduced to a stunned and sickly silence.

First she asked me for a cigarette, then another. And now, in a rather low whisper – THOUGH NO ONE ELSE EXISTED AT TWO MINUTES BEYOND THE FIFTEEN – she asked me about, of all things, my hair. It was a sincere question, she assured me, in the lowest of tones imaginable . . . I tell you, it was almost like a dream: first the dogs and now this question! The darkness, at once so full of possibility and now so utterly claustrophobic; now so haunted by moments not all that long ago past! And I thought: I am going to explode; there is nothing to stop this now, and by god, it will not be a pretty sight. I will splatter somewhere between the airlessness of that goddam good and the innocence of this bad.

I could not look at her. She repulsed me. She repulsed me even more than I repulsed myself, though perhaps it was just because the air stood eerily at bay, more dead than alive. Well, who could be certain of *that*? she repulsed me in any event. Bitterly.

I spat out at her, 'And for what? And for how long! these thousands of deaths! . . . And you ask about hair?' I demanded of her to account for herself, to account for it all, enraged and sickened by the battle, the battle we had for so long fought . . . and had lost. For I saw it all too clearly now: we were the Failures, the Woman-Nigger-Jew in a very phobic world and (I tell you, this is exactly how it happened), I spat out against her, and cursed the whole, bloody, thing . . . Spinning round, turning, my head filled with all the projectiles of my rage . . . I searched for the right word . . . I was so very much inside it. I simply could not say one more thing or I would have surely burst right then and there . . .

She laughed.

She laughed, now, low and hard and, indeed, began to bellow and wheeze, barely able to get the words out, so funny did she find my stand. The philosopher in her made its way out: 'Lift a rock, find a goddam romantic', she eventually proclaimed, 'oh for the sex goddeses of t'day to understand the story of Lot's wife!' and demanded another smoke.

A-ha! Stung into life, I crawled from under that rock: 'A stupid, morally indefensible tale!' I shrieked back against the envelope of this night, delirious and almost swept away (though moving not an inch). 'A stupid tale! you stupid whore! (who really ought to know!); an utterly, completely and without reservation, indefensible in its rot . . .'

She blew a large bubble, popped it and pretending not to hear my words – though she must have heard them, I WAS NOT DREAMING – she pulled out a neatly folded gum wrapper from way beneath her skirt, and proceeded to recite the four lines of verse written therein:

> I have never seen no flower
> bloom without the aid of water;
> And I wouldn't touch no
> human skin cut off from blood and oil.

171

> Lot's Wife no tale of sex
> and slime or other moral *sin*
> just how we gotta eat it
> all, if we're to live, a'gin.

The old whore folded the gum wrapper and stuffed it in my pocket, right next to the (now utterly useless) tit clamps. I shut my eyes and watched myself watch Lot's Wife: poor LW! Stricken at the grisly sounds of a hell-fire curdling the bloodlines of that city – her city – turns to catch the last bit of wretched commotion, of life itself standing before the void, standing at the very precipice of the present tense as it explodes into the past – whereupon and despite Lot's infamous warnings, she is transformed into a pillar of salt.

For the blinding sight of the deep flash when the living goes to dead – the very transformation of Sodom and Gomorrah into the past tense of total annihilation – was precisely 'history', now; her history-now; exactly her memory, and, as such, it set the boundary over which she could not possibly leap. As she swirls backward to re-live the impossible, as she tries in vain to hold onto a reality tangible only as memory-past, she condemns herself to an endless immobility, a static hell infinitely attempting to retrieve that which no longer exists.

Not surprisingly, the whore knew that poetry, well. It had not one whit to do with morality; there was not, contrary to the popular reading of this tale, a moral reason preventing Lot's Wife from re-living or maintaining the past. There was only one reason, and it was a practical one: she could not – nor could anyone else for that matter – attempt to sustain a present or future life endlessly rooted in the land of the dead. That would condemn any 'survivor' to a tearful emptiness so profound as to become no life at all. For to re-live forever the very instant of that memory – the very instant of a life gone by – would manage only to squeeze interminably the very juice from one's limbs. It would always-already dry us right up – embodying the pristine absence of the future in the un-deadness of our gaze. And it would monumentalize us precisely (as the global fairy tale so eloquently named it) as a pillar of salt.

Paralysed.

Is it no wonder that the rawness of possibility and change in the face of – rather than in spite of – all the mad pleasures and damnations and decay, begins with taking the memories of them: ALIVE; by carrying those memory figments forward and as close to the body parts as possible, playing with them, re-inventing them and, in the most profane and moist sense of the phrase, of 'never looking back'.

So David died last week . . . Before his death, it was Lorne; Michael (a flaming queen) a couple of days earlier . . . I used to borrow Ricky's leather jacket: now I've inherited it. Danny, Andrew, Teddy, Sam (we called him 'Daddy') . . . The funeral Alan prepared for himself was particularly riveting (made me think that I, too, should have Gregorian chants and naked people carrying white lit candles, solemnly and in step when my death-time comes) . . .

A long, slow, and very hot bath. Starched white shirt buttoned exact and to the collar. Cuff links (silver, I should think, and very plain). Hair in a sharply angled cut. Fine leather boots. Oh yes, and of course: the gum wrapper, neatly folded and held between the tongues of those lovely little clamps, with their perfect weighted chains leaning right up next to my body. Wouldn't dream of buying the Book without them: the task is too delicate; each name's inscription, too extreme.

Sue Golding, 'The Address Book' (original publication).

From a Dictionary of the Bible, 1893

SODOM . . . Jerome vacillates between singular and plural, noun and adjective. He employs all the following forms, *Sodoman, in Sodomis, Sodomorum, Sodomæ, Sodomitæ*. One of the most ancient cities of Syria, whose name is now a synonym for the most disgusting and opprobrious of vices. It is commonly mentioned in connexion with Gomorrah, but also with Admah and Zeboim, and on one occasion (Gen. xiv.) with Bela or Zoar. Sodom was evidently the chief town in the settlement. Its king takes the lead and the city is always named first in the list, and appears to be the most important. The four are first named in the ethnological records of Gen. x. 19, as belonging to the Canaanites . . .

Without questioning that the narrative of Gen. xix. is strictly historical throughout, we are not at present in possession of sufficient knowledge of the topography and of the names attached to the sites of this remarkable region, to enable any profitable conclusions to be arrived at on this (the site of Sodom) and other kindred questions connected with the destruction of the five cities.

SODOMITES (*scortator, effeminatus*). This word does not denote the inhabitants of Sodom (except only in 2 Esdr. vii. 36) nor their descendants; but is employed in the A.V. of the Old Testament for those who practised as a religious rite the abominable and unnatural vice from which the inhabitants of Sodom and Gomorrah have derived their lasting infamy. It occurs in Deut. xxiii. 17; 1 K. xiv. 24. 12, xxii. 46; 2 K. xxiii. 7; and Job xxxvi. 14 (margin). The Hebrew word *Kadesh* is said to be derived from a root *kadash*, which (strange as it may appear) means 'pure,' and thence 'holy'. The words *sacer* in Latin, and 'devoted' in our own language, have also a double meaning, though the subordinate signification is not so absolutely contrary to the principal one as it is in the case of *kadesh*. 'This dreadful "consecration", or rather desecration, was spread in different forms over Phoenicia, Syria, Phrygia, Assyria, Babylonia. Ashtaroth, the Greek Astarte, was its chief object.' It appears also to have been established at Rome where its victims were called Galli (not from Gallia, but from the river Gallus in

Bithynia), there is an instructive note on the subject in Jerome's *Cómm.* on Hos. iv. 14.

SODOMITISH SEA, THE (*Mare Sodomiticum*), 2 Esdr. v. 7; meaning the Dead Sea. It is the only instance in the Books of the Old Testament, New Testament, or Apocrypha, of an approach to the inaccurate modern opinion which connects the salt lake with the destruction of Sodom. The name may, however, arise here simply from Sodom having been situated near the lake..

Sir William Smith, D.C.L., LL.D., ed., *A Dictionary of the Bible: Comprising its Antiquities, Biography, Geography and Natural History*, vol. 3, London, John Murray, 1893. Entries on 'Sodom', 'Sodomites' and 'Sodomitish Sea, The'.

A Day-Trip to Sodom

It turns out that an ingenious travel agency could organize fairly passable day-trips to Sodom on behalf of gay tourists, assuming – a big assumption – the Israeli authorities wouldn't soon put an outraged stop to it. There'd be quite a lot to look at, and even more to think about while looking; a heavy tan to be got; and a float (for you can't really swim in it) in the Dead Sea.

I got foiled this September 5 in efforts I made to get really close to the site where the town stood. All I could do was take the coach-tour out of Jerusalem to Masada, which is 10 miles or so to the north of the site. From Masada, the high fortified rock where in AD 73 Jewish defendants killed themselves rather than surrender to the besieging Roman army, you look down on the great expanse of the Dead Sea burning under the sun. And you can look, from that height, at where Sodom once was.

Sodom, and Gomorrah, and three more towns. For there were five Cities of the Plain (says Genesis), which God destroyed (Gen. 18.20) 'because the cry of Sodom and Gomorrah is great and because their sin is very grievous'. Since the probable dating of the historical destruction of the Cities is around 1900–2000 BC, and the land-area they covered was very small, they'll have been tiny, scarcely more than villages in our terms.

I worked out, from the information I could get hold of, what sort of a day out the Guided Tour to Sodom would be. For a start, on Israeli prices, it would be about £20 a head, for an air-conditioned coach leaving Jerusalem by the Mont of Olives at 8 am, and returning to Jerusalem round about 5 in the afternoon. Lunch of some sort would be thrown in for that, and if enough tourists became interested, the price would tumble. The Dead Sea is about the size of Lake Geneva, so the tour means a 10 mile eastward descent from Jerusalem to the northern start of the Sea, and then a 40 mile run along the western (Israeli) shore to 'Sedom' at the southernmost end. Sedom, a name which is of course a memory of Sodom, is dry ground, with salt mines

176

and salt factories, but also a youth-camp and picnic site and a Sedom post-office stamp. So post-cards could be written home from Sodom . . .

But the Sedom of today, though worth its place on the tour for the pillars of salt that still stand there, is the name of a region, and not – probably – exactly where the cities themselves once stood. The likeliest place for the vanished original Sodom is under the waters which lap the baking dry ground of modern Sedom: under the southernmost waters of the Dead Sea, which are shallow. So rowing boats, or preferably glass-bottomed boats, would be needed.

The gays (and others along for the ride) get into the boats and will see 'something quite fantastic. Some distance from the shore, and clearly visible under the surface of the water, stretch the outlines of forests which the extraordinarily high salt content of the Dead Sea has kept in preservation. The trunks and roots in the shimmering green depths must be very ancient indeed. Once upon a time, when they were in blossom and green foliage covered their twigs and branches, perhaps the flocks of Lot grazed under their shadow . . .'*

No buildings, no trace of human existence, but trees. For the Bible doesn't at all describe Sodom and Gomorrah as Babylonish places, but says they lay in a valley 'well-watered everywhere . . . even as the garden of the Lord, like the land of Egypt'. It was a paradise, a beautiful and fertile small land.

Geologists estimate that $c.$1900 BC there was an earthquake, and the Dead Sea burst its former southern boundary, and collapsed onto the subsiding floor of what had been the townships in the valley.

There'll be no getting out of the boats to snorkel, unless with very good equipment. Dead Sea water can cause temporary blindness if the eyes are exposed to it, and nausea and vomiting for days if it's swallowed. The best you can do is to gingerly let yourself into it – or, from the shore, wade out into it – and float cautiously on your back, in sunglasses and preferably a hat as well. The heat is like the Sahara or Arizona.

And what kind of information would the tour-guide be handing out to anyone who wasn't fast asleep or chatting on board the bus? Nothing very earnest or scholarly, for who could be pedantic in front of about

---

* The quote is from Werner Keller, *The Bible as History*, London, Hodder & Stoughton, 1969, p. 94.

60 gay tourists doing a Guided Tour to Sodom in holiday mood – but there could be a booklet, for anyone who wanted to settle down and read. I see it as dedicated to the Rev. Ian Paisley for his Save Ulster from Sodomy campaign, and giving a revised history of the town and of the reputation it has been given. Something perhaps by John Boswell . . .

The imaginary Handbook to Sodom would show that there isn't a shred of historical justification for thinking that Sodom and Gomorrah or the other settlements were havens for gay people, till disaster overtook them. It would show how the Old Testament writers (Ezekiel, Isaiah, Jeremiah) not only contradict one another in what they say about Sodom, but make no mention of homosexuality. In fact it would show what an indescribable number of lies have been told about a farming valley that was swept away long before Moses brought the Jewish people to Canaan.

But many of us would still, I think, take the Guided Tour of Sodom if anyone ever gets it going. Legend too is a kind of fact, and if the imagination can blaze at the site of Troy with thoughts of Achilles and Patroclus, or at Knossos from thoughts of the labyrinth, or indeed in Jerusalem at the host of religious sites – then sprawling in the bottom of a boat on the Dead Sea staring through glass at the preserved woodlands of Sodom, deep beneath the water, ought to be good for a solemn moment or two.

Andrew Lumsden, 'A Day-Trip to Sodom', *Gay News*, 252, 28 October–10 November 1982.

The Dead Sea
(Encyclopaedia Entry, Nineteenth
Century)

DEAD SEA, the largest lake in Palestine, and physically, as well as historically, among the most remarkable in the world. It is called in Scripture *The Salt Sea* (Gen. xiv. 3), *The Sea of the Plain*, or more correctly of the *Arabah* (Deut. iii. 17), and *The East Sea* (Ezek. xlvii. 18). Josephus calls it the *Asphaltic Lake*, a name adopted by classic writers in allusion to the bitumen, or asphaltum, which abounds in its basin. Jerome gave it the name *Dead Sea* because its waters are so fatal to animal life, and in the Talmud it is called the *Sea of Sodom*. Its common name among the inhabitants of Palestine is *Baheiret Luî*, 'The Sea of Lot.'

The sea is 46 miles long, and varies from 5 to 9 in breadth. Its bed is the lowest part of the great valley of the Jordan; and its surface has a depression of no less than 1308 feet beneath the level of the ocean. . . . At the north-west curve of the sea are extensive salt marshes, and at the south-west is a range of hills of rock salt, 7 miles long and 300 feet high, called *Khashm Usdom*, 'The ridge of Sodom.'

. . . Lying in a deep cavity, shut in by naked white hills, exposed during the long summer to the burning rays of an unclouded sun, nothing could be expected on the shores of the Dead Sea but sterility. Yet here and there on the low plains to the north and south, and on the eastern and western sides, wherever a little fountain springs up, or a mountain streamlet flows, there are thickets of willow, tamarisk, and acacia, among which the birds sing as sweetly as in more genial climes. The Arab also pitches his tent beside them, and sometimes cultivates a few patches of grain and tobacco. The heat causes such excessive evaporation that though the Jordan and other smaller streams fall into the lake the water seems to be gradually decreasing. The marshes along the shore, especially to the north and south, emit pestilential exhalations, during summer and autumn which are fatal to strangers, and which make the inhabitants of Jericho, and the few poor tribes who pitch their tents in the surrounding territory, weak and sickly. They are degraded and immoral also, as were their progenitors in the 'cities of the plain'.

The only ruin of note close to the Dead Sea is the fortress of Masada, on a cliff on the western shore, opposite the peninsula of Lisân. It was the scene of the final struggle between the Jews and the Romans after the destruction of Jerusalem by Titus. At Engedi there are a few ruins; and also at Ain-el-Feshkhah on the north-west, and on a little peninsula near the mouth of the Jordan. The ruins of Sodom and Gomorrah have entirely disappeared. Their site is disputed, for some hold that they stood near the northern end of the lake, while others affirm that they must have been situated at the southern end . . .

The presence of so much saline matter is accounted for by the washings of the salt range of Sodom, the numerous brackish springs along the shore, and the great evaporation. The reports of early travellers, however, regarding the Dead Sea were to a great extent fabulous. They represented it as an infernal region, its black and fetid waters always emitting a noisome vapour, which being driven over the adjoining land destroyed all vegetation; they also stated that no birds could fly over it. All this is untrue; the water is as transparent as that of the Mediterranean, and a bath in it is both pleasant and refreshing.

The historical notices of the Dead Sea extend back nearly 4000 years. When Lot looked down from the heights of Bethel, he 'beheld all the plain of the Jordan that it was well watered, before the Lord destroyed Sodom, even as the garden of the Lord' (Gen. xiii. 10). The region is further described as a 'deep valley' (*Emek*, Gen. xiv. 3, 8), distinguished by 'fertile fields' (*Siddim*). The aspect now is entirely different. There must have been a lake then as now; but it was smaller, and had a margin of fertile plain, especially on the southern end, 'as thou comest unto Zoar.' In the narration of the capture of the cities of the plain by the Eastern Kings, it is said that they were situated in the 'vale of Siddim,' which was full of 'bitumen (slime) pits.' When the cities were destroyed, 'the Lord rained upon Sodom and Gomorrah brimstone and fire from the Lord out of heaven;' and Abraham from the mountain ridges 'looked toward Sodom, and toward all the land of the plain, and, lo, the smoke of the country went up as the smoke of a furnace' (Gen. xix. 24, 28). The sacred writer further asserts regarding the whole of Siddim that it became the Salt Sea, or was submerged; and consequently it now forms part of the bed of the lake.

These events entirely changed, as it would seem, both the political and physical condition of the whole region. Upon the plains originally existing round the sea Gentile and Jewish records combine in placing the earliest seat of Phoenician civilization. 'The Tyrians,' says Justin, 'first dwelt by the Syrian lake before they removed to Sidon.' Sodom and Gomorrah are mentioned as the first cities of the Canaanites; and when Lot went down from Bethel 'the cities of the plain' formed a nucleus of civilized life before any city, except Hebron and perhaps Jerusalem, had sprung up in central Palestine. The great catastrophe in the days of Abraham changed the aspect of the country, and gave a death-blow to its prosperity. With the exception of the village of Engedi, and the small town of Jericho, the circuit of the Dead Sea appears to have remained ever afterwards almost without settled inhabitants.

Recent researches, especialy those of M. Lartet, the Duc de Luynes, and Canon Tristram, have contributed greatly to our knowledge of the physical geography of the Dead Sea basin . . .

Many traces of volcanic action, both remote and recent, have been observed in the basin of the Dead Sea, such as trap dykes, and hot sulphur and brackish springs. Tristram describes a valley at the northern end of the salt range of Sodom, in which there are 'large masses of bitumen mingled with gravel. These overlie a thick stratum of sulphur, which again overlies a thicker stratum of sand so strongly impregnated with sulphur that it yields powerful fumes on being sprinkled over a hot coal. The bitumen, unlike that which we pick up on the shore, is strongly impregnated with sulphur. Above all, it is calcined, and bears the marks of having been subjected to extreme heat. So far as I can understand this deposit, if there be any physical evidence left of the catastrophe which destroyed Sodom and Gomorrah, or of similar occurrences, we have it here. The whole appearance points to a shower of hot sulphur, and an irruption of bitumen upon it, which would naturally be calcined and impregnated with its fumes; and this at a geological period quite subsequent to all the diluvial and alluvial action of which we have such abundant evidence. The catastrophe must have been since the formation of the valley, and while the water was at its present level, – therefore, probably during the historic period.' (*Land of Israel*, pp. 355, sq.)

Tristram applies the above-observed facts to the solution of the great historical question about the destruction of the cities of the plain in the following manner:

'Setting aside all preconceived notions, and taking the simple record of Genesis xix. as we find it, let us see whether the existing condition of the country throws any light on the Biblical narrative. Certainly we do observe by the lake sulphur and bitumen in abundance. Sulphur springs stud the shores, sulphur is strewn, whether in layers or in fragments, over the desolate plains; and bitumen is ejected in great floating masses from the bottom of the sea, oozes through the fissures of the rocks, is deposited with gravel on the beach, or appears with sulphur to have been precipitated by some convulsion. We know that at the time of earthquakes bitumen seems to be detached from the bottom of the lake. Everything leads to the conclusion that the agency of fire was at work. The kindling of such a mass of combustible material, either by lightning from heaven, or by other electrical agency, combined with an earthquake ejecting other bitumen or sulphur from the lake, would soon spread devastation over the plain, so that the smoke of the country would go up as the smoke of a furnace.' (*Land of Israel*, p. 359).

Here we have to do only with physical facts and appearances. A mass of burning sulphurous matter might be ejected from some open crater, as is often the case with Vesuvius; and this, falling upon the cities and the bituminous plain around them, would produce just such a form of conflagration as Abraham is stated to have seen. The valley may then have sunk a few feet, and become submerged. This, it is true, is mere theory; it is a theory, however, suggested, and to a large extent confirmed, by the physical aspect of the country, and the careful observations of travellers around the lake. The subject is not one for vague speculation, and much less for dogmatic assertion. The problems which the Dead Sea presents must be solved, if they are ever to be solved, by scientific research.

It is not strange that the Dead Sea has never been navigated to any extent. It seems probable from the statement of Josephus (*Ant.* ix. 1, 2) that the Moabites crossed it to invade Judah; and he tells us the Romans used boats against the fugitive Jews (*B.J.* iv. 7, 6). Costigan was the first in modern times to navigate it, going from the mouth of the Jordan to the peninsula of Lisân in the boat by which he had come from Tiberias. He afterwards died of fatigue and exhaustion. In 1837 Moore and

Beck conveyed a little boat from Joppa, and visited some points. Ten years later Lieutenant Molyneux took a boat to the peninsula, and his life was also sacrificed. The expedition of Lynch was far more successful, and he was the first thoroughly to examine the shores, and to determine the depths by soundings. Several of his party took the fever which is so fatal, and one died. Winter is the proper season for such researches. Rain seldom falls; and the air during the depth of winter is fresh, and cold almost unknown.

Professor J.L. Porter, Entry on the Dead Sea, *Encyclopaedia Britannica*, vol. 7, 9th Edition, 1877.

VOLTAIRE

Asphalt

ASPHALTUS is a Chaldæan word, signifying a species of bitumen. There is a great deal of it in the countries watered by the Euphrates; it is also to be found in Europe, but of a bad quality. An experiment was made by covering the tops of the watch-houses on each side of one of the gates of Geneva; the covering did not last a year, and the mine has been abandoned. However, when mixed with rosin, it may be used for lining cisterns; perhaps it will some day be applied to a more useful purpose.

The real asphaltus is that which was obtained in the vicinity of Babylon, and with which it is said that the Greek fire was fed. Several lakes are full of asphaltus, or a bitumen resembling it, as others are strongly impregnated with nitre. There is a great lake of nitre in the desert of Egypt, which extends from lake Mœris to the entrance of the Delta; and it has no other name than the Nitre Lake.

The Lake Asphaltites, known by the name of Sodom, was long famed for its bitumen; but the Turks now make no use of it, either because the mine under the water is diminished, because its quality is altered, or because there is too much difficulty in drawing it from under the water. Oily particles of it, and sometimes large masses, separate and float on the surface; these are gathered together, mixed up, and sold for balm of Mecca.

Flavius Josephus, who was of that country, says that, in his time, there were no fish in the lake of Sodom, and the water was so light that the heaviest bodies would not go to the bottom. It seems that he meant to say heavy instead of so light. It would appear that he had not made the experiment. After all, a stagnant water, impregnated with salts and compact matter, its specific matter being then greater than that of the body of a man or a beast, might force it to float. Josephus's error consists in assigning a false cause to a phenomenon which may be perfectly true.

As for the want of fish, it is not incredible. It is, however, likely that this lake, which is fifty or sixty miles long, is not all asphaltic; and that while receiving the waters of the Jordan it also receives the fishes of that river; but perhaps the Jordan, too, is without fish, and they are to be found only in the upper lake of Tiberias.

Josephus adds, that the trees which grow on the borders of the Dead Sea bear fruits of the most beautiful appearance, but which fall into dust if you attempt to taste them. This is less probable; and disposes one to believe that Josephus either had not been on the spot, or has exaggerated according to his own and his countrymen's custom. No soil seems more calculated to produce good as well as beautiful fruits than a salt and sulphurous one, like that of Naples, of Catania, and of Sodom.

The Holy Scriptures speak of five cities being destroyed by fire from heaven. On this occasion natural philosophy bears testimony in favor of the Old Testament, although the latter has no need of it, and they are sometimes at variance. We have instances of earthquakes, accompanied by thunder and lightning, which have destroyed much more considerable towns than Sodom and Gomorrah.

But the River Jordan necessarily discharging itself into this lake without an outlet, this Dead Sea, in the same manner as the Caspian, must have existed as long as there has been a River Jordan; therefore, these towns could never stand on the spot now occupied by the lake of Sodom. The Scripture, too, says nothing at all about this ground being changed into a lake, it says quite the contrary: 'Then the Lord rained upon Sodom and upon Gomorrah brimstone and fire, from the Lord out of heaven. And Abraham got up early in the morning, and he looked toward Sodom and Gomorrah, and toward all the land of the plain, and beheld; and lo, the smoke of the country went up as the smoke of a furnace.'

These five towns, Sodom, Gomorrah, Zeboin, Adamah, and Segor, must then have been situated on the borders of the Dead Sea. How, it will be asked, in a desert so uninhabitable as it now is, where there are to be found only a few hordes of plundering Arabs, could there be five cities, so opulent as to be immersed in luxury, and even in those shameful pleasures which are the last effect of the refinement of the debauchery attached to wealth? It may be answered that the country was then much better.

Other critics will say – how could five towns exist at the extremities of a lake, the water of which, before their destruction, was not potable? The Scripture itself informs us that all this land was asphaltic before the burning of Sodom: 'And the vale of Sodom was full of slime-pits; and the kings of Sodom and Gomorrah fled and fell there.'

Another objection is also stated. Isaiah and Jeremiah say that Sodom and Gomorrah shall never be rebuilt; but Stephen, the geographer, speaks of Sodom and Gomorrah on the coast of the Dead Sea; and the 'History of the Councils' mentions bishops of Sodom and Segor. To this it may be answered that God filled these towns, when rebuilt, with less guilty inhabitants; for at that time there was no bishop *in partibus*.

But, it will be said, with what water could these new inhabitants quench their thirst? All the wells are brackish; you find asphaltus and corrosive salt on first striking a spade into the ground.

It will be answered that some Arabs still subsist there, and may be habituated to drinking very bad water; that the Sodom and Gomorrah of the Eastern Empire were very wretched hamlets, and that at that time there were many bishops whose whole diocese consisted in a poor village. It may also be said that the people who colonized these villages prepared the asphaltus, and carried on a useful trade in it.

The arid and burning desert, extending from Segor to the territory of Jerusalem, produces balm and aromatic herbs for the same reason that it supplies naphtha, corrosive salt and sulphur.

It is said that petrifaction takes place in this desert with astonishing rapidity; and this, according to some natural philosophers, makes the petrifaction of Lot's wife Edith a very plausible story.

But it is said that this woman, 'having looked back, became a pillar of salt.' This, then, was not a natural petrifaction, operated by asphaltus and salt, but an evident miracle. Flavius Josephus says that he saw this pillar. St. Justin and St. Irenæus speak of it as a prodigy, which in their time was still existing.

These testimonies have been looked upon as ridiculous fables. It would, however, be very natural for some Jews to amuse themselves with cutting a heap of asphaltus into a rude figure, and calling it Lot's wife. I have seen cisterns of asphaltus, very well made, which may last a long time. But it must be owned that St. Irenæus goes a little too far when he says that Lot's wife remained in the country of Sodom no longer in corruptible flesh, but as a permanent statue of salt, her feminine nature still producing the ordinary effect: '*Uxor remansit in Sodomis, jam non caro corruptibilis sed statua salis semper manens, et per naturalia ea quæsunt consuetudinis hominis ostendens.*'

St Irenæus does not seem to express himself with all the precision of a good naturalist when he says Lot's wife is no longer of corruptible flesh, but still retains her feminine nature.

In the poem of Sodom, attributed to Tertullian, this is expressed with still greater energy:

> Dicitur et vivens alio sub corpore se us,
> Mirifice solito dispungere sanguine menses.

This was translated by a poet of the time of Henry II., in his Gallic style:

> *La femme à Loth, quoique sel devenue,*
> *Est femme encore; care elle a sa menstrue.*

The land of aromatics was also the land of fables. Into the deserts of Arabia Petræa the ancient mythologists pretend that Myrrha, the granddaughter of a statue, fled after committing incest with her father, as Lot's daughters did with theirs, and that she was metamorphosed into the tree that bears myrrh. Other profound mythologists assure us that she fled into Arabia Felix; and this opinion is as well supported as the other.

Be this as it may, not one of our travellers has yet thought fit to examine the soil of Sodom, with its asphaltus, its salt, its trees and their fruits, to weigh the water of the lake, to analyze it, to ascertain whether bodies of greater specific gravity than common water float upon its surface, and to give us a faithful account of the natural history of the country. Our pilgrims to Jerusalem do not care to go and make these researches; this desert has become infested by wandering Arabs, who range as far as Damascus, and retire into the caverns of the mountains, the authority of the pasha of Damascus having been inadequate to repress them. Thus the curious have but little information about anything concerning the Asphaltic Lake.

As to Sodom, it is a melancholy reflection for the learned that, among so many who may be deemed natives, not one has furnished us with any notion whatever of this capital city.

Entry on 'ASPHALTUS. Asphaltic Lake – Sodom', in *The Works of Voltaire: A Contemporary Version. A Philosophical Dictionary*, vol. 3, Pt 2. Translated by William F. Fleming. New York, Dingwall-Rock, Ltd., 1927.

EDWIN FEY

Summer in Sodom

Ted didn't see either Eileen or Ian all the next day. Mostly he didn't see them because he lay on his bed staring up at the ceiling all through the hot, sticky morning and afternoon.

Once with Ian he could have explained to himself. He *had* explained it to himself by saying it was an accident brought on by his over-excited state and by the frustration of his relations with Eileen. But last night had showed that explanation up for what it was . . . a fantasy. There was more to his relationship with Ian than he had thought. He had to face the fact that here was something about him, Ted, that responded to other than normal sexual desires.

He had to face it, but could he? The men and boys he had seen at the Golden Onion haunted him and he rejected the idea that he was like them. He had found the bar itself boring and their talk and manners offensive. Surely he couldn't be one of them! Then what was he? My God, what was he?

It wasn't one of Ted's better days and by four o'clock he decided to get up and get out of his room before he went absolutely crazy. He dressed quickly in clean jeans and a pullover shirt that fitted smoothly over the well-developed muscles in his chest and arms. Then he ran a comb through his red hair and stalked from the room. He was supposed to meet Ian at eight. The big blond had mentioned a cabin that belonged to some friend of his and suggested going there tonight, but that was at eight and it was only four now. He couldn't just sit around until then, he was too restless and upset. Maybe if he went on into town, he'd feel better.

He crossed the lawn, glad no one was anywhere in sight, particularly Eileen or Ian. For some obscure reason, he didn't feel up to facing either of them right now. In fact, he didn't even want to face himself. That was why he was hurrying off into town.

A few minutes later he was striding along the road, enjoying the feel of the sun on the back of his neck. The powerful muscles in his legs stretched the fabric of the jeans almost to breaking point, but it felt good to be out in the air doing something, even if it was only walking.

This time Ian was waiting for him when he entered the Golden Onion at seven-thirty.

'Well, you're early,' Ian greeted him with his sunniest smile.

'And you're already here,' Ted said, feeling the familiar excitement flow through him as it always did in Ian's presence.

'Do you want a drink or shall we go?' Ian asked.

'I think I'd like to go,' Ted said with a grin. For some reason he was feeling feckless, all his doubts and fears buried for the time being. 'I'm anxious to see this fabulous beach cabin of yours.'

'Not mine,' Ian said. 'I only wish it were.'

'Well, it'll be ours for tonight,' Ted said and was pleased when the words brought a slight flush to Ian's cheeks.

Then they were on their feet and he was following Ted down the dark hallway that led to the rear entrance of the Golden Onion . . .

Ian unlocked the door and looked back impatiently. 'Come on, Ted. Don't stand there mooning at the lake all night.'

'I'm coming . . . I was just looking at the moonlight on the water.'

'My, my, aren't you the romantic one tonight.'

Ted looked at the handsome face in the pale light. 'Don't you ever stop and think about things . . . wonder what life is all about . . . wonder if you're doing the right thing?'

'Not if I can avoid it,' Ian said, 'and I manage to avoid it quite easily most of the time.'

They went inside and Ian turned on the light. 'Nice, huh?' he said. 'How'd you like to have a pad like this all to yourself?'

'It's real nice,' Ted agreed. Sure, he'd like to have a place like this, but would he want it all to himself? Wouldn't it be fun to share it with someone? Someone like Eileen . . . or Ian . . . or . . . well just someone else. Maybe if he sold his mother's house he could . . .

'Wait till you see the bedroom,' Ian said, pouring them each a drink, 'it's really something!' The look in his eyes left no doubt in Ted's mind as to what would happen in the bedroom.

For a second Ted thought of telling him he didn't want to see the bedroom, then he decided that would sound childish and silly. They both knew why he had come here tonight. It wasn't like the other times;

his eyes were wide open now and he knew what he was doing. If he tried to back out now, Ian would think he was a silly little boy. 'Okay,' he said taking his drink and downing half of it in one swallow, 'let's go see the bedroom.'

Ian laughed and led the way up the stairs. Ted followed, his eyes glued to the smooth rippling of the blond's hip and thigh muscles. Ian certainly was a beautiful hunk of male, the most beautiful he had ever seen, but what else was there to him? Did they have anything in common except sex?

His thoughts broke off abruptly as he stepped across the threshold of the room and found himself locked in Ian's arms. They stood there swaying, their bodies pressed tightly together, their lips hotly demanding. Then Ian's hands were up under his shirt, running like fingers of fire over the expanse of his chest, caressing his shoulders and back and finally pulling the shirt off altogether.

'You've got such a marvelous body, Ted,' Ian whispered, 'such a marvelous body . . . anyone would want you . . . male or female.'

Ted felt the wild excitement Ian was always able to arouse roaring through him, and he didn't even try to keep from responding to the tingling caresses.

Ian's hands were growing bolder and Ted felt his belt buckle opened and his jeans being shoved down over his hips. 'I'm going to love you like you've never been loved before,' Ian said, 'I'm going to teach you things you never even imagined.'

'I love you, Ian . . . I love you,' Ted whispered under the compulsion of the raging desire surging through his veins.

'Prove it to me,' Ian said. 'Come on over on the bed and prove it to me!'

They moved toward the big round bed and Ian pulled back the spread and pushed Ted down on the black sheets. Ted watched the blond undress and opened his arms as he joined him on the bed.

From then on the night was filled with burning, flaming passion and Ted hardly noticed when Ian reached and turned on the tall lamp on the bedside table. He merely blinked a little and sank back into blissful sensations as Ian whispered, 'I want to see you while I love you . . . I want to see your face . . . I want to see all of you!'

From Edwin Fey, *Summer in Sodom*, New York, Paperback Library Edition, 1965.

TERTULLIAN [?]

A Strain of Sodom

Already had Almighty God wiped off
By vengeful flood (with waters all conjoined
Which heaven discharged on earth and the sea's plain
Outspued) the times of the primeval age:
Had pledged Himself, while nether air should bring
The winters in their course, ne'er to decree,
By *liquid* ruin, retribution's due;
And had assigned, to curb the rains, the bow
Of many hues, sealing the clouds with band
Of purple and of green, Iris its name
The rain-clouds' proper baldric.
        But alike
With mankind's second race impiety
Revives, and a new age of ill once more
Shoots forth; allotted now no more to *showers*
For ruin, but to *fires*: thus did the land
Of SODOM earn to be by glowing dews
Upburnt, and typically thus portend
The future end. There wild voluptuousness
(Modesty's foe) stood in the room of law;
Which prescient guest would shun, and sooner choose
At Scythian or Busirian altar's foot
'Mid sacred rites to die, and, slaughtered, pour
His blood to Bebryx, or to satiate
Libyan palæstras, or assume new forms
By virtue of Circæn cups, than lose
His outraged sex in Sodom.
        At heaven's gate
There knocked for vengeance marriages commixt
With equal incest common 'mong a race
By nature rebels 'gainst themselves; and hurts
Done to man's name and person equally.
But God, forewatching all things, at fix'd time

Doth judge the unjust; with patience tarrying
The hour when crime's ripe age – not any force
Of wrath impetuous – shall have circumscribed
The space for waiting.
                              Now at length the day
Of vengeance was at hand. Sent from the host
Angelical, two, youths in form, who both
Were ministering spirits, carrying
The Lord's divine commissions, come beneath
The walls of Sodom. There was dwelling Lot,
A transplantation from a pious stock;
Wise, and a practiser of righteousness,
He was the only one to think on God:
As oft a fruitful tree is wont to lurk,
Guest-like, in forests wild. He, sitting then
Before the gate (for the celestials scarce
Had reached the ramparts), though he knew not them
Divine, accosts them unsolicited,
Invites, and with ancestral honour greets;
And offers them, preparing to abide
Abroad, a hospice. By repeated prayers
He wins them; and then ranges studiously
The sacred pledges on his board, and quits
His friends with courteous offices. The night
Had brought repose: alternate dawn had chased
The night, and Sodom with her shameful law
Makes uproar at the doors. Lot, suppliant-wise,
Withstands: 'Young men, let not your new-fed lust
Enkindle you to violate this youth!
Whither is passion's seed inviting you?
To what vain end your lust? For such an end
No creatures wed: not such as haunt the fens;
Not stall-fed cattle; not the gaping brood
Subaqueous; nor they which, modulant
On pinions, hang suspended near the clouds;
Nor they which with forth-stretchèd body creep
Over earth's face. To conjugal delight
Each kind its kind doth owe: but female still
To all is wife; nor is there one that has

A mother save a female one. Yet now,
If youthful vigour holds it right to waste
The flower of modesty, I have within
Two daughters of a nuptial age, in whom
Virginity is swelling in its bloom,
Already ripe for harvest – a desire
Worthy of men – which let your pleasure reap!
Myself their sire, I yield them; and will pay,
For my guests' sake, the forfeit of my grief!'
Answered the mob insane: 'And who art thou?
And what? and whence? to lord it over us,
And to expound us laws? Shall foreigner
Rule Sodom, and hurl threats? Now, then, thyself
For daughters and for guests shalt sate our greed!
One shall suffice for all!' So said, so done:
The frantic mob delays not. As, whene'er
A turbid torrent rolls with wintry tide,
And rushes at one speed through countless streams
Of rivers, if, just where it forks, some tree
Meets the swift waves (not long to stand, save while
By her root's force she shall avail to oppose
Her tufty obstacles), when gradually
Her hold upon the underminèd soil
Is failing, with her barèd stem she hangs,
And, with uncertain heavings to and fro,
Defers her certain fall; not otherwise
Lot in the mid-whirl of the dizzy mob
Kept nodding, now almost o'ercome. But power
Divine brings succour: the angelic youths,
Snatching him from the threshold, to his roof
Restore him; but upon the spot they mulct
Of sight the mob insane in open day, –
Fit augury of coming penalties!
Then they unlock the just decrees of God:
That penalty condign from heaven will fall
On Sodom; that himself had merited
Safety upon the count of righteousness.
'Gird thee, then, up to hasten hence thy flight,
And with thee to lead out what family

Thou hast: already we are bringing on
Destruction o'er the city.' Lot with speed
Speaks to his sons-in-law; but their hard heart
Scorned to believe the warning, and at fear
Laughed. At what time the light attempts to climb
The darkness, and heaven's face wears double hue
From night and day, the youthful visitants
Were instant to outlead from Sodoma
The race Chaldean, and the righteous house
Consign to safety: 'Ho! come, Lot! arise,
And take thy yokefellow and daughters twain
And hence, beyond the boundaries be gone,
Preventing Sodom's penalties!' And eke
With friendly hands they lead them trembling forth,
And then their final mandates give, 'Save, Lot,
Thy life, lest thou perchance should will to turn
Thy retroverted gaze behind, or stay
The step once taken: to the mountain speed!'
Lot feared to creep the heights with tardy step,
Lest the celestial wrath-fires should o'ertake
And whelm him: therefore he essays to crave
Some other ports; a city small, to wit,
Which opposite he had espied. 'Hereto,'
He said, 'I speed my flight: scarce with its walls
'Tis visible; nor is it far, nor great.'
They, favouring his prayer, safety assured
To him and to the city; whence the spot
Is known in speech barbaric by the name
Segor. Lot enters Segor while the sun
Is rising, the last sun, which glowing bears
To Sodom conflagration; for his rays
He had armed all with fire: beneath him spreads
An emulous gloom, which seeks to intercept
The light; and clouds combine to interweave
Their smoky globes with the confusèd sky:
Down pours a novel shower: the ether seethes
With sulphur mixt with blazing flames: the air:
Crackles with liquid heats exust. From hence
The fable has an echo of the truth

Amid its false, that the sun's progeny
Would drive his father's team; but nought availed
The giddy boy to curb the haughty steeds
Of fire: so blazed our orb: then lightning reft
The lawless charioteer, and bitter plaint
Transformed his sisters. Let Eridanus
See to it, if one poplar on his banks
Whitens, or any bird dons plumage there
Whose note old age makes mellow!
                    Here they mourn
O'er miracles of metamorphosis
Of other sort. For, partner of Lot's flight,
His wife (ah me, for woman! even then
Intolerant of law!) alone turned back
(At the unearthly murmurs of the sky)
Her daring eyes, but bootlessly: not doomed
To utter what she saw! and then and there
Changed into brittle salt, herself her tomb
She stood, herself an image of herself,
Keeping an incorporeal form: and still
In her unsheltered station 'neath the heaven
Dures she, by rains unmelted, by decay
And winds unwasted; nay, if some strange hand
Deface her form, forthwith from her own store
Her wounds she doth repair. Still is she said
To live, and 'mid her corporal change, discharge
With wonted blood her sex's monthly dues.

Gone are the men of Sodom; gone the glare
Of their unhallowed ramparts; all the house
Inhospitable, with its lords, is gone:
The champaign is one pyre; here embers rough
And black, here ash-heaps with hoar mould, mark out
The conflagration's course: evanishèd
Is all that old fertility which Lot,
Seeing outspread before him, . . .

No ploughman spends his fruitless toil on glebes
Pitchy with soot: or if some acres there,
But half consumed, still strive to emulate

195

Autumn's glad wealth, pears, peaches, and all fruits
Promise themselves full easely to the eye
In fairest bloom, until the plucker's hand
Is on them: then forthwith the seeming fruit
Crumbles to dust 'neath the bewraying touch,
And turns to embers vain.
                              Thus, therefore (sky
And earth entombed alike), not e'en the sea
Lives there: the quiet of that quiet sea
Is death! – a sea which no wave animates
Through its anhelant volumes; which beneath
Its native Auster sighs not anywhere;
Which cannot from its depths one scaly race,
Or with smooth skin or cork-like fence encased,
Produce, or curlèd shell in single valve
Or double fold enclosed. Bitumen there
(The sooty reek of sea exust) alone,
With its own crop, a spurious harvest yields;
Which 'neath the stagnant surface vivid heat
From seething mass of sulphur and of brine
Maturing tempers, making earth cohere
Into a pitch marine. At season due
The heated water's fatty ooze is borne
Up to the surface; and with foamy flakes
Over the level top a tawny skin
Is woven. They whose function is to catch
That ware put to, tilting their smooth skiffs down
With balance of their sides, to teach the film,
Once o'er the gunnel, to float in: for, lo!
Raising itself spontaneous, it will swim
Up to the edge of the unmoving craft;
And will, when pressed, for guerdon large, ensure
Immunity from the defiling touch
Of weft which female monthly efflux clothes.
Behold another portent notable,
Fruit of the sea's disaster: all things cast
Therein do swim: gone is its native power
For sinking bodies: if, in fine, you launch
A torch's lightsome hull (where spirit serves

For fire) therein, the apex of the flame
Will act as sail; put out the flame, and 'neath
The waters will the light's wreckt ruin go!

Such Sodom's and Gomorrah's penalties,
For ages sealed as signs before the eyes
Of unjust nations, whose obdurate hearts
God's fear have quite forsaken, will them teach
To reverence heaven-sanctioned rights, and lift
Their gaze unto one only Lord of all.

'A Strain of Sodom' (and a strain to read); author (and much of the meaning)
uncertain but sometimes attributed to Tertullian. Translated by the Rev. S.
Thelwall, in *The Writings of Quintus Sept. Flor. Tertullianus*, vol. 3, Edinburgh, T.
& T. Clark, 1870.

JONATHAN D. SPENCE

The Memory Palace of Matteo Ricci

Ricci [a Jesuit missionary in China] left four religious pictures, each with a caption in his calligraphy and three of them embellished with his own commentaries: these were of Christ and Peter at the Sea of Galilee, of Christ and the two disciples at Emmaus, of the men of Sodom falling blinded before the angel of the Lord, and of the Virgin Mary holding the Christ Child. That these pictures have been preserved is due to Ricci's friendship with the publisher and inkstone connoisseur Cheng Dayue, who was introduced to him by a mutual friend in Peking in 1605. Cheng, who was about to publish a collection of Chinese calligraphy and graphics under the title of 'The Ink Garden,' was eager to include samples of Western art and handwriting, and requested Ricci to contribute some. Though Ricci, elaborately self-deprecating, confessed to Cheng that only 'one ten-thousandth part' of Western culture could be of any interest to the erudite Chinese, he nevertheless consented, with the result that the following year his four pictures appeared along with his commentaries in Cheng's elegant volume. Such religious pictures could be confidently expected to fix in Chinese minds the details of dramatic passages from the Bible, whether these were from moments in Christ's life or from antecedents in the book of Genesis.

For the third picture that will be placed in Cheng Dayue's book, Ricci chooses one of a series of prints telling the story of Lot's life, made by Crispin de Pas the Elder in Antwerp. De Pas illustrated Lot's life through four pictures. In the first, the Lord, having heard of the sin of Sodom, announces he will destroy the city. In the second, he blinds the men of Sodom as they strive to break into Lot's house to abuse the men (in fact they are angels) who have been sheltered there. In the third, Lot, his wife and his two daughters flee the city under the angels' protection, just before the city is destroyed and Lot's wife, who has turned to look back, is transformed into a pillar of salt. In the fourth, the two daughters get their father to drink himself to dizziness and then sleep with him, so as to perpetuate their family line.

Ricci wants the Chinese to be aware of the sin of Sodom and of the city's fate. . . . Unfortunately . . . there is the slight problem that none of the four pictures available quite fits what Ricci wants to say. In the event he chooses the second picture from the de Pas cycle, because it shows the turmoil of the moment best: the angel stretching out his hand to blind the men of Sodom; Lot, hands clasped, pleading with them to desist; the men themselves tumbling to the ground or still reaching to seize the stranger, under the distant towers of their proud city. To make his point Ricci gives the story a clarity the Bible version does not contain, and though he has not spelled out the names of the Sea of Galilee or of Emmaus in his first two pictures, in this one he includes the closest transcription he can manage to the word 'Sodom' so that the Chinese will have a focus for future discussion with the Jesuit fathers. He is careful, of course, that the syllable 'ma' he uses to render the *m* sound at the end of Sodom is quite different from the 'ma' of his own Chinese name. He titles his essay 'Depraved sensuality and vileness bring on themselves heavenly fire':

> In ancient times the people of So-do-ma gave themselves up to depraved sensuality, and the Lord of Heaven turned away from them. Among them lived one pure man named Lo, so the Lord of Heaven sent his angles to get [Lo] to leave the city and go to the mountains. Then down from heaven rained a great fire of consuming flame, men and animals and insects were all burned up and nothing was left, even the trees and rocks were turned to ash and sank into the ground. From the mire was formed a lake that brought forth stinking waters and still today serves as a testimony to how greatly the emperor of heaven hates unnatural sensuality and perverse lusts.
>
> Lo was able to keep himself pure amidst the perversity, so heaven blessed him. Most people can behave well in the presence of goodness; but to stay pure and upright in the midst of unnatural customs, that truly calls for a courage that is rarely encountered. The wise man is happy when amongst good customs, and uses them to strengthen himself; he is also happy among evil practices, and uses them as a sharpening-stone for his own character. He can trust his own guidance in any circumstances.

When one places this text of Ricci's next to the picture, one gets an even stronger effect than de Pas has intended. For it is these people whose faces we can study, these lofty domes and towers etched so sharply against the stormy sky that are going to be destroyed in the fire.

It is across this piazza that will spread the noisome, eternal lake. And since the picture has only Lo and the angel, without the daughters and the wife, much cumbersome exegesis can be saved. Why the wife became a pillar of salt, or why the daughters slept with their father in these texts of long ago – the explanation of such problems can be left to another time and place . . .

Ricci . . . wrote that the young actors of China were 'the vilest and most vicious people in this whole country,' . . . it is likely that these heavily made-up young male singers enforced the agitation that he felt at the presence of male prostitutes in Peking, and at the obvious extent of male homosexuality there:

> That which most shows the misery of these people is that no less than the natural lusts they practice unnatural ones that reverse the order of things: and this is neither forbidden by law, nor thought to be illicit, nor even a cause for shame. It is spoken of in public, and practiced everywhere, without there being anyone to prevent it. And in some towns where this abomination is most common – as in this capital city of the country – there are public streets full of boys got up like prostitutes. And there are people who buy these boys and teach them to play music, sing, and dance. And then, gallantly dressed and made up with rouge like women these miserable men are initiated into this terrible vice.

These lines were written in 1609 or 1610, near the end of Ricci's life, but he had expressed similar sentiments in 1583, when he had been in China only a few weeks, writing to Valignano about 'the horrible sin to which everyone here is much given, and about which there seems to be no shame or impediment.' In taking this position before he can have had much evidence one way or the other, and in reinforcing it a quarter of a century later after detailed observation, Ricci was expressing a moral outrage totally in line with his times. Indeed, the two men who had published accounts of China before Ricci travelled there had both written in similar terms. Galeote Pereira wrote of the Chinese that 'the greatest fault we do find in them is sodomy, a vice very common in the meaner sort, and nothing strange among the best.' Friar Gaspar da Cruz said much the same, adding that this 'unnatural vice' was 'in no wise reproved among them,' and that the Chinese expressed surprise when he spoke against it, claiming, 'that they had never had any who told them that it was a sin, nor an evil thing done.' Da Cruz ascribed the vengeance that God took on certain Chinese cities in the late 1550s, in the form of terrible earthquakes followed by lightning bolts that destroyed whole communities, to the prevalence of this vice. He emphasized the point by noting that the Chinese man who brought the news of these catastrophes 'was so frightened that it appeared to him as if the whole province of Sanxi was desolated, just as the daughters of Lot, seeing the destruction of Sodom and Gomorrah, thought that the whole world had perished.' And da Cruz concluded that this catastrophe and its causes might indeed portend the coming of the Antichrist . . .

In the first version of the Ten Commandments, which Ricci and Ruggieri translated together in 1584, instead of translating the sixth commandment in its simple form as 'Thou shalt not commit adultery,' they wrote, 'Thou shalt not do depraved, unnatural, or filthy things.'

From Jonathan D. Spence, *The Memory Palace of Matteo Ricci*, London, Faber & Faber, 1985.

Perverts in Paradise

The conquerors called the Indians 'buggers' or 'heathens'. The first term (from the Middle Ages) and the second (from the Bible) were applied indifferently to the heretic and to the practitioner of sodomy – for the 'abominable sin' was almost always associated with the greater sin of disbelief or heresy. But if the Europeans professed horror at pagan debauchery, they also became fascinated by it in that it symbolised liberation from their guilt. For the colonists who came from a Europe being decimated by rival doctrines and under the strict watch of the Inquisition, 'the passionate temperaments, the immoral customs and all the unremitting growth of virgin nature were an invitation to a dissolute and unrestrained life in which everything was permitted' – in the words of the historian Paulo Prado. For Simão de Vasconcelos, a Portuguese chronicler, the seventeenth-century colonists were in no way different from the Indians, 'because although they are Christian, they live as the heathens do'. Pierre Moreau, a French traveller in Brazil in the same century, stated that during the short period of Dutch colonisation of Pernambuco, 'everyone led a scandalous life: Jews, Christians, Portuguese, Dutch, English, French, Germans, blacks, Brazilians, mestizos, mulattos, mamelukes and creoles'.

The truth is that among foreigners who came to Brazil there was a – perhaps silent – consensus which transcended nationality and doctrine: it was that of *infra equinoxialem nihil peccari* – 'there is no sin below the equator'. It seemed that the tropics placed Christian moral duties in parentheses. Thus in the seventeenth century the city of Recife (capital of Pernambuco) was considered the largest centre of prostitution in the Americas; its brothels were frequented by sailors and soldiers, but also by local dignitaries, councillors and members of the colonial administration. Many of the prostitutes of the time were famous: Sara Hendricx from Holland, for example, who is said to have arrived by ship dressed as a man to escape the vigilance of Calvinist preachers. Pierre Moreau wrote that the incidence of incest and unnatural sin, 'for which many Portuguese were condemned to death', was high there.

The same author refers to the case of a Dutch captain who, convicted of practising sodomy, was first exiled to the island of Fernando de Noronha (off the Brazilian coast), then sent to prison in Amsterdam. Such facts were, moreover, confirmed by Vincent Soler, a Calvinist preacher who lived in Recife in the same period and who claimed in a letter: 'I seem to be in Sodom, or even worse.'

João S. Trevisan, from Chapter One, 'Brazil Seen From the Moon', in *Perverts in Paradise*. Translated by Martin Foreman. London, GMP, 1986.

Carella and King Kong

In the middle of the Brazilian political upheaval of 1961–62, a gigantic
Argentinian gentleman, almost 2 metres tall and with childlike eyes,
arrived in the city of Recife to take up his post as teacher of Stage and
Design at the theatre school of the local University. His name was Tulio
Carella, a teetotaller of about forty who had left his wife in Buenos
Aires to plunge, as he put it, 'into the land of burning coal' –
recollecting that the name *Brasil* comes from brazil-wood, a native
wood so called because it produces a resin as red as coal.* The facts and
impressions of his journey were scrupulously noted down in his diary
(later published), which constitutes one of the most disturbing accounts
of the sudden transformation (or madness) of a stranger in the tropics.
Carella, a Catholic and a profound believer in mysticism, thought that
the Powers of Fire, with their dual aspect of destruction and purifi-
cation, simultaneously producing light and darkness, were in a process
of development in Brazil. Poetically, he proposed that the name of the
country be the United States of Fire. Such reflections seem truly
prophetic when his diary is read, as the following extracts show.

Carella had already been seduced on Brazilian territory, by a woman
who burst into his hotel room on one of the stop-overs of his flight. In
Recife he dived into a reality where poverty, luxury and revolution
were inextricably bound together – in the country's poorest and most
explosive region. In his diary he wrote: 'What is noticeable in this town
is the mixture of the metropolitan and the wild, the progressive and the
archaic.' His elegant bearing, foreign clothes and unusual height,
together with the different language he spoke – Spanish – made
Carella an object of curiosity in the streets. Men, especially blacks and
mulattos, greedily pursued and tried to touch him. At first he was
afraid. He saw eyes undressing him. He felt the urgent shock of the
stranger in Sodom solicited by its inhabitants. However, he did not
exactly consider himself the Messenger Angel in the Biblical story of

---

* *Brasa* (Span. & Port.) means both 'burning coal' and 'ardour' [Trans. note].

Lot. On the contrary, he was a stranger who wanted to break out of his shell and surrender to this tropical Sodom's enchantments. He believed that there, 'as among the birds, the male is the more attractive.' Above all, he was fascinated by the black men. They 'have shining skulls, the colour of polished steel; they are lascivious and cruel. The sea's aphrodisiac air makes them gentle and bloodthirsty. . . . For me they are an inexhaustible source of wonder. To have one near me produces a kind of happiness and at that moment I want nothing else. . . . This is Africa in America.'

The city's sensual heat seemed to dilute his blood; the air had the scent of honey and was 'splendid for the sex glands'. The university professor with pretensions to philosophy noted that merely to think of bodily functions made him aware of needs that had previously been forbidden. He went for a walk along the quays in the port. The youths of every skin colour walked by, fingering their sexes or displaying their backsides under their tight trousers. They argued over him among themselves. While he was watching a religious procession in the street, men groped and pinched him. A black gently took his hand and whispered flirtations in his ear. Carella became alarmed; he was discovering that these pursuits pleased him. He fled into a bar. Harassed, he went into the toilet, and found several men displaying their erections. He fled again, although even more fascinated, and entered the toilet of another bar. There a blond youth sucked his cock. That produced in Carella a change that was both physical and mental; he felt lighter and happier. 'My existence has been lost or changed. I seem to be someone else. I begin to feel myself a prisoner of a series of attractions that I have never imagined before.' He remembered an inscription he had seen in the ruins of the whorehouse in Pompeii: 'Here happiness reigns.' And he associated it with Recife, where 'everthing is erotic energy, bodily contact. Venus reclining and Uranus at street corners'.

Carella was fascinated by the prescence of blacks more than anything else. They 'walk as if dancing'. The very word *negro* acquired an erotic connotation. 'If I repeat it constantly it is because I hear it like a musical note, a lulling sound, an embrace. . . . I think that not blood but sunlight, the vital substance of the tropics, runs in the veins of blacks. . . . Here they resemble swans and wear their rags with an indescribable majesty.' He was also fascinated by the blond negroes typical of north-eastern Brazil and known locally as *sararás* – they have the characteristic physiognomy and woolly hair of blacks, but due to a congenital abnormality characterised by the absence of pigmentation, their skin is light and their hair blond.

Carella learnt that there were boarding-houses 'only for men' in the city and he was persistently invited to them. He was, however, afraid. He tried to find his earlier peace of mind, which had been shattered by the insolence of those men. He went into a church where three masses were being celebrated at the same time. He only found a temporary peace. Trying to pray, he found he could not: the negroes stuck in his mind. He went to a post office, sat in a bar, entered a shop; in each of these places men importuned him. Watching a television in a shop window, a group of men positioned themselves strategically; Carella followed the manoeuvre of a handsome negro fondling the buttocks of a youth apparently absorbed by the screen. Returning to his room, Carella rediscovered a pleasure from infancy – he stripped completely. 'To be nude is one of the ways to regain Paradise.'

So the streets of Sodom became the paths of Paradise. Carella began to surrender to the men's opportuning, already feeling part of it all. From the notes in his diary it seems that his erotic interest became more important than anything else he had come to do in the city.

> . . . In the pissoir at the Market an old man with a beard smokes a pipe and shakes a great rod as if he wanted to excite a casual spectator.

> A television shop window. A young lad leaves an old man and stands next to me while a delicious little negro sighs and pants on the other's side. A third watches me, signing with his arm that I should follow him . . . Going down the stairs he embraces me, kisses me, rubs against me, pulls out his dick, which he puts into my hand, and ejaculates. He admits that it is the second time he has come. The first time was when he showed me his penis in the dark street.

When he had an attack of diarrhea, Tulio Carella considered it God's punishment. As soon as he was cured, however, he could not resist returning to the streets. . . . It was then that he met a young *sarará* of 22, whose nickname, from his herculaean manner and body, was King Kong . . . Carella took him to his room on Good Friday. . . . He gave himself to the centaur while a procession passed outside singing hymns. In his diary Carella wrote some of the most beautiful pages of homosexual erotica that I know. (He writes in the third person, calling himself Lúcio Ginarte, perhaps from some vain precaution.)

King Kong proceeds with caution. Little by little he slides down Lúcio's back until meeting a convex prominence where he settles. His stroking is at first gentle, then harder, becoming alive, deliberate. . . . With a boldness that astounds Lúcio, he unbuttons his shirt and pulls it off, then does the same with his trousers. He is completely naked and displays himself with pride, knowing it would be difficult to find a body more perfect than his own. And because Lúcio hesitates, he pulls him up, helps him undress. Lúcio sees his own body and King Kong's in a dressing-table mirror. The meagre light is enough to delineate hills and valleys. They compare members, which are almost the same size. But King Kong does not understand prolonged foreplay: he wants to screw immediately. He turns Lúcio round so that his back is to him and, without wasting time, lays the glans against the naked flesh. Lúcio, who has been distracted for a moment by the bodies in the mirror, rebels; he could never take that prick. He tries to pull away, but King Kong holds him as he continues pushing uselessly into the narrow entry. Lúcio squirms in pain and succeeds in getting away, but is pulled back by the indisputable strength of those steel muscles. A second attempt fails and Lúcio suffers and refuses, but he can no longer control the excited male who holds him with one hand as the other rubs spit on his penis. King Kong enters again; his fingers have become iron pincers. Lúcio feels both fear and attraction. Will this cylinder of hard flesh succeed in penetrating his body? Some of King Kong's great lust communicates itself to him. King Kong is now an obsessed monster, possessed by an angry erotic passion, implacable, unable to control his reactions. He is blind and dumb except for some guttural noises and heavy breathing, the indication of his unyielding purpose. Only the sense of touch means anything and in the contact of mucous membranes he seeks the return of lost tranquility. He has to enter this pale, alien body in order to communicate with the white gods who inhabit it, even if he has to tear it and make it bleed. He applies more saliva, spreads the buttocks and takes him with his stiff member. It seems unlikely he will achieve his goal. Lúcio gives a cry and pulls away. King Kong roars, seizes his victim again, puts his rod in the right place, pushes, pushes harder when he realises the flesh is beginning to give. It dilates slightly before the continuing pressure, allowing the hope that the act might be completed. He breathes deeply and pushes with a terrible violence; Lúcio, feeling himself invaded, strangles a cry. The rapist's hands drive into his chest, producing a new pain which in no way distracts from the other; they counterbalance, complement and cancel each other. He is totally infected by King Kong's violent lust. He forgets his modesty, prudence and morality. He is compelled to surrender, anxious to feel and enjoy this gigantic instrument. He relaxes and helps the stallion penetrating his entrails with movements that hurt and do not hurt. First the glans, then the rest, all slowly disappear past the dilated anal sphincter. One last thrust completes the work; King Kong owns and subdues his body. King Kong knows he has touched the depths and triumphed. His claws turn to silk; instead of grasping, he caresses Lúcio's chest, his back and his belly. Resting his face on one of Lúcio's shoulders he relishes his partner's groans more clearly. Lúcio suffers, but through some interaction in the order established for each sensation the suffering is also delight. The rapist begins to move, at first slowly and then with greater force and speed until he reaches a steady and accelerating rhythm. The interlocked bodies can be seen in the mirror moving in cadence, with the long, piston-like withdrawal and entry of the huge virile member which is tearing him apart yet making him experience previously unknown sensations. The silence becomes stronger (their panting is part of that silence), jubilant and grows into something like song. Lúcio reaches out behind to stroke that marvellous body, to appreciate it better and more. At that moment King Kong groans and, immobile, reaches orgasm. Lúcio, unable to tolerate any more, masturbates and shares the other's pleasure. Their breathing slows. Their hands, no longer possessive or caressing, slip away, tired and grateful. Happily they let the tension drain, staying quiet together for a few moments before separating. King Kong withdraws his member – it has lost its rigidity but not its length. Lúcio sighs with relief and nostalgia. They wash in the basin and dress. . . . King Kong's face is lit with a pleasant smile. Sitting down, he picks up the pencil again and asks if Lúcio is content. Lúcio answers, omitting half the truth: 'It hurt a lot.' With a proud expression, the other writes: 'It hurt *but* you liked it.'

Guilt-ridden, Carella argued with himself. Afterwards, he sought out King Kong again. . . . He gave King Kong money, which he spent on prostitutes, returning with a sore. Unable to have sex, he asked Carella to hold his prick discreetly in the street at each shop window where they stopped. Carella held back from the more stable relationship that he wanted because he was still being importuned and fought over by the men of the town. 'I am followed by a great train of youths and men as a bridal gown is followed by a great train.' . . . He learnt that the average human lifespan in the region was 37 years and that infant mortality reached 75%. . . . He saw that life passed 'as lightly as a spark in those ephemeral bodies' and concluded that 'perhaps awareness of this brevity disposes them to pleasure and they take advantage of it when they can'. So did he, Carella, take advantage when he could, perhaps driven by this sense of fatality. 'I turn slowly. He kisses my back, then sinks and kneels again, kisses my buttocks, spreads them with his hands and voraciously licks my hole. It is not the first time that I have been caressed this way, but it has never been done with such enthusiasm, perfection, constancy and duration – more than half an hour of licking and sucking.' He also learnt sado-masochistic pleasure; he struck and was struck. Bodies disfigured by the diseases of squalor began to attract him and he was fascinated by the monstrous testicles of those with elephantiasis. There was no longer a distinction between beauty and horror for him.

Perhaps because his presence in the city at a politically explosive period was too noticeable, Carella was arrested by the Brazilian military, on suspicion of smuggling arms from Cuba for the rebellious farm-workers of Pernambuco. He was interrogated and tortured for a long time, and once taken up in a plane where they threatened to throw him out if he would not confess his subversive crimes. The police had received information that he often walked the quaysides at night and met people suspected of being subversives or guerillas. Looking through his apartment, they came across his diary and read it carefully. Then they saw their mistake; they had arrested a queer instead of a Cuban guerilla. Carella was released and warned to say nothing about his arrest, or obscene extracts from the photocopy of his diary that they were keeping would be published. Shortly afterwards he was called in by the university rector and dismissed from his post. The rector, who had been informed of everything by the police, was not inclined to accept in his school someone who 'lived chasing men and, what is worse, negroes'. Humiliated, Carella returned to Buenos Aires at once, where it was said that he fell sick with nostalgia for Brazil. It was 1962. It is vaguely known that he separated from his wife and that he died from heart failure in 1979. Apart from the first volume of his *Diary* published in Portuguese translation, there is an edition of Tulio Carella's poems dedicated to the city of Recife, the Sodom which had welcomed him so hospitably.

João S. Trevisan, from Chapter One, 'Brazil Seen from the Moon', in *Perverts in Paradise*. Translated by Martin Foreman. London, GMP, 1986.

The Travels of Dr Jacobus X

As may readily be understood, we have studied Pederasty more particularly in France, and in Paris above all. But it would be an error to suppose that it exists only in Paris. Our good friends the English, who are perhaps the chief Pederasts in the world, for in all the Colonies and countries which I have visited I have met with English Pederasts, have wished to create a diversion by calling Paris the Modern Babylon. We may answer them that London might truly be called the Modern Sodom. Raffalovich gives us valuable information upon this head. It is well known that in Italy the taste for Sodomy and Pederasty has always been widely spread. Rome and Naples are far greater centres of Pederastic prostitution than Paris. What traveller in Naples, Messina or in any district in Italy has not had proposals made to him by some Italian ruffian, offering for his choice, *abatino*, a *piccolo bambino*, a *bella ragazza* or a *bello ragazzo*.

In Germany especially, Pederasty is very widely spread. We are acquainted with Casper's studies, with the case of Count Caylus, the organizer and chief of a band of Pederasts in Berlin, and with the writings of Heinrich Ulrichs. Moll and Krafft Ebing's works, from which we have made such interesting quotations, confirm Casper's statements.

Tarnowsky informs us that in Russia Pederasty is far from being common and is looked upon by the people as an *aristocratic game for gentlemen*.

Elsewhere we find Pederasty in Turkey, the North of Africa, Persia, India, China, Japan, in short, throughout the whole world.

Dr Jacobus X (author of 'Untrodden Fields of Anthropology,' 'Genital Laws,' etc., etc.), *Crossways of Sex: A Study in Eroto-Pathology*, vol. 2, Paris, British Bibliophiles' Society, 1904. Privately Issued For The Subscribers.

The Arabian Nights

Pornography

To those critics who complain of these raw vulgarisms and puerile indecencies in The Nights I can reply only by quoting the words said to have been said by Dr. Johnson to the lady who complained of the naughty words in his dictionary – 'You must have been looking for them, Madam!'

But I repeat, there is another element in The Nights and that is one of absolute obscenity utterly repugnant to English readers, even the least prudish. It is chiefly connected with what our neighbours call *Le vice contre nature* – as if anything can be contrary to nature which includes all things. Upon this subject I must offer details, as it does not enter into my plan to ignore any theme which is interesting to the Orientalist and the Anthropologist. And they, methinks, do abundant harm who, for shame or disgust, would suppress the very mention of such matters: in order to combat a great and growing evil deadly to the birth-rate – the mainstay of national prosperity – the first requisite is careful study ... I proceed to discuss the matter sérieusement, honnêtement, historiquement; to show it in decent nudity not in suggestive fig-leaf or feuille de vigne.

Pederasty

The 'execrabilis familia pathicorum' first came before me by a chance of earlier life. In 1845, when Sir Charles Napier had conquered and annexed Sind, despite a fraction (mostly venal) which sought favour with the now defunct 'Court of Directors to the Honourable East India Company,' the veteran began to consider his conquest with a curious eye. It was reported to him that Karáchi, a townlet of some two thousand souls and distant not more than a mile from the camp, supported no less than three lupanars or bordels, in which not women but boys and eunuchs, the former demanding nearly a double price, lay for hire. Being then the only British officer who could speak Sindi, I was asked indirectly to make enquiries and to report upon the subject . . .

Subsequent enquiries in many and distant countries enabled me to arrive at the following conclusions:

1. There exists what I shall call a 'Sotadic Zone,' bounded westwards by the northern shores of the Mediterranean (N. Lat. 43°) and by the southern (N. Lat. 30°). Thus the depth would be 780 to 800 miles including meridional France, the Iberian Peninsula, Italy and Greece, with the coast-regions of Africa from Marocco to Egypt.

2. Running eastward the Sotadic Zone narrows, embracing Asia Minor, Mesopotamia and Chaldæa, Afghanistan, Sind, the Punjab and Kashmir.

3. In Indo-China the belt begins to broaden, enfolding China, Japan and Turkistan.

4. It then embraces the South Sea Islands and the New World where, at the time of its discovery, Sotadic love was, with some exceptions, an established racial institution.

5. Within the Sotadic Zone the Vice is popular and endemic, held at the worst to be a mere peccadillo, whilst the races to the North and South of the limits here defined practise it only sporadically amid the opprobrium of their fellows who, as a rule, are physically incapable of performing the operation and look upon it with the liveliest disgust.

Before entering into topographical details concerning Pederasty, which I hold to be geographical and climatic, not racial, I must offer a few considerations of its cause and origin. We must not forget that the love of boys has its noble sentimental side. The Platonists and pupils of the Academy, followed by the Sufis or Moslem Gnostics, held such affection, pure as ardent, to be the beau idéal which united in man's soul the creature with the Creator. Professing to regard youths as the most cleanly and beautiful objects in this phenomenal world, they declared that by loving and extolling the chef-d'œuvre, corporeal and intellectual, of the Demiurgus, disinterestedly and without any ad-mixture of carnal sensuality, they are paying the most fervent adoration to the Causa causans. They add that such affection, passing as it does the love of women, is far less selfish than fondness for and admiration of the other sex which, however innocent, always suggests sexuality, and Easterns add that the devotion of the moth to the taper is purer and more fervent than the Bulbul's love for the Rose. Amongst the Greeks of the best ages the system of boy-favourites was advocated on considerations of morals and politics. The lover undertook the education of the beloved through precept and example, while the two were conjoined by a tie stricter than the fraternal . . .

The only physical cause for the practice which suggests itself to me and that must be owned to be purely conjectural, is that within the Sotadic Zone there is a blending of the masculine and feminine temperaments, a crasis which elsewhere occurs only sporadically. Hence the male *féminisme* whereby the man becomes patiens as well as agens, and the woman a tribade, a votary of mascula Sappho, Queen of Frictrices or Rubbers. Prof. Mantegazza claims to have discovered the cause of this pathological love, this perversion of the erotic sense, one of the marvellous list of amorous vagaries which deserve, not prosecution but the pitiful care of the physician and the study of the psychologist. According to him the nerves of the rectum and the genitalia, in all cases closely connected, are abnormally so in the pathic who obtains, by intromission, the venereal orgasm which is usually sought through the sexual organs . . . it is a medical question whose discussion would be out of place here . . .

The origin of pederasty is lost in the night of ages; but its historique has been carefully traced by many writers . . . Pederastía had in Greece, I have shown, its noble and ideal side: Rome, however borrowed her malpractices, like her religion and polity, from those ultra-material Etruscans and debauched with a brazen face . . .

From Rome the practise extended far and wide to her colonies especially the Provincia now called Provence. . . . Roman civilisation carried pederasty also to Northern Africa, where it took firm root, while the negro and negroid races to the South ignore the erotic perversion, except where imported by foreigners into such kingdoms as Bornu and Haussa. In old Mauritania, now Marocco, the Moors proper are notable sodomites; Moslems, even of saintly houses, are permitted openly to keep catamites, nor do their disciples think worse of their sanctity for such license: in one case the English wife failed to banish from home 'that horrid boy.'

Yet pederasty is forbidden by the Koran. In chapter iv. 20 we read: 'And if two (men) among you commit the crime, then punish them both,' the penalty being some hurt or damage by public reproach, insult or scourging. There are four distinct references to Lot and the Sodomites in chapters vii. 78; xi. 77–84; xxvi. 160–174 and xxix. 28–35. In the first the prophet commissioned to the people says, 'Proceed ye to a fulsome act wherein no creature hath foregone ye? Verily ye come to men in lieu of women lustfully.' We have then an account of the rain which made an end of the wicked and this judgement on the Cities of the Plain is repeated with more detail in the second reference. Here the angels, generally supposed to be three, Gabriel, Michael and Raphael, appeared to Lot as beautiful youths, a sore temptation to the sinners and the godly man's arm was straitened concerning his visitors because he felt unable to protect them from the erotic vagaries of his fellow townsmen. He therefore shut his doors and from behind them argued the matter: presently the riotous assembly attempted to climb the wall when Gabriel, seeing the distress of his host, smote them on the face with one of his wings and blinded them so that all moved off crying for aid and saying that Lot had magicians in his house. Hereupon the 'cities' which, if they ever existed, must have been Fellah villages, were uplifted: Gabriel thrust his wing under them and raised them so high that the inhabitants of the lower heaven (the lunar sphere) could hear the dogs barking and the cocks crowing. Then came the rain of stones: these were clay pellets baked in hell-fire, streaked white and red, or having some mark to distinguish them from the ordinary and each bearing the name of its destination like the missiles which destroyed the host of Abrahat al-Ashram. Lastly the 'Cities' were turned upside down and cast upon earth. These circumstantial unfacts are repeated at full length in the other two chapters; but rather as an instance of Allah's power than as a warning against pederasty, which Mohammed seems to have regarded with philosophic indifference. The general opinion of his followers is that it should be punished like fornication unless the offenders made a public act of penitence. But here, as in adultery, the law is somewhat too clement and will not convict unless four credible witnesses swear to have seen rem in re. I have noticed (vol. i 211) the vicious opinion that the Ghilmán or Wuldán, the beautiful boys of paradise, the counterparts of the Houris, will be lawful catamites to the True Believers in a future state of happiness; the idea is nowhere countenanced in Al-Islam; and, although I have often heard debauchees refer to it, the learned look upon the assertion as scandalous.

As in Marocco so the Vice prevails throughout the old regencies of

Algiers, Tunis and Tripoli and all the cities of the South Mediterranean seaboard, whilst it is unknown to the Nubians, the Berbers and
the wilder tribes dwelling inland. Proceeding Eastward we reach
Egypt, that classical region of all abominations which, marvellous to
relate, flourished in closest contact with men leading the purest of lives,
models of moderation and morality, of religion and virtue. Amongst
the ancient Copts Le Vice was part and portion of the Ritual and was
represented by two male partridges alternately copulating . . .

Syria and Palestine, another ancient focus of abominations, borrowed from Egypt and exaggerated the worship of Androgynic and
hermaphroditic deities . . .

We find the earliest written notices of the Vice in the mythical
destruction of the Pentapolis (Gen. xix.), Sodom, Gomorrah (=
'Amirah, the cultivated country), Adama, Zeboïm and Zoar or Bela.
The legend has been amply embroidered by the Rabbis who make the
Sodomites do everything à l'envers: e.g. if a man were wounded he was
fined for bloodshed and was compelled to fee the offender; and if one
cut off the ear of a neighbour's ass he was condemned to keep the
animal till the ear grew again. The Jewish doctors declare the people to
have been a race of sharpers with rogues for magistrates, and thus they
justify the judgement which they read literally. But the traveller cannot
accept it. I have carefully examined the lands at the North and at the
South of that most beautiful lake, the so-called Dead Sea, whose
tranquil loveliness, backed by the grand plateau of Moab, is an object of
admiration to all save patients suffering from the strange disease 'Holy
Land on the Brain.' But I found no traces of craters in the neighbourhood, no signs of vulcanism, no remains of 'meteoric stones': the
asphalt which named the water is a mineralised vegetable washed out
of the limestones, and the sulphur and salt are brought down by the
Jordan into a lake without issue. I must therefore look upon the history
as a myth which may have served a double purpose. The first would be
to deter the Jew from the Malthusian practices of his pagan prede-
cessors, upon whom obloquy was thus passed, so far resembling the
scandalous and absurd legend which explained the names of the
children of Lot by Pheiné and Thamma as 'Moab' (Mu-ab) the water or
semen of the father, and 'Ammon' as mother's son, that is, bastard. The
fable would also account for the abnormal fissure containing the lower
Jordan and the Dead Sea, which the late Sir R.I. Murchison used
wrong-headedly to call a 'Volcano of Depression': this geological

feature, that cuts off the river-basin from its natural outlet the Gulf of Eloth (Akabah), must date from myriads of years before there were 'Cities of the Plains.' But the main object of the ancient lawgiver, Osarsiph, Moses or the Moseidae, was doubtless to discountenance a perversion prejudicial to the increase of population. And he speaks with no uncertain voice, Whoso lieth with a beast shall surely be put to death (Exod. xxii. 19); If a man lie with mankind as he lieth with a woman, both of them shall have committed an abomination: they shall surely be put to death; their blood shall be upon them (Levit. xx. 13; where v. v. 15–16 threaten with death man and woman who lie with beasts). Again, There shall be no whore of the daughters of Israel nor a sodomite of the sons of Israel (Deut. xxii. 5).

The old commentators on the Sodom-myth are most unsatisfactory *eg.* Parkhurst, *s.v.* Kadesh. 'From hence we may observe the peculiar propriety of this punishment of Sodom and of the neighbouring cities. By their sodomitical impurities they meant to acknowledge the Heavens as the cause of fruitfulness independently upon, and in opposition to Jehovah; therefore Jehovah, by raining upon them not genial showers but brimstone from heaven, not only destroyed the inhabitants, but also changed all that country, which was before as the garden of God, into brimstone and salt that is not sown nor beareth, neither any grass groweth therein.' It must be owned that to this Pentapolis was dealt a very hard measure for religiously and diligently practising a popular rite which a host of cities even in the present day, as Naples and Shiraz, to mention no others, affect for simple luxury and affect with impunity. The myth may probably reduce itself to very small proportions, a few Fellah villages destroyed by a storm, like that which drove Brennus from Delphi.

The Sotadic Zone covers the whole of Asia Minor and Mesopotamia now occupied by the 'unspeakable Turk,' a race of born pederasts . . . Le Vice of course prevails more in the cities and towns of Asiatic Turkey than in the villages; yet even these are infected; while the nomad Turcomans contrast badly in this respect with the Gypsies, those Badawin of India. The Kurd population is of Iranian origin, which means that the evil is deeply rooted: I have noted in The Nights that the great and glorious Saladin was a habitual pederast. . . . Entering Persia we find the reverse of Armenia; and despite Herodotus, I believe that Iran borrowed her pathologic love from the peoples of the Tigris Euphrates Valley and not from the then insignificant Greeks. But whatever may be its origin, the corruption is now bred in the bone. It begins in boyhood and many Persians account for it by paternal severity. Youths arrived at puberty find none of the facilities with which Europe supplies fornication. Onanism is to a certain extent discouraged by circumcision, and meddling with the father's slave-girls and concubines would be risking cruel punishment if not death. Hence they use each other by turns, a 'puerile practice' known as Alish-Takish, the Lat. facere vicibus or mutuum facere. Temperament, media, and atavism recommend the custom to the general; and after marrying and begetting heirs, Paterfamilias returns to the Ganymede. Hence all the odes of Hafiz are addressed to youths. . . . Chardin tells us that houses of male prostitution were common in Persia whilst those of women were unknown: the same is the case in the present day and the boys are prepared with extreme care by diet, baths, depilation, unguents and a host of artists in cosmetics. Le Vice is looked upon at most as a peccadillo and its mention crops up in every jest-book.

Resuming our way Eastward we find the Sikhs and the Moslems of the Panjab much addicted to Le Vice, although the Himalayan tribes to the north and those lying south, the Rájputs and Marathás ignore it . . .

Yet the Hindus, I repeat, hold pederasty in abhorrence and are as much scandalised by being called Gánd-márá (anus-beater) or Gándú (anuser) as Englishmen would be. During the years 1843–1844 my regiment, almost all Hindu Sepoys of the Bombay Presidency, was stationed at a purgatory called Bandar Ghárrá, a sandy flat with a scatter of verdigris-green milk-bush some forty miles north of Karáchi the head-quarters. The dirty heap of mud-and-mat hovels, which represented the adjacent native village, could not supply a single woman; yet only one case of pederasty came to light and that after a tragical fashion some years afterwards. A young Brahman had connection with a soldier comrade of low caste and this had continued till, in an unhappy hour, the Pariah patient ventured to become the agent. The latter, in Arab. Al-Fá'il = the 'doer,' is not an object of contempt like Al-Mafúl = the 'done'; and the high-caste sepoy, stung by remorse and revenge, loaded his musket and deliberately shot his paramour. He was hanged by court martial at Hyderabad and, when his last wishes were asked he begged in vain to be suspended by the feet; the idea being that his soul, polluted by exiting 'below the waist,' would be doomed to endless transmigrations through the lowest forms of life.

Beyond India, I have stated, the Sotadic Zone begins to broaden out embracing all China, Turkistan and Japan. The Chinese, as far as we know them in the great cities, are omnivorous and omnifutuentes: they are the chosen people of debauchery and their systematic bestiality with ducks, goats and other animals is equalled only by their pederasty. . . . For the islands north of Japan, the 'Sodomitical Sea' and the 'nayle of tynne' thrust through the prepuce to prevent sodomy, see Lib 11. chap 4 of Master Thomas Caudish's Circumnavigation, and vol. vi of Pinkerton's Geography translated by Walckenaer.

Passing over to America we find that the Sotadic Zone contains the whole hemisphere from the Behring's Straits to Magellan's. This prevalence of 'mollities' astonishes the anthropologist, who is apt to consider pederasty the growth of luxury and the especial product of great and civilised cities, unnecessary and therefore unknown to simple savagery where the births of both sexes are about equal and female infanticide is not practised. In many parts of the New World this perversion was accompanied by another depravity of taste – confirmed cannibalism. . .

I have remarked that the Tupi races of the Brazil were infamous for cannibalism and sodomy; nor could the latter be only racial as proved by the fact that the colonists of pure Lusitanian blood followed in the path of the savages. Sr. Antonio Augusto da Costa Aguiar is outspoken upon this point. 'A crime which in England leads to the gallows, and which is the very measure of abject depravity, passes with impunity amongst us by the participating in it of almost all or of many (*de quasi todos, ou de muitos*). Ah! if the wrath of Heaven were to fall by way of punishing such crimes (*delictos*), more than one city of this Empire, more than a dozen, would pass into the category of the Sodoms and Gomorrahs' . . .

The negro race is mostly untainted by sodomy and tribadism. Yet Joan dos Sanctos found in Cacongo of West Africa certain 'Chibudi, which are men attyred like women and behaue themselves womanly, ashamed to be called men; are also married to men, and esteem that vnnaturale damnation an honor.' Madagascar also delighted in dancing and singing boys dressed as girls. In the Empire of Dahomey I noted a corps of prostitutes kept for the use of the Amazon-soldieresses.

North of the Sotadic Zone we find local but notable instances. Master Christopher Burrough describes on the western side of the Volga 'a very fine stone castle, called by the name Oueak, and adioyning to the same a Towne called by the *Russes, Sodom,* . . . which was swallowed into the earth by the iustice of God, for the wickednesse of the people' . . .

Dr. Gaspar, a well-known authority on the subject . . . found it flourishing in Palermo, the Louvre, the Scottish Highlands and St. Petersburg, to name only a few places. Frederick the Great is said to have addressed these words to his nephew, 'Je puis vous assurer, par mon expérience personelle, que ce plaisir est peu agréable à cultiver.' This suggests the popular anecdote of Voltaire and the Englishman who agreed upon an 'experience' and found it far from satisfactory. A few days afterwards the latter informed the Sage of Ferney that he had tried it again and provoked the exclamation, 'Once a philosopher: twice a sodomite!' . . .

Those who have read through these ten volumes (of The Nights) will agree with me that the proportion of offensive matter bears a very small ratio to the mass of the work. In an age saturated with cant and hypocrisy, here and there a venal pen will mourn over the 'Pornography' of The Nights, dwell upon the 'Ethics of Dirt' and the 'Garbage of the Brothel;' and will lament the 'wanton dissemination (!) of ancient and filthy fiction.' This self-constituted Censor morum reads Aristophanes and Plato, Horace and Virgil, perhaps even Martial and Petronius, because 'veiled in the decent obscurity of a learned language'; he allows men Latinè loqui; but he is scandalised at stumbling-blocks much less important in plain English. To be consistent he must begin by bowdlerising not only the classics, with which boys' and youths' minds and memories are soaked and saturated at schools and colleges, but also Boccaccio and Chaucer, Shakespeare and Rabelais; Burton, Sterne, Swift and a long list of works which are yearly reprinted and republished without a word of protest. Lastly why does not this inconsistent puritan purge the Old Testament of its allusions to human ordure and the pudenda; to carnal copulation and impudent whoredom, to adultery and fornication, to onanism, sodomy and bestiality? But this he will not do, the whited sepulchre! . . . It appears to me that when I show to such men, so 'respectable' and so impure, a landscape of magnificent prospects whose vistas are adorned with every charm of nature and art, they point their unclean noses at a little heap of muck here and there lying in a field-corner.

'The Terminal Essay' by Richard F. Burton in his A Plain and Literal Translation of the Arabian Nights' Entertainments, Now Entituled: The Book of The Thousand Nights and A Night (Volume X). Printed by the Burton Club for Private Subscribers Only. Illustrated Benares Edition, issued by the Burton Club, for private circulation among its members, and strictly limited to one thousand sets. London (1886).

ALDO BUSI

Sodomies in Elevenpoint

I am immensely fond of being alone. The hours pass in contemplation and I do not wish to be distracted by anything. Here there are residues of hippies with rotten teeth and filthy hands who look at you as if you are usurping their Sixties paradises of which I didn't have the right to 'discover' the holy of holies. I detest *travel journals* and travel literature. People who discover nothing usually discover geography.

The unreadability of literature taken from literature – travel and sex – when it is long-drawn-out. Unreadability also of Italian writers who emulate Henry James: 'I don't go to Crete otherwise I wouldn't be able to set a story there.' How many detestable little works *du regard italien*. An industry for the aesthetics of ways of asphyxiating nicely. The soul of the *self* who writes does not permit stylistic compromises between within and without: in order to have need of them, one must forget about them and not take their name in vain as if they really existed. For the sublime to take off you have to attach ballast. Anyone who does not venture into the vanity of large undertakings should abstain from putting his hand to the vanity of writing.

Here there is a little hollow smoothed out by the wind across the millennia which now blows a little less strongly. Little shepherd girls with a sheep, old men walking along the hilltracks, shameless voyeurs, a French designer. He has been coming to the same place for sixteen years and is fifty-three. For sixteen years he has lived through the same approaches and consequent disenchantment but the enchantment never ends – it is like being at a needlework school run by the nuns. It is not by chance that *high* literature has not dealt much with everyday sodomy; there is no story to tell because there is no *development*. A prick in the arse is legible in its direct contingent dynamism – transposed on to the page and the inside of a novel it loses any aesthetic friction. The characters become 'all those poor things' (a weary dandy on the subject of gays in *The Standard Life*). The same goes for pricks in cunts: either it is pornography or it is Mills and Boon. In Proust, there is neither sex nor love, only images of the erotic bestiary in order to narrate the words demanded by the representation of what cannot be represented. Swann's passion for Odette is seen as a sarabande of the mediocrity of the desired object faced by the desire of the words set in motion by this banal pre-text (there is nothing to give between them – it is the same legal-linguistic shorthand as is adopted for scenes of homosexual love including lesbian ones). Truly *high* literature as an end in itself with all the consequences that flow from it – see Walter Benjamin* – does not deal with the common sexual desires whether satisfied or denied, but with the unleasing of frustration in the character and how it reverberates in its customs and social surroundings. The great passions in the novel are always a metaphor for political sickness – there is no intimacy in the adultery of *Anna Karenina* or in that of *Madame Bovary* – they are therefore either examples like a monument (to the fallen, to those who will fall) or they are not *interesting*, they do not add to what is specifically literary.

Translating is a skill and one learns it; it therefore improves with each book translated; writing is not (otherwise there would be no explaining why the first work usually remains the best of a writer who continues to give us works). One day (after you have been writing, let's say, for twenty years without any appreciable results – and you know it) you get out of bed and write and find yourself thinking once again: THIS IS LITERATURE. That is what it is all about. But one does not ever learn to write *better* once this passage from dilettantism to professionalism in obsession has taken place: writing changes the writer (as reading does the reader), but the contrary does not happen. Therefore, I repeat, it is not by chance that the best works of minor writers are their youthful ones; for the others, myself included, aware that maturity is a positive sign where writing is concerned, they are all synchronous, all *first and last works*, works per se, *without parentage*, unable to be related to each other, evading any hierarchy of quality. We cannot teach ourselves something which cannot even be learned from anyone else.

I have burned masses of papers in which I had celebrated every haemorrhoid because, believing I was doing good by giving an epic quality to the arse, I had ended up by confusing my little sultana-raisins with the literary *theme par excellence*, since they were the two princessly topics of sentimental gay literature: *sin* and *pain* – that is to say good

* No poem addresses the reader, no picture the spectator, no symphony the listeners.

excuses which would have enabled me to make reassuring *serials*. for well-bred ladies but never works of art as I aspired to do decade after decade – and not for *any reader*.

Only continual practice with words gives you the measure of all the words you discard because they do not fit into your favourite *theme-tune from Dr. Zhivago*. By observing this accumulation of words which have never made themselves heard, one succeeds finally in discovering in filigree a consciousness – *through the looking-glass* – of what we have not yet understood we are and what we want to be in order *to write*. The miracle of literature happens when you understand that the totality of language is *the theme* of the writer and nothing else, while everything else may or may not be a part of it, but without prejudice or particular predilection. I knew only one thing confusedly about myself as a writer – I did not want – no and again no! – to become a *homosexual writer* but as it were a real writer, that is a writer. It is possible, in retrospect, to hazard the guess that I resolved my homosexuality in great style and with great beating of drums precisely to avoid the error of making it *the* theme, the *souhaitable* theme of my literature, which was also homage to my real homosexuality. One cannot delegate one's arsehole to anyone other than oneself: by liberating it in life and freeing it from the word, so that it might enjoy itself in pure adventures of its own, I have not condensed it within a linguistic grid to compensate for the *impossibility of living with it*, which never was there. As a reward, I finally found myself face to face with *the* subject *par excellence* of language: language.

From Aldo Busi, *Sodomies in Elevenpoint*. Translated by Stuart Hood. London, Faber & Faber, 1992.

On Sodomy

(Twelfth Century)

The sin of Sodom was 'abundance of bread and proudness of life and excess of wine.' In condemning this sin the Lord says, 'But the men of Sodom were very evil, and sinned greatly before the Lord.' And the Lord said, 'Because the cry of Sodom and Gomorrah is great, and because their sin is very grievous, I will go down now, and see whether they have done altogether according to the cry of it, which is come unto me' [Gen. 18: 20:21, KJV]. The novelty of a sin so great and unheard of evokes astonishment and wonder in the hearer. Whence the Lord is introduced as if marveling and amazed at such a crime, saying, 'I will go down and see . . .'

In fact it seems incredible to me that men could have perpetrated such a crime. A sin 'speaks' when it involves an action which is barely noticeable; it 'cries out' when it is perpetrated openly with the clear commission of a crime. Of only two sins is it said that their gravity 'cries out' to heaven from earth: murder and sodomy. Thus, it is written, the Lord complains that he 'created them male and female for the multiplication of men,' but murderers and sodomites destroy and slay them as mortal enemies and adversaries of God and the human race, as if to say, 'You have created men that they might be multiplied, but we shall strive to undermine and wreck your labor.'

Furthermore, when the Lord assigns the punishments to be inflicted for various sins, he seems to abandon his native patience and kindness with this one, not waiting for the Sodomites to come to justice but, rather, punishing them temporarily with fire sent from heaven, as he will ultimately exact justice through the fires of hell.

The Lord formed man from the slime of the earth on the plain of Damascus, later fashioning woman from his rib in Eden. Thus in considering the formation of woman, lest any should believe they would be hermaphrodites, he stated 'Male and female created he them,' as if to say, 'There will not be intercourse of men with men or women with women, but only of men with women and vice versa.' For this reason the church allows a hermaphrodite – that is, someone with the organs of both sexes, capable of either active or passive functions – to use the organ by which (s)he is most aroused or the one to which (s)he is more susceptible.

If (s)he is more active [literally, 'lustful'], (s)he may wed as a man, but if (s)he is more passive, (s)he may marry as a woman. If, however, (s)he should fail with one organ, the use of the other can never be permitted, but (s)he must be perpetually celibate to avoid any similarity to the role inversion of sodomy, which is detested by God.

Furthermore, in Romans we read, 'Wherefore God gave them over to the desires of their hearts, to uncleanness, so that they might afflict their own bodies with disrespect, in ignominious passions. For their women changed the natural use into that which is unnatural. Likewise the males, abandoning the natural use of the female, burned in their lusts, males doing evil with males, abandoned to reprobate sensibilities, so that they do things which are unbecoming' [paraphrase of Rom. 1: 26–27].

Similarly Jude 7: 'Even as Sodom and Gomorrah and the cities about them in the like manner, giving themselves over to fornication and going after strange flesh,' males doing evil with males, women with women.

The flesh of a man and wife is one; so [the sodomites] are made an example, sustaining the penalty of eternal fire in the present. Compare Leviticus 18 [:23]: 'You shall not lie with a male as with a female, for it is an abomination,' ignominious and unspeakable. Intercourse with a male incurs the same penalty – death – as intercourse with an animal. Whence Leviticus 20 [:13]: 'If a man also lie with mankind, as he lieth with a woman, both of them have committed an abomination: they shall surely be put to death; their blood shall be upon them' [KJV].

But how is it that these have fallen into disuse, so that what the Lord punished severely the church leaves untouched, and what he treated lightly she punishes harshly? I fear that one may result from avarice and the other from the coldness of charity. These enemies of man are like Onan, who spilled his seed on the ground, refusing to raise children to his brother, who was struck by God. These, as Isaiah says in Chapter I (Isa. 1:9?], are as Sodom and Gomorrah, silent in the praise of God and hardened in the enormity of their sins. Likewise in I Timothy I and Colossians 3 [:5]: 'Mortify therefore your members which are upon the earth' [KJV]. And Joshua 6 [:26]: 'Cursed be the man before the Lord, that riseth up and buildeth this city Jericho: he shall lay the foundation thereof in his firstborn, and in his youngest son shall he set up the gates of it' [KJV]. Much more cursed is he who raises up the sin of Sodom, thus losing the first and last of his children, i.e. faith and humility, even for wickedness.

In his contempt for this sin God even turned against the land, changing the Pentapolis into the Dead Sea, in which no fish can live and upon which no ship bearing humans may sail. In that land there are trees bearing fruit which crumbles at the touch into dust and ashes. For just one look back at Sodom, Lot's wife was changed into earth and a pillar of salt, as if the Lord were saying, 'I wish that no memory of this crime should remain, no reminder, no trace of its enormity.'

Such men, spastic and feeble, who change themselves from males to females, abusing feminine coitus, are kept as women by the pharaoh for his pleasure. They are imitators of Sardanapalus, a man who was more corrupt than any woman. Jeremiah also, at the end of the Lamentations, adds to his long lament and sorrow over the ruin and captivity of the city a complaint and groan about sodomy, saying, 'They abused the young men indecently, and boys have perished on wood.' Such men were struck not only dumb but blind knocking on Lot's door at noon, so that seeing, they did not see. So Isaiah 66 [:17]: 'Those that sanctify themselves and think themselves pure in gardens behind a gate, or inside behind a door . . .' So Joel 3 [:3]: 'They have placed a boy [in a brothel].' So also, 'When a man marries as a woman, let the laws be armed, let justice come forth.'

Peter Cantor (d. 1192), 'On Sodomy' (*De vitio sodomitico*). Translated by John Boswell in his *Christianity, Social Tolerance and Homosexuality: Gay People in Western Europe from the Beginning of the Christian Era to the Fourteenth Century.* Chicago, University of Chicago Press, 1980.

Fanny Hill

For presently the eldest unbutton'd the other's breeches, and removing the linen barrier, brought out to view a white shaft, middle sized, and scarce fledg'd, when after handling and playing with it a little, with other dalliance, all received by the boy without other opposition than certain wayward coynesses, ten times more alluring than repulsive, he got him to turn round, with his face from him, to a chair that stood hard by; when knowing, I suppose, his office, the Ganymede now obsequiously lean'd his head against the back of it, and projecting his body, made a fair mark, still covered with his shirt, as he thus stood in a side view to me, but fronting his companion, who presently unmasking his battery, produc'd an engine that certainly deserved to be put to a better use, and very fit to confirm me in my disbelief of the possibility of things being pushed to odious extremities, which I had built on the disproportion of parts; but this disbelief I was now to be cured of, as by my consent all young men should likewise be, that their innocence may not be betray'd into such snares, for want of knowing the extent of their danger: for nothing is more certain than that ignorance of a vice is by no means a guard against it.

Slipping, then, aside the young lad's shirt, and tucking it up under his cloaths behind, he shewed to the open air those globular fleshly eminences that compose the Mount Pleasants of *Rome*, and which now, with all the narrow vale that intersects them, stood displayed and exposed to his attack; nor could I without a shudder behold the dispositions he made for it. First, then, moistening well with spittle his instrument, obviously to make it glib, he pointed, he introduced it, as I could plainly discern, not only from its direction and my losing sight of it, but by the writhing, twisting and soft murmur'd complaints of the young sufferer; but, at length, the first straights of entrance being pretty well got through, every thing seem'd to move and go pretty currently on, as on a carpet road, without much rub or resistance; and now, passing one hand round his minion's hips, he got hold of his red-topt ivory toy, that stood perfectly stiff, and shewed, that if he was like his mother behind, he was like his father before; this he diverted himself with, whilst, with the other he wanton'd with his hair, and leaning forward over his back, drew his face, from which the boy shook the loose curls that fell over it, in the posture he stood him in, and brought him towards his, so as to receive a long-breathed kiss after which, renewing his driving, and thus continuing to harass his rear, the height of the fit came on with its usual symptoms, and dismissed the action.

From volume 2 of the first edition of John Cleland's *Memoirs of a Woman of Pleasure* (Fanny Hill), 1748. The scene was excluded from almost all later editions.

Sodom
(Seventeenth Century)

DRAMATIS PERSONAE

Bolloxinian	King of Sodom
Cuntigratia	Queen
Pricket	Prince
Swivia	Princess
Buggeranthos	General of the Army
Pockenello	Prince, Colonel and Favourite of the King
Borastus	Buggermaster general
Pine	Two Pimps of honour
Twely	
Fuckadilla	
Officina	Maids of honour
Cunticula	
Clitoris	
Flux	Physician to the King
Virtuoso	Merkin and Dildoe maker to the Royal Family

Boys, Rogues, Pimps and Other Attendants

The curtain rises upon 'an Antechamber hung round with *Aretine's Postures.*' The King is surrounded by Borastus, Pockenello, Pine and Twely.

BOLLOXINIAN

Thus in the zenith of my lust, I reign;
I eat to swive, and swive to eat again;
Let other monarchs who their sceptres bear
To keep their subjects less in love than fear
Be slaves to crowns; my nation shall be free;
My pintle only shall my sceptre be,
My laws shall act more pleasure than command,
And with my prick I'll govern all the land.

POCKENELLO

Your Grace at once has from the powers above
A knightly wisdom and a princely love
Who doth permit your nation to enjoy
That freedom which a tyrant would destroy.
By this your royal tarse will purchase more
Than all the riches of the kings of Zoar.

BORASTUS

May your most gracious prick and cods be still
As boundless in their pleasure as your will,
May plentiful delights of cunt and arse
Be never wanting to your royal tarse,
May lust endue your prick with flame and spright
Ever to fuck with safety and delight.

BOLLOXINIAN

My Lord Borastus, your judgement and your care
Is now required in a nice affair.

BORASTUS

My duty's still my service to prepare.

BOLLOXINIAN

You are our council all –

BORASTUS

                     The bliss we own.

BOLLOXINIAN

But this advice belongs to you alone.
Borastus! I do no longer cunt admire;
The drudgery has worn out my desire.

BORASTUS

Your Grace may soon to human arse retire.

* * *

BOLLOXINIAN

My prick no more shall to bald cunts resort,
Merkins rub off, and sometimes spoil the sport . . .

230

BORASTUS

I would advise you, Sire, to make a pass
Once more at Pockenello's Royal arse;
Besides, Sire, Pine has such a gentle skin,
'Twould tempt a Saint to thrust his pintle in.

The King chooses Pockenello and Twely.

BOLLOXINIAN

Henceforth, Borastus, set the nation free,
Let conscience have its right and liberty:
I do proclaim that bugg'ry may be us'd
Through all the land, so cunt be not abus'd
That's the proviso . . .
To Buggeranthos let this charge be given,
And let them bugger all things under heaven.

Exeunt Borastus and Pine. Pockenello now reveals to the King that
Pine has been familiar with the Queen; and Twely adds that 'he swiv'd
her in the time of term'; but Bolloxinian takes no offence.

BOLLOXINIAN

With crimes of this sort I shall now dispense,
His arse shall suffer for his prick's offence;
In roopy seed my spirit shall be sent,
With joyful tidings, to his fundiment.
Come, Pockenello, o're my pintle burns,
In, and untruss, I'll bugger you by turns.

With the King bent on buggery Cuntigratia, the Queen, feels frus-
trated: 'I can command all but my cunt's relief'. Officina suggests that
the royal cunt should 'claim a subject's liberty'.

OFFICINA

Buggeranthos to a hair your cunt would rick.

CUNTIGRATIA

The gen'ral! Oh, I long to see his prick.
They say he fucks all women to a trance.

FUCKADILLA

Madam, you'll say so when you see his lance.

CLITORIS

He is a man no doubt . . .

While waiting for Buggeranthos, the Queen is discovered 'in a chair of state, frigged by the Lady Officina. All the rest pull out their dildoes and frigg in point of honour.' Cuntigratia complains that Officina friggs 'as if afraid to hurt'. Officina blames it on the tool, Virtuoso, she claims, has crafted the dildo too small. The women while away the time with bawdy song and dance. The plot meanders and an episode of heterosexual incest follows from the Princess Swivia's examination of her young brother:

SWIVIA

. . . let's see how much 'tis grown.
By Heavens a neat one! Now we are alone,
I'll shut the door and you shall see my thing.

She shows.

PRICKET

Strange how it looks, methinks it smells of ling,
It has a beard too, and the mouth's all raw,
The strangest creature that I ever saw;
Are these the beards that keep men in such awe?

SWIVIA

'Twas such as these, philosophers have taught,
That all mankind into the world have brought;
'Twas such a thing the King, our sire, bestrid,
Out of whose womb we came.

PRICKET

The Devil we did!

SWIVIA

This is the workhouse of the world's chief trade,
On this soft anvil all mankind was made;
Come, 'tis a harmless thing, draw near and try,
You will desire no other death to die.

PRICKET

Is't death then?

SWIVIA
          Ay! But with such pleasant pain,
That straight it tickles you to life again.

PRICKET
I feel my spirits in an agony.

SWIVIA
These are the symptoms of young lechery.

Cunticula joins in and tries to rouse the boy to further action. Over-eager, she receives her reward in her hand. The Queen meanwhile is pleased with her Borastus experiment, but less so when he's too exhausted to perform twice, 'with prick too weak to act with my desire'. She dismisses him as a 'pampered lecher'.

We return to the King, Borastus and Pockenello. They extoll the joys of sodomy. Buggeranthos reports how the soldiery is taking to the new regime.

BUGGERANTHOS
My liege, the General.

BOLLOXINIAN
                    – Brave man of war,
How fares the Camp –

BUGGERANTHOS
Great sir, the soldiers are
In double duties to your favour bound.
They own it all, they swear and tear the ground,
Protest they'll die with drinking of your health
And creep into the other world by stealth,
Intending there among the Gods to vye
Our Sodom's King to immortality.

BOLLOXINIAN
How are they pleased with what I did proclaim?

BUGGERANTHOS
They practise it in honour of your name;
If lust present, they want no woman's aid,
Each buggers with content his next comrade.

BOLLOXINIAN

They know 'tis chargeable with cunts to play?

BUGGERANTHOS

It saves them, Sire, at least a fortnight's pay.

BOLLOXINIAN

Then arse they fuck, and bugger one another
And live like man and wife, sister and brother?

Buggeranthos relates how the women have fared without men. One craved the stately yard of a stallion, but the stallion drew back. Twely enters to announce the arrival of forty striplings, sent by Tarse-hole, King of Gomorrah. Bolloxinian selects a boy.

BOLLOXINIAN

Come my soft flesh of Sodom's dear delight,
To honour'd lust thou art betray'd to-night.
Lust with thy beauty cannot brook delay,
Between thy pretty haunches I will play.

We return to the women. They interrogate Virtuoso.

OFFICINA

Let's see the great improvement in your art,
The simple dildoes are not worth a fart.

FUCKADILLA

This is not stiff.

CUNTICULA

The muscle is too small,
Not long enough.

CLITORIS

It is no good at all.

OFFICINA

Lord! Virtuoso, wherefore do you bring
So weak and simple bauble of a thing?

VIRTUOSO

True philosophical dimension!
These are invented with a full intention
To satisfy the most retentive veins
That lust or blood or seed in womb retains.

OFFICINA

Oh, fie! they scarce extend a virgin's span,
Art should exceed what Nature gave to man.

FUCKADILLA

I'll hold a fucking, if the truth were known
He made them by the measure of his own.

VIRTUOSO

Madam, 'tis done, and I'll be judg'd by all,
The copy doth exceed th' original.

Virtuoso unveils the original. The women declare his member superior
to any 'silly dildoe'.

The last scene is set in 'a grove of cypress and other trees cut in the
shape of pricks with a banqueting-house', etc.

Flux reports on the current state of the nation. There is much
discontent, disease and despair. The Queen is dead, Pricket has the
clap, and the Princess has gone raving mad.

BOLLOXINIAN

Curse upon fate, to punish us for nought.
Can no redress nor remedy be sought?

FLUX

To Love and Nature all their rights restore
Fuck women, and let bugg'ry be no more,
It doth the procreative end destroy,
Which Nature gave with pleasure to enjoy;
Please her, and she'll be kind, – if you displease
She turns into corruption and disease.

BOLLOXINIAN

How can I leave my most beloved son
Who has so long my dear companion been?

FLUX

Sire, 'twill prove the short'ning of your life.

BOLLOXINIAN

Then must I go to the old whore my wife?
Why did the Gods, who gave me leave to be
A King, not give me immortality?

To be a substitute to heaven at will,
I scorn the gift, I'll reign and bugger still.

The clouds burst, then fiery demons rise and sing. They vanish, and the ghost of Cunticula rises. Dreadful shrieks and groans are heard, and horrid apparitions are seen.

POCKENELLO
Pox on these sights I'd rather have a whore.

BOLLOXINIAN
Or cunt's rival.

FLUX
       For heaven's sake no more;
Nature puts on me a prophetic fear,
Behold, the heavens all in flame appear.

BOLLOXINIAN
Let heav'n descend and set the world on fire,
We to some darker cavern will retire.

Fire, brimstone and clouds of smoke rise.

The curtain falls.

Sodom, attributed to John Wilmot, the Earl of Rochester, 1684(?). From various sources (there is no definitive text). Link passages freely adapted from the notes of H.S. Ashbee, in *Centuria Librorum Absconditorum* (Bibliography of Prohibited Books), London, 1879.

Jolly Hockey-Sticks

Summing up in Birmingham's 'Jolly Hockey-Sticks' blue films trial last week, a High Court judge reminded his jury that they had seen:

> The unnatural and horrible offence of sodomy . . . if you have but a passing acquaintance with the Bible, you will know what happened in Sodom when Jehovah called forth fire and brimstone to punish the inhabitants for their unnatural practises. It has always been in this country, and in every civilised country, a serious offence to commit sodomy, which is punishable by life imprisonment. It is as serious as committing manslaughter, or grievous bodily harm. So that you can be aware of the seriousness of the offence, it is right that you should know how the law classifies it.

The law – or rather the judges who made the law – first classified heterosexual anal intercourse as a crime in 1718, a time when sexual superstition was so rife that bestiality was declared illegal because 'a great lady had committed buggery with a baboon and conceived by it' (Coke, 3 Institutes, p. 59). Enlightenment had still not dawned by 1956, when Section 12(1) of the Sexual Offences Act echoed the ancient taboos: 'It is an offence for a person to commit buggery with another person or with an animal.' The 1967 homosexual reform enabled males over 21 to be lawfully penetrated: consenting ladies and their lovers were left liable to life imprisonment. The offence might be worth preserving for arcane amusement, were it not for the fact that it is actually being used to imprison consenting adults and to outlaw publications which seek to discuss an aspect of sexual behaviour.

Even in the 1930s the late Dr Eustace Chesser discovered that 30 per cent of the happily married women he surveyed in Manchester had experienced anal intercourse. Last year the scenario of *Last Tango in Paris* was authenticated by a comprehensive survey of French sexual behaviour, which found that 19 per cent of males and 15 per cent of females (especially educated and sophisticated Parisians) frequently indulged in the practice. This year Dr Michael Schofield and Mr Maurice Jaffé discovered that 40 per cent of a 3,600 sample of *Forum* readers had committed this serious crime, and a further 14.5 per cent looked forward to doing so.

If the law on sodomy is an ass, police, prosecutors and judges have been reluctant to recognise the fact. A few years ago a photographer named Ronald Harris enjoyed a sexual engagement with one of his models, who subsequently complained to the police that he had stolen her watch. His house was raided, and photographs showing their consensual anal intercourse were discovered. Harris was charged on two counts: theft of the watch, and buggery. He was acquitted of theft, but convicted of an offence against Section 12(1), and jailed for 18 months. The court of appeal approved this sentence, stating that although married men who returned home drunk might commit the crime with their wives by mistake, deliberate acts (involving *mens rea*) ought not to be encouraged. The judgement provoked not a single protest from the liberal establishment.

At St Albans Crown Court in June a spray painter was jailed for nine months (suspended for two years) for heterosexual sodomy committed in the course of a blue film (the director, producer and cameraman received similar sentences for 'aiding, abetting, counselling, procuring' him). During the committal proceedings, a local policeman was questioned about prosecuting practices:

'Surely the police don't usually bring this charge to court?'

'When the people are married we do not usually take action. But this is a crime, and as a member of the Bushey police force I have a duty to investigate all crime reported in the area.'

'So if you hear of a couple buggering in Bushey, you go right in there after them?'

'Yes sir.'

Several recent obscenity prosecutions have hinged upon the illegality of heterosexual sodomy. The DPP argument – that couples who indulge in anal intercourse are depraved and corrupted, and any written or visual encouragement of them to do so is therefore obscene – was first formulated by Warden Sparrow in the wake of the *Lady Chatterley's Lover* trial. For the prosecution, Mr (now Judge) Mervyn Griffith-Jones Q.C. had read to the jury:

'It was a night of sensual passion, in which she was a little startled and almost unwilling: yet it pierced again with piercing thrills of sensuality, different, sharper, more terrible than the thrills of tenderness, but at the moment, more desirable. Though a little frightened, she let him have his way . . .'

'Not very easy, sometimes,' mused Mr Griffith-Jones, 'to know what in fact he is driving at in that passage.' Warden Sparrow claimed to know precisely what was meant and devoted an article in *Encounter* to demonstrate that had the jurors shared his knowledge, they would have convicted.

But in 1972 an Old Bailey jury rejected the allegation that a detailed and arousing description of anal intercourse published in the magazine *In Depth* would deprave and corrupt, after hearing three eminent psychiatrists testify that disseminating information about the practice was for the public good.

Despite the acquittal of *In Depth*, lawyers are reluctant to approve publications about anal intercourse, because they fear obscenity or incitement prosecution – perhaps with good reason. Last year the DPP tried to stop the Schofield/Jaffé research by prosecuting *Forum* for sending their questionnaire to readers who had volunteered to answer it. The very question 'Have you had anal intercourse?' was alleged to be indecent, and hence an affront to Her Majesty's mails. Some newspapers, reporting the evidence in the Birmingham blue films case, felt obliged to employ the euphemism 'an unusual sex practice' whenever buggery was mentioned.

The existing law against consensual heterosexual buggery offends against John Stuart Mill's philosophy that criminal law in a civilised community should punish only harmful practices, and against the Wolfenden Committee conclusion that 'it is not the function of law to intervene in the private lives of citizens, or to seek to enforce any particular pattern of behaviour'. In a tolerant society, where one man's obscenity is another man's bed-time reading, what is 'unnatural' is that the criminal law should intrude upon couples who want to decide for themselves who should do what and to whom. Lawyers may still believe in the abominable crime of buggery; others may be more attracted to Dr Anthony Storr's view that 'the chief interest which attaches to both sodomy and bestiality is not the practice of those acts but the savage penalties which the law attaches to them. Man's cruelty to man is surely more remarkable and shocking a phenomenon than his various forms of sexual activity'.

Geoffrey Robertson, 'The Abominable Crime', *New Statesman*, 1 November 1974.

The Tryal of Mervin Lord Audley,
1631

There were three Indictments found at Salisbury in Wiltshire against the Earl, the Wednesday preceding Easter, before the Lord Chief Justice Hyde, the Lord Chief Justice Richardson, and Baron Denham, Justices of Assize for that Circuit, and special Commissioners in that matter. One indictment was for a Rape upon his own Wife; for holding her by Force, while one of his Minions forcibly, against her Will, had carnal Knowledge of her: So that he was indicted as *Praesens, Auxilians, and Confortans*; and therefore a Principal. The other two Indictments were for Buggery with a Man.

The Arraignment

The Lord Coventry, Lord Keeper of the Great Seal of England, was appointed Lord High-Steward for that Day; who, having Orders for the said Tryal from his Majesty, gave Directions for the same.

The Lords the Peers took their Places about Eight of the Clock in the Morning, and were seated on Benches on each side of a large Table, cover'd with Green Cloth; and below them were the Judges placed, and the Kings learned Counsel, and the Officers of the Court. And having dispos'd of themselves in their several Places, the Lord Steward about Nine of the Clock enter'd the Hall uncover'd, with seven Maces carried before him by seven Serjeants at Arms, and was attended upon by Sir John Burroughs, Garter Principal King of Arms, and Mr. James Maxwel, Usher of the Black Rod.

. . . the Lord High Steward, after a solemn Precognizance, commanded the Indictments to be certified and brought in; and then, by a Serjeant at Arms, the Lieutenant of the Tower was called to bring forth the Prisoner, (who until that time was kept in a little Room by the *Common-pleas*) and the Lieutenant brought him to the Bar, with divers of the Guard attending on him, and when he had a Place in manner of a

Pew, lin'd with Green, in which he stood; and the Lieutenant had another of the same Form for him to rest in, adjoining to it. And when he had done his Obeysance to the Lord High-Steward and the Peers, (who all resaluted him again) the Lord High Steward spake to him in the manner following:

The Lord High Steward's Speech

My Lord Audley,
The King hath understood, both by Report and the Verdict of divers Gentlemen of Quality in your own Country, that you stand impeach'd of sundry Crimes of a most high and heinous nature; and to try whether they be true or not, and that Justice may be done accordingly, his Majesty brings you this day to your Tryal, doing herein like the mighty King of Kings, in the 18th of *Genesis*, ver. 20, 21, who went down to see whether their Sins were so grievous as the Cry of them: *Because the Cry of* Sodom and Gomorrah *is great, and their Sins grievous, I will go down* (saith the Lord) *and see whether they have done altogether according to the Cry of it*. And Kings on Earth can have no better Pattern to follow than the King of Heaven; and therefore our Sovereign Lord the King, God's Vicegerent here on Earth, hath commanded that you shall be here tried this day, and to that end, hath caus'd these Peers to be assembled: and the Desire of his Majesty is, that your Tryal shall be as equal as Equity and Justice it self; and therefore these noble Men your Peers (whose Hearts are as full of Integrity, Justice and Truth, as their Veins full of noble Blood) are this Day to try you . . .

Mr. Attorney:
May it please your Grace, there are three Indictments against Mervin Lord Audley; the first for a Rape, the other two for Sodomy.

The Person is honourable; the crimes of which he is indicted dishonourable; which if it fall out to be true (which is to be left to Tryal) I dare be bold to say, never Poet invented, nor Historian writ of any Deed so foul. And although *Suetonius* hath curiously set out the Vices of some of the Emperors who had absolute Power, which might make them fearless of all manner of Punishment, and besides were Heathens, and knew not God; yet none of these came near this Lord's Crimes. The one is a Crime, that I may speak it to the Honour of our Nation is of such Variety, that we seldom or never knew of the like; but they are all of such a pestilential Nature, that, if they be not punish'd, they will draw from Heaven a heavy Judgment upon this Kingdom.

Whereupon (Mr. Attorney digressing from the Matter) the Lord *Audley* would have interrupted him, and requir'd to hold him to the Points in the Indictments. But the Lord High Steward desir'd his Lordship to be patient, and assur'd him he should be heard in fit time at full. Whereupon Mr. Attorney proceeded again in his charge as followeth:

May it please your Grace,
For the *Crimen Sodomiticum*, our Law had no knowledge of it till the 15th of *Hen.* VIII. by which Statute it was made Felony; and in this there is no more question, but only, whether it be *Crimen Sodomiticum, sine Penetratione*; and the Law of 15 *Eliz.* sets it down in general Words: and where the Law does not distinguish, neither must we. And I know you will be cautious how you will give the least Mitigation to so abominable a Sin, which brought such Plagues after it, as we may see in *Gen.* 17. *Levit.* 18. *Judg.* 19. *Rom.* 1. But (my Lord) it seem'd to me strange at the first, how a Nobleman of his Quality should fall to such abominable Sins; but when I found he had given himself over to Lust, and that *Nemo repente sit pessimus*, and if once Men habit themselves in ill, it is no marvel if they fall into any Sins; and that he was constant to no Religion, but in the Morning he would be a Papist and go to Mass, and in the Afternoon a Protestant and go to a Sermon. When I had consider'd these Things, I easily conceiv'd, and shall be bold to give your Grace a Reason why he became so ill. He believ'd not God; he had not the Fear of God before his Eyes; he left God, and God left him to his own Wickedness: and what may not a Man run into? What Sin so foul, what Thing so odious, which he dares not adventure? But I find in him Things beyond all Imagination; for I find his ill Imagination and Intentions bent to have his Wife naught with the wickedest Man that ever I heard of before: for who would not have his Wife virtuous and good, how bad soever himself be? And I find him Bawd to his own Wife. If she loved him, she must love Skipwith, (whom he honour'd above all) and not any honest Love, but in a dishonest Love; and he gives his Reason by Scripture, *She was now made subject to him*; and therefore if she did ill at his Command, it was not her Fault but his, and he would answer it. His irregular Bounty towards Skipwith was also remarkable. He lets this Skipwith

(whom he calls his Favourite) spend of his Purse 500 *l. per Annum*; and if his Wife or Daughter would have any thing, tho never so necessary, they must lie with Skipwith, and have it from him, and not otherwise; also telling Skipwith and his Daughter-in-Law, he had rather have a Child by him than any other. But for these things, I had rather they should come forth of the Witnesses Mouths than from me: and thereupon desir'd that the Proofs might be read.

The Deposition of Walter Bigg

Walter Bigg depos'd, That Amptil was a Page to Sir H. Smith, and had no more Means when he came to my Lord Audley, but the Mare he rode on. He entertain'd him as his Page eight Years, and afterwards let him keep Horses in my Lord's Grounds, by which I think he enrich'd himself 2000 *l.* but he never sat at Table with my Lord till he had marry'd his Daughter, and then gave him to the Value of 7000 *l.*

That Skipwith was sent from Ireland to be my Lady's Page; and that his Father and Mother were very poor Folks there. He spent of my Lord's purse, *per annum*, 500 *l.* and he gave him at one time 1000 *l.* and hath made divers Deeds of Land unto him.

My Lord was at first a Protestant; but after, by buying of Founthill, he turn'd his Religion.

That *Henry Skipwith* had no Means when he came to him, and that he had given him 1000 *l.* and that Skipwith lay with him when he was straiten'd in Rooms; and that he gave a Farm of 100 *l. per Annum* to Amptil that married his Daughter, and at other times to the value of 7000 *l.* and that there was one Blandina in his House fourteen Days, and bestowed an ill Disease there, and therefore he sent her away.

The Countess of Castlehaven's *Examination*.

That shortly after the Earl marry'd her, *viz.* the first or second Night, Amptil came to the Bed's-side, whilst she and her Husband were in Bed, and the Lord Audley spake lasciviously to her, and told her, *That now her Body was his, and that if she lov'd him she must love Amptil; and that if she lay with any other Man with his Consent, it was not her Fault, but his; and that if it was his Will to have it so, she must obey, and do it.*

That he attempted to draw her to lie with his Servant Skipwith; and that Skipwith made him believe he did it, but did it not.

That he would make Skipwith come naked into his Chamber, and delighted in calling up his Servants to shew their Privities, and would make her look on, and commended those that had the largest.

That one Night, being a-bed with her at *Founthill*, he call'd for his Man Brodway, and commanded him to lie at his Bed's Feet; and about Midnight (she being asleep) call'd him to light a Pipe of Tobacco. Brodway rose in his Shirt, and my Lord pull'd him into Bed to him and her, and made him lie next to her; and Brodway lay with her, and knew her carnally, whilst she made Resistance, and the Lord held both her Hands, and one of her Legs the while: and that as soon as she was free, she would have kill'd herself with a Knife, but that Brodway forcibly took that Knife from her; and before that Act of Brodway, she had never done it.

That he delighted to see the Act done; and made Skipwith to come into Bed with them, and lie with her whilst he might see it; and she cried out to have sav'd herself.

The Examination of Fitz-Patrick *was then read, the Truth of which he then again confirm'd upon Oath.*

That the Earl had committed Sodomy twice upon his Person; that Henry Skipwith was the special Favourite of my Lord Audley, and that he usually lay with him; and that Skipwith said, that the Lord Audley made him lie with his own Lady; and that he saw Skipwith in his sight do it, my Lord being present: and that he lay with Blandina in his sight, and four more of the Servants, and afterwards the Earl himself lay with her in their sights.

Then Skipwith *was produc'd and sworn, and his Examination read, which he again confirm'd upon Oath, and deposeth,* viz.

That the Earl often sollicited him to lie with the young Lady, and persuaded her to love him; and to draw her thereunto, he urg'd that his Son lov'd her not; and that in the end he usually lay with the young Lady, and that there was Love between them both before and after; and that my Lord said, he would rather have a Boy of his own begetting than any other; and that she was but twelve Years of Age when he first lay with her, and that he could not enter her Body without Art; and that the Lord Audley fetch'd Oil to open her Body, but she cry'd out, and he could not enter; and then the Earl appointed Oil the second time; and then Skipwith enter'd her Body, and he knew her carnally; and that my Lord made him lie with his own Lady, but he knew her not, but told his Lord he did.

That he spent 500 *l. per Annum* of the Lord's Purse, and, for the most part, he lay with the said Earl.

That the Earl gave him his House at *Salisbury*, and a Mannor of 600 *l. per Annum*.

That Blandina lay in the Earl's house half a year, and was a common Whore.

Fitz-Patrick's *Second Examination*.

That the Lord Audley made him lie with him at Founthill and at Salisbury, and once in the Bed, and emitted between his Thighs, but did not penetrate his Body; and that he heard he did so with others.

That Skipwith lay with the young Lady often, and ordinarily; and that the Earl knew it, and encourag'd him in it, and wish'd to have a Boy by him and the young Lady.

That Blandina liv'd half a year in my Lord's House, and was a common Whore.

Then was read the young Lady Audley's *Examination*.

That she was marry'd to her Husband by a Romish Priest in the Morning, and at Night by a Prebend at Kilkenny; that she was first tempted to lie with Skipwith by the Earl's Allurements; and that she had no Means but what she had from Skipwith; but she would not lie with Pawlet; he sollicited her also to lie with one Green.

That the Earl himself saw her and Skipwith lie together divers times; and nine Servants of the House had also seen it.

When the Earl sollicited her first, he said, that upon his Knowledge, her Husband lov'd her not; and threatend, that he would turn her out of Doors, if she did not lie with Skipwith; and that if she did not, he would tell her Husband she did.

That she being very young, he us'd Oil to enter her Body first: and afterwards he usually lay with her, and it was with the Earl's Privity and Consent.

Brodway's *Examination, who confesseth,*

That he lay at the Earl's Bed's Feet, and one Night the Earl call'd to him for Tobacco; and as he brought it in his Shirt, he caught hold of him, and bid him come to Bed, which he refus'd; but to satisfy my Lord, at last he consented, and came into the Bed on my Lord's Side; then my Lord turn'd him upon his Wife, and bid him lie with her, which he did; and the Earl held one of her Legs, and both her Hands, and at the last (notwithstanding her Resistance) lay with her.

That the Earl us'd his Body as the Body of a Woman, but never pierc'd it, only emitted between his thighs.

He hath seen Skipwith lie with the young Lady in Bed together; and when he had got upon her, the Earl stood by and encourag'd him to get her with Child: and that he hath made him the said Brodway kiss his own Lady, and often sollicited him to lie with her, telling him, that he himself should not live long, and that it might be his Making; and that he hath said the like to Skipwith.

The Earl's Second Examination

The Earl desir'd To be pardon'd of those Things whereof he must accuse himself, and said, *That Condemnation should not come out of his own Mouth.*

These Testimonies being read, Mr. Attorney press'd things very earnestly, and in excellent Method against the Earl, and said,

My Lords,
You have seen the Clearness of the Proofs, and I know your Wisdoms to be such (as you well know) in so dark a Business clearer Proofs cannot possibly be had; for let a Man be never so wicked, or never so impudent, he will not call Witnesses to see his Wickedness, yet you see here this Point fully proved.

Then he shew'd how both the Laws of God and Man were against Sodomy, and cited *Levit.* 18 towards the end, *That by these Abominations* the Land is defil'd; and therefore the Lord doth visit this Land for the Iniquity thereof. And then concludes, that God may remove and take away from us his Plagues, let this wicked Man (saith he) be taken away from amongst us.

The Earl answer'd (having first made a solemn Protestation of his Innocency, but nevertheless implor'd the Mercy of God and the King) That he had nothing more to say, but left himself to God and his Peers, and presented to their consideration three *Woes*:

1. *Woe* to that Man, whose Wife should be a Witness against him!
2. *Woe* to that Man, whose Son should persecute him, and conspire his Death!
3. *Woe* to that Man, whose Servants should be allow'd Witnesses to take away his Life!

And he willed the Lords to take this into their Consideration; for it might be some of their Cases, or the Case of any Gentleman of Worth, that keeps a Footman, or other, whose Wife is weary of her Husband, or his son arriv'd to full Age, that would draw his Servants to conspire his Father's Death.

He said further, his Wife had been naught in his Absence, and had had a Child, which he conceal'd to save her Honour.

That his Son was now become 21 Years old, and he himself old and decay'd; and the one would have his Lands, and the other a young Husband; and therefore, by the Testimony of them, and their Servants added to their own, they had plotted and conspired his Destruction and Death.

Then the Peers withdrew themselves; and after two Hours Debate, and several Advices and Conferences . . . at the last they return'd to their Places: and then the Lord Steward ask'd them one by one, beginning at the lowest, and so ascending;

1. Whether the said Earl of Castlehaven was Guilty of the Rape whereof he stood indicted, or not? And they all gave him Guilty.

2. Whether the said Earl of Castlehaven was Guilty of the Sodomy with which he was charged, or not? And fifteen of the Lords condemned him, and the other eleven freed him.

When the Verdict was thus given, the Lieutenant of the Tower was again commanded to bring the Prisoner to the Bar, to hear his Sentence; and after he was brought in, the Lord Steward said unto him:

Forasmuch as thou Mervin Lord Audley, Earl of Castlehaven, hast been indicted for divers Felonies, by three several Indictments; one for a Rape, the other two for Sodomy; and hast pleaded Not Guilty to them all, and for thy Tryal thou hast put thy self upon God and thy Peers; which Tryal thou hast had, and they found thee guilty of them all: What canst thou say for thy self, why the Sentence of Death should not be pronounced against thee?

Whereupon he answered, He could say no more, but referred himself to God and the King's Mercy.

Then the Lord Steward said, My Heart grieveth for that which my Tongue must utter; but Justice is the way to cut off Wickedness, and therefore hear thy Sentence.

Thou must go from hence to the Prison from whence thou camest, and from thence to the place of Execution, there to be hang'd by the Neck till thou be dead, and the Lord have Mercy on thy Soul.

The Lord Steward's Exhortation.

Oh think upon your Offences! which are so heinous and so horrible, that a Christian Man ought scarce to name them, and such as the deprav'd Nature of Man (which of itself carries a Man to all Sin) abhorreth! And you have not only offended against Nature, but the Rage of a Man's Jealousy! And altho you die not for that, that you have abused your own Daughter! And having both Honour and Fortune to leave behind you, you would have had the impious and spurious Offspring of a Harlot to inherit! Both these are horrid Crimes. But my Lord, it grieves me to see you stand out against the Truth so apparent; and therefore I will conclude with this Admonition, That God might have taken you away when you were blinded in your Sins, and therefore hope he hath reserved you as a Subject of his Mercy: and as he sends you to see this Day of Shame, that you may return unto him, so thereby in a manner he lovingly draws you to him: therefore spend the remainder of your Time in Tears and Repentance; and this Day's Work, I hope, will be a Correction from many Crimes and Corruptions.

Whereupon, at last, the Earl descended to a low Petition to the Lords, and very humbly besought them to intercede with his Majesty, that he might not suddenly cut him off, but give him Time of Repentance. And then he desired their Lordships Pardons, in that he had been so great a Stain to Honour and Nobility.

Then a Proclamation being made by a Serjeant, declaring, That the Lord High Steward's Pleasure was, that all such as had attended this Day's Service might depart; the Lieutenant of the Tower carried the Earl away, and so the Court broke up.

Excerpts from 'The Tryal of Mervin Lord Audley, (Earl of Castlehaven) for a Rape and Sodomy, on the 25th of April, 1631 in the Sixth Year of King Charles the First', in *A Compleat Collection of State-Tryals and Proceedings Upon Impeachments for High Treason and Other Crimes and Misdemeanours: From the Reign of King Henry the Fourth to the End of the Reign of Queen Anne*, London 1719, 4 vols.

MARQUIS DE SADE

The One Hundred and Twenty
Days of Sodom

Four accomplished procuresses to recruit women, and a similar number of pimps to scout out men, had the sole duty to range both the capital and the provinces and bring back everything, in the one gender and in the other, that could best satisfy their sensuality's demands. Four supper parties were held regularly every week in four different country houses located at four different extremities of Paris. At the first of these gatherings, the one exclusively given over to the pleasures of sodomy, only men were present; there would always be at hand sixteen young men, ranging in age from twenty to thirty, whose immense faculties permitted our four heroes, in feminine guise, to taste the most agreeable delights. The youths were selected solely upon the basis of the size of their member, and it almost became necessary that this superb limb be of such magnificence that it could never have penetrated any woman; this was an essential clause, and as naught was spared by way of expense, only very rarely would it fail to be fulfilled. But simultaneously to sample every pleasure, to these sixteen husbands was joined the same quantity of boys, much younger, whose purpose was to assume the office of women. These lads were from twelve to eighteen years old, and to be chosen for service each had to possess a freshness, a face, graces, charms, an air, an innocence, a candor which are far beyond what our brush could possibly paint. No woman was admitted to these masculine orgies, in the course of which everything of the lewdest invention in Sodom and Gomorrah was executed.

It is commonly accepted amongst authentic libertines that the sensations communicated by the organs of hearing are the most flattering and those whose impressions are the liveliest; as a consequence, our four villains, who were of a mind to have voluptuousness implant itself in the very core of their beings as deeply and as overwhelmingly as ever it could penetrate, had, to this end, devised something quite clever indeed.

It was this: after having immured themselves within everything that was best able to satisfy the senses through lust, after having established this situation, the plan was to have described to them, in the greatest detail and in due order, every one of the debauchery's extravagances, all its divagations, all its ramifications, all its contingencies, all of what is termed in libertine language its passions. There is simply no conceiving the degree to which man varies them when his imagination grows inflamed; excessive may be the differences between men that is created by all their other manias, by all their other tastes, but in this case it is even more so, and he who should succeed in isolating and categorizing and detailing these follies would perhaps perform one of the most splendid labors which might be undertaken in the study of manners, and perhaps one of the most interesting. It would thus be a question of finding some individuals capable of providing an account of all these excesses, then of analyzing them, of extending them, of itemizing them, of graduating them, and of running a story through it all, to provide coherence and amusement. Such was the decision adopted. After innumerable inquiries and investigations, they located four women who had attained their prime – that was necessary, experience was the fundamental thing here – four women, I say, who, having spent their lives in the most furious debauchery, had reached the state where they could provide an exact account of all these matters; and, as care had been taken to select four endowed with a certain eloquence and a fitting turn of mind, after much discussion, recording, and arranging, all four were ready to insert, each into the adventures of her life, all the most extraordinary vagaries of debauch . . .

Wherewith, having said this much, I advise the overmodest to lay my book aside at once if he would not be scandalized, for 'tis already clear there's not much of the chaste in our plan, and we dare hold ourselves answerable in advance that there'll be still less in its execution.

Adjacent to this room was an assembly chamber intended for the storytellers' narrations. This was, so to speak, the lists for the projected jousts, the seat of the lubricious conclaves, and as it had been decorated accordingly, it merits something by way of a special description.

Its shape was semicircular; set into the curving wall were four niches whose surfaces were faced with large mirrors, and each was provided with an excellent ottoman; these four recesses were so constructed that each faced the center of the circle; the diameter was formed by a throne, raised four feet above the floor and with its back to the flat wall, and it was intended for the storyteller; in this position she was not only well before the four niches intended for her auditors, but, the circle being small, was close enough to them to insure their hearing every word she said, for she was placed like an actor in a theater, and their audience in their niches found themselves situated as if observing a spectacle in an amphitheatre. Steps led down from the throne, upon them were to sit the objects of debauchery brought in to soothe any sensory irritation provoked by the recitals; these several tiers, like the throne, were upholstered in black velvet edged with gold fringe, and the niches were furnished with similar and likewise enriched material, but in color dark blue. At the back of each niche was a little door leading into an adjoining closet which was to be used at times when, having summoned the desired subject from the steps, one preferred not to execute before everyone the delight for whose execution one had summoned that subject. These closets were provided with couches and with all other furnishings required for every kind of impurity. On either side of the central throne an isolated column rose to the ceiling; these two columns were designed to support the subject in whom some misconduct might merit correction. All the instruments necessary to meting it out hung from hooks attached to the columns, and this imposing sight served to maintain the subordination so indispensable to parties of this nature, a subordination whence is born almost all the charm of the voluptuousness in persecutors' souls.

Statutes

. . . The salon shall be heated to an unusual temperature, and illuminated by chandeliers. All present shall be naked: storytellers, wives, little girls, little boys, elders, fuckers, friends, everything shall be pell-mell, everyone shall be sprawled on the floor and, after the example of animals, shall change, shall commingle, entwine, couple incestuously, adulterously, sodomistically, deflowerings being at all times banned, the company shall give itself over to every excess and to every debauch which may best warm the mind. When 'tis time for these deflowerings, it shall be at this moment and in these circumstances that

those operations shall be performed, and once a child shall be initiate, it shall be available for every enjoyment, in all manner and at all times.

The slightest religious act on the part of any subject, whomsoever he be, whatsoever be that act, shall be punished by death.

Messieurs are expressly enjoined at all gatherings to employ none but the most lascivious language, remarks indicative of the greatest debauchery, expressions of the filthiest, the most harsh, and the most blasphemous.

The name of God shall never be uttered save when accompanied by invectives or imprecations, and thus qualified it shall be repeated as often as possible.

Any friend who fails to comply with any one of these articles, or who may take it into his head to act in accordance with a single glimmer of common sense or moderation and above all to spend a single day without retiring dead drunk to bed, shall be fined ten thousand francs.

And now, friend-reader, you must prepare your heart and your mind for the most impure tale that ever has been told since our world began, a book the likes of which are met with neither amongst the ancients nor amongst us moderns. Fancy, now, that all pleasure-taking either sanctioned by good manners or enjoined by that fool you speak of incessantly, of whom you know nothing and whom you call Nature; fancy I say, that all these modes of taking pleasure will be expressly excluded from this anthology, or that whenever peradventure you do indeed encounter them here, they will always be accompanied by some crime or colored by some infamy.

Many of the extravagances you are about to see illustrated will doubtless displease you, yes, I am well aware of it, but there are amongst them a few which will warm you to the point of costing you some fuck, and that, reader, is all we ask of you; if we have not said everything, analyzed everything, tax us not with partiality, for you cannot expect us to have guessed what suits you best. Rather, it is up to you to take what you please and leave the rest alone, another reader will do the same, and little by little, everyone will find himself satisfied. It is the story of the magnificent banquet: six hundred different plates offer themselves to your appetite; are you going to eat them all?

Simple Passions

Madame Duclos was she to whom they entrusted the relating of the one hundred and fifty simple passions . . .

Said Duclos, taking up the thread of her narrative:

Next, with the most scrupulous attention he examined my ass, with one hand screening his eyes to avoid any glimpse of my cunt whereof, it appeared, he was in mortal terror . . . And then, taking a stool and placing it between my legs, he sat down in such a way that his prick, which he now dragged from his breeches and began to vibrate, was as it were at a level with the hole upon which he was to offer a libation. His movements now grew more rapid, with one hand he frigged himself, with the other he separated my buttocks, and a few adulatory commendations seasoned with a quantity of hard language constituted his speech, 'Ah, bugger the Almighty, here 'tis, the lovely ass,' he cried, 'the sweet little hole, and how I'm going to wet it.' He kept his word. I felt myself soaked; his ecstasy seemed to annihilate the libertine. Ah, how true it is that the homage rendered at this temple is always more ardent than the incense which is burned at the other . . .

Madame Duclos: *This abbot of mine, much less phlegmatic, as he used one hand to spread my buttocks, used the other to frig himself very voluptuously, and as he discharged he drew my anus to his face with such violence and tickled it so lubriciously that my ecstasy coincided with his. When he was finished, he spent another moment scrutinizing my buttocks, staring at that hole he'd just reamed wider, and couldn't prevent himself from gluing his mouth to it for one last time . . .*

For six months he came to visit me three or four times a week, regularly performing the same operation to which I became so thoroughly accustomed that each time he excecuted his little project, I all but expired with delight – an aspect of the rite about which he appeared to care very little, for, as best I could judge, he had no inclination to find out whether or no my work pleased me; that did not seem to matter to him. And indeed, who can tell? Men are extraordinary indeed; had he known of it, my pleasure might even have displeased him.

Madame Duclos: *The hero of the adventure was an old brigadier in the King's army; he had to be stripped to the skin, then swaddled like an infant; when he was thus prepared, I had to shit while he looked on, bring him the plate and, with the tops of my fingers, feed him my turd as if it were pap. Everything is done according to prescription, our libertine swallows it all and discharges in his swaddling clothes, the while simulating a baby's cry.*

150 Complex Passions (Draft)

Champville assumes the task of story-telling . . .

7. *He has his valet depucelate the maid, aged ten to twelve, before his eyes, and during the operation touches them nowhere save upon the ass. He now fondles the girl's, now the valet's. Discharges upon the valet's ass . . .*

The Duc recounts – but his anecdote cannot be numbered amongst the stories because, Messieurs being unable to duplicate it, it does not compose a passion – the Duc recounts, I say, that he once knew a man who fucked his three children he had by his mother, amongst whom there was a daughter whom he had marry his son, so that in fucking her he fucked his sister, his daughter and his daughter-in-law, and thus he also constrained his son to fuck his own sister and mother-in-law.

38. *He has four streetwalkers besot themselves with wine and then fight each other while he looks on; and when they are thoroughly drunk, they one after another vomit into his mouth. He favors the oldest and ugliest women.*

150 Criminal Passions (Draft)

20. *In order to combine incest, adultery, sodomy and sacrilege, he embuggers his married daughter with a Host.*

34. *Embuggers a swan after having popped a Host up into its ass; then strangles the bird upon discharging.*

151. *He gives her copiously to drink, then sews up her cunt, her asshole and her mouth as well, and leaves her thus until the water bursts through its conduits, or until she dies.*

(Determine why there is one too many; if one is to be deleted, suppress the last, for I believe I have already used it.)

150 Murderous Passions (Draft)

Their sufferings were long, cruel and various . . .
    With what regards the tortures and deaths of the last twenty subjects, and life such as it was in the household until the day of departure, you will give details at your leisure and where you see fit, you will say, first of

all, that thirteen of the sixteen survivors (three of whom were cooks) took all their meals together; sprinkle in whatever tortures you like.

The Marquis de Sade, *The 120 Days of Sodom*. Translated by Austryn Wainhouse and Richard Seaver. New York, Grove Press, 1966.

La Colère de Samson

(Samson and Delilah are in their tent in the desert. Samson sings Delilah to sleep with a *chant funèbre et douloureux* in Hebrew, which she does not understand.) The song:

An eternal struggle, at all times and in all places, is waged on Earth, in the sight of God, between the goodness of Man and the guile of Woman, for woman is a being impure in body and soul.

Man always needs caresses and love; his mother surrounds him with them from the moment he is born, and her arms are the first to rock him to sleep and give him the taste for love and indolence. Disturbed in his actions, disturbed as he tries to plan, he will dream wherever he is of the warmth of her breast, of the songs of night and the kisses of dawn, of the burning lips which his lips devour, and of the loose hair flowing over her face, and as he walks, fond memories of bed will follow him.

He will go into the town and there, the foolish virgins will catch him in their toils as soon as he speaks. The stronger he is born, the more completely he will be conquered, for the greater a river is the more turbulently it flows. When the battle which God ordained for his creature against its fellows and against Nature forces Man to seek a bosom to rest on, when his eyes are filled with tears, he needs a kiss. But his task is not finished: now comes another battle more secret, treacherous and cowardly which is fought under the shadow of his arm, of his heart; for always, more or less, woman is DELILAH.

She laughs and triumphs; in her knowing coldness, among her sisters, she waits and boasts that she feels nothing of the fire. To her fairest friend she confesses it: she makes men love her without herself loving. She fears a master. What she loves is pleasure: Man is rough and takes it without knowing how to give it. The sacrifice of a great heart causes wonder and sets off better than any gold her beauty, which produces such marvels and sprinkles blood where her feet are to pass.

– So, then, Lord, what I have dreamed of does not exist! – She towards whom our love goes and from whom comes life, Woman, in her Pride, has become our enemy. Woman is now worse than in those times when God, looking on men, said 'I repent'. Soon, withdrawing into a hideous kingdom, Woman will have Gomorrah and Man will have Sodom: and, casting angry looks upon each other from a distance, the two sexes will die, each on its own side.

Alfred de Vigny, 'La Colère de Samson', 1839, unpublished in his lifetime. Translated by Carol Clark, 1993.

JOHN MILTON
An Outline for a Tragedy

Sodom. – the title Cupids funeral pile. Sodom Burning – the Scene before Lots gate

[T]he Chorus consists of Lots Shepherds com n to the citty about some affairs await in the evening thire maisters return from his evenin[g] walk toward the citty gates, he brings with him 2 yong men or youth of noble form after likely discourses præpares for thire entertainmen[t] by then Supper is ended, the Gallantry of the town passe by in Processi[on] with musick and song to the temple of Venus Urania or Peor and understanding of tow noble strangers arriv'd they send 2 of thire choysest youth with the preist to invite them to thire citty solemnities it beeing an honour that thire citty had decreed to fair *per*sonages, as being Sacred to thir goddesse. the angels being askt by the preist whence they are say they are of Salem the preist inveighs against ye strict raigne of melchizedeck Lot that knows thire drift answers thwartly at last of which notice give[n] to the whole assembly they hasten thither taxe him of præsumption, singularity, breach of citty customs, in fine offer violence, the chorus of Shephe[rds] præpare resistance in thire maisters defence calling the rest of the serviture, but beeing forc't to give back, the Angels open the dore rescue Lot, discover them selves, warne him to gather his freinds and sons in Law out of ye citty, he goes and returns as having met with some incredulous, some other freind or son in law out of the way when Lot came to his house, overtakes him to know his buisnes, heer is disputed of incredulity of divine judgements & such like matter, at last is describ'd the parting from the citty the Chorus depart with thir maister, the Angels doe the deed with all dreadfull execution, the K. and nobles of the citty may come forth and serve to set out the terror a Chorus of Angels concluding and the Angels relating the events of Lots journy, & of his wife. the first Chorus beginning may relate the course of the citty each evening every one with mistresse, or Ganymed, gitterning along the streets, or solacing on the banks of Jordan, or

259

down the stream. at the preists inviting yᵉ Angels to yᵉ Solemnity the Angels pittying thir beauty may dispute of Love & how it differs from lust seeking to win them in the last scene to yᵉ king and nobles when the firie thunders begin aloft the Angel appeares all girt with flames which he saith are the flames of true love & tells the K. who falls down with terror his just suffering as also Athanes id est Gener lots son in law for dispising yᵉ continuall admonitions of Lots then calling to yᵉ thunders lightnings & fires he bids them heare the call and command of god to come & destroy a godlesse nation he brings them down with some short warning to all other nations to take heed.

From John Milton, *Complete Prose Works*, ed. Maurice Kelley, vol. 8, New Haven and London, Yale University Press, 1982.

The Grape-Gatherers of Sodom

When the day dawned, the land was fuming like a fermenter filled with the grapes of wrath. The vineyard surrounded by the vast and troubled plain shone redly in the fierce light of the sun – a sun as bright as the hot fires which were used to start the grapes fermenting, and which made the huge pips burst out of them like black eyes popping out of their sockets. The vineyard seemed, for a while, to be set at the bottom of a pit seething bitumen. While it displayed its own red-and-gold foliage to the sky, a seeming abundance of monstrous riches, the ground all around it gave vent to writhing plumes of grey smoke, which glittered in the sunlight like molten metal.

As the luscious fruits of the vineyard were ripening, so the softened red clay of the carnal earth was yielding its own produce of poisonous volcanic gas. Like an over-fecund beast released from its tethers in order to drop its litter, the land threw out her vaporous garlands: imploring arms held out towards the newly-risen sun, delirious with sinfully ecstatic joy. As the sun-baked surface cracked here and there, hot liquids oozed out of her like thick tears. These irruptions gradually condensed into lustrous brown masses: prodigious fruits of the earth's womb, distilled by volcanic fire, their dark hue suggestive of satanic sugar. And from some of these clustered and half-rotted fruits there continued to ooze a gentle and abominable liquor whose gaseous exhalation intoxicated the bees which swarmed about the vineyard, tempting them to their deaths.

Between the clouds, so red that one would have thought them all afire, and the plain, so yellow that one might have believed it powdered with saffron, no creature stirred nor bird sang. Only the vineyard was alive, possessed by a dull humming of busy insects like the gentle vibration of a simmering kettle.

In the midst of that forest of golden boughs, on the rim of the primitive fermenting vat – a huge trough of raw granite, crudely hollowed-out, like an altar of human sacrifice – there sat a fabulous lizard clad in sparkling viridian scales, with darting eyes the colour of hyacinths; it stretched itself out enigmatically, occasionally raising its silvery belly as it took a deep breath. It, too, was intoxicated by the drifting vapours, almost to the point of death.

Little by little, as the day progressed, the incendiary glow reflected in the clouds became fainter; they gradually paled, became opalescent, and slowly dissipated. The sky's hot light was gradually concentrated into that solitary blaze which was the sun; the clear sky took on the appearance of the blue sheen which metal has when it has been seared by a fierce torch.

The land of the tribes of Israel extended as far as the eye could see, faintly dappled by the shadows of the slender fig-trees. Every one of those puny trees trailed its palmate leaves as though dissatisfied with its lot, and their lighter branches, all entwined, were ringed by unnatural excrescences of sap like amber bracelets. Their trunks had been deformed by the unfortunate combination of the fire above and the fire below, their pliant contours twisted and warped.

Far away, beyond the most distant of these clumps of trees, there stood the protective wall of a town. Behind the wall loomed a tall tower made of stone as white as ivory or bleached bone, whose spire stood out sharply against the vivid colour of the sky, like a road into the infinite or a spiralling flock of great white birds in search of a place to roost.

There emerged from the walled town a party of Sodomites, heading for the vineyard.

The party was headed by a gloomy old man, perhaps a centenarian twice over, whose bony and tremulous head was devoid of hair and who had long since lost all his teeth. He was dressed in a linen tunic which was loosely gathered about his rickety limbs, hanging upon him like a shroud. He was the father, chief and patriarch of the party which he led, and as he marched before them his stern forehead shone with reflected sunlight like a rectangular star as bright as the moon. He directed his charges by signalling to them with his staff, having long since given up speech.

On either side of the patriarch marched his eldest sons: huge and robustly healthy men with luxuriant black beards. One of them, whose name was Horeb, carried suspended from his leathern belt several shining metal cups, which struck one another melodiously as he strode along.

Behind this leading group there came a group of younger sons, headed by one Phaleg, a nearly-naked giant whose smooth flesh was like veined marble, whose beard was rust-red, and who carried on his head a stack of wicker baskets, some of which contained wheat-cakes.

Further behind, keeping a respectable distance, came playful adolescents who were clad in short robes girdled with ornately-embroidered sashes; their fair girlish tresses streamed behind them as they capered about. The most handsome of these was a child with lips the colour of ripe plums or the blurred violet of the distant horizon; his name was Sinéus, and he had innocently dressed his half-open goatskin tunic with plucked flowers. When Sinéus entered the vineyard, the bees swarmed about him, taking him for some mysterious honey-bearer because of his golden appearance, but they did him no harm.

After singing a celebratory hymn the grape-gatherers began to work, using baskets to carry the grapes from the vines to the fermenting-vat. The older ones, as measured and efficient in their movements as they always were, reached up to take the best grapes; the younger ones hurriedly grabbed those which came most easily to hand, crying out with excitement all the while. After a time the old man, who had set himself down on the rim of the stone trough, stood up and raised his staff to signal that everyone should gather round to admire the full baskets; then he sat down again and the work of emptying the baskets into the stone vat began.

As they worked, some of them were accidentally splashed about the legs by the ruddy juice, others smeared it haphazardly upon their clothing. Sinéus fervently set about treading the grape-harvest, occasionally mixing in with it a handful of wild roses. Beneath the hot sun their labour was very tiring, and when they had filled the stone trough they lay down around it to sleep. The old patriarch remained on the rim of the vat, still sitting up but quite immobile, looming over the liquefied mass of the trampled grapes like an image of some long-dead king preserved in stone.

After a while, there emerged furtively from the shade of the nearest clump of fig-trees a very strange creature: a girl.

She was thin and wan, and naked – but she was burnished by the sun, and covered with a light down of fair hair; so that it seemed as if she were clothed in linen embroidered with filamentous threads of gold. Her forehead struck such a contrast with the blue of the sky that it gleamed like a polished spear-head. Her long yellow hair was gathered up into a sheaf; her heels were as round as peaches, bouncing off the ground as she danced forward like a delighted animal; but the two nipples upon her breasts were very dark, almost black – as if they had been badly burned.

The girl approached the sleeping Sinéus, who slept very soundly, having eaten abundantly of those grapes which he had gathered and trodden. She too ate greedily, and having done so she lay down beside the boy, entwining herself about him in a serpentine fashion. It was not long before her writhing caused the boy to wake, and he awoke groaning lamentably because he felt that some impure sensation was working within his flesh. He got up expeditiously, crying out to wake his brothers; they responded with roars of their own.

The old man awoke too, stretching forth his staff against the intruder with a deathly gleam in his eye. The girl was quickly surrounded by the entire company.

The girl was one of many who had been condemned as temptresses, and driven out of Sodom at the behest of the priests. In a mad fit of righteous wrath, the assembly of the men of God had decreed that the town must be relieved of the evil passions which haunted it from twilight until dawn. The girls of Sodom, they had decided, had been so badly guided by their lax mothers that they had become voluptuous vessels of iniquity which sapped the strength of the men of the town – strength which would be needed for the harvest, and must be conserved by rigid chastity.

In the grip of this madness, the men of Sodom had repudiated their wives and cast out their sisters; these women had been thrown into the streets, beaten and bruised, their clothes torn from their bodies, and chased by dogs into the wilderness without the walls. Driven into the desert, the women had been forced to cross the burning sands to seek refuge in Gomorrah. Many had died in the furnace of the noonday heat; a few had kept themselves alive by plundering the vineyards. But none of these accursed creatures had been brought to repentance, for their flesh was still inflamed by insensate desires, which took nourishment from the fiery heat of the sun and lusted also after those secret fires which were hidden beneath the surface of the plain.

Now, here was one of these bitches, driven by her appetite for the flesh of men to inflict her attentions upon a child no older than herself.

'Who are you?' Horeb demanded of her.

'I am Sarai!'

Sinéus buried his face in the crook of his elbow, hiding his eyes.

'What do you want?' said Phaleg.

'I am thirsty!'

Oh yes! It was evident to them all that she had a thirst in her!

The sons looked at one another, uncertain what to do, but their grim-faced father raised his staff to issue a command, and each one bowed down obediently to take hold of a stone.

The woman, her golden skin glistening in the sunlight, extended her arms like two beams of light.

She cried out, in a voice so strident that they recoiled.

'A curse upon you all!'

'Oh yes,' said Horeb then, 'I recognise you. One night you came to steal the very best of my metal cups.'

'I know you too,' said Phaleg. 'You have tempted me to sin on the Sabbath.'

'As for me,' cried Sinéus, with tears glimmering beneath his eyelids, 'I do not know you at all, nor have I the slightest wish to know you!'

The old man brought down his staff.

'She must be stoned!' they roared in unison.

The woman had no opportunity to escape. Thirty stones were hurled at her all at once.

Her breasts were lacerated and splashed with red; her forehead was wreathed with bands of vermilion. She fell back, writhing desperately, her long hair was loosed, but it clung to her like binding ropes; she tried to make herself very small, and tried to crawl away after she fell, squirming like a snake; but she slipped and tumbled into the great vat where the grape-juice was fermenting. She groped feebly at the crushed clusters, but soon became inert, augmenting the blood of the grapes with the exquisite wine of her own veins. The brief convulsion of her death pulled her down into the depths of the trough, among the burst and trodden grapes which spurted out their black pips – but reflected in her rolling eyes, there was an expression of supreme malediction.

That evening, having completed their task in the saintly fashion required of them, the grape-gatherers distributed the wheat-cakes which they had brought with them, and filled their cups. They had not taken the trouble to remove the cadaver from the trough, and they were already drunk – more intoxicated by the killing than by the vintage which they had prepared. They continued to utter blasphemies against the luckless girl while they drank more of the horrible liquor they had made, saturated with poisonous love.

That same night – while unknown beasts howled in the distance all around them, and the atmosphere they breathed was heavy with the odour of sulphur, and the giant tower in the city took on a skeletal pallor beneath the dismal light of the moon – these men of Sodom committed for the first time their sin against nature, in the arms of their young brother Sinéus, whose soft shoulders somehow seemed to be flavoured with honey.

Rachilde (Marguerite Eymery), 'The Grape-Gatherers of Sodom', in Brian Stableford, ed., *The Dedalus Book of Decadence (Moral Ruins)*. Translated by Brian Stableford. First published in *Mercure de France*, March 1893.

HENRI D'ARGIS
Sodome

Cautious as regards his own temptations, Soran was but rarely alone, well knowing how harmful solitude might be to him. One night he chanced to be crossing the Champs Elysées as he was slowly making his way home.

It was hardly ten o'clock and the place displayed a peculiar appearance. Here and there, gleams of light and sounds of music were issuing from a few *café-concerts*, while all around them was plunged in silence and obscurity. Jacques walked on without looking about him and perhaps scarcely thinking, when a passer-by lightly brushed against him. He paid no attention, thinking it had been done through carelessness, when a little further on, he again came across the same individual whom he had looked at mechanically a short time before. Soran was struck by his appearance. He had curly hair, his face was painted, his neck bare, and his waist squeezed in; he had projected hips and he cast at Jacques an effeminate look which struck him as being strange. His hand was working to and fro in a disgusting way, while he protruded a portion of his nether garment in a provocative manner which could not escape Jacques' attention, and like some filthy nightmare he was clearly offering his girl-like body for a monstrous satisfaction. Jacques Soran shuddered at this strange obstinacy of fate. The enormous temptation of this protean Sodomy which had shown itself to him in such numerous shapes was again before his eyes.

He thought of Giraud whose ripe yet childish ways had perhaps sown in him the germs of a disease which he felt growing within. And now, in this retreat where he had thought to find shelter, had appeared . . . Jacques had force enough to drive this image from his mind; he still thought of his first fall, the foretaste of delights now fully and completely offered to him. His feelings of curiosity held him to the spot, when he ought to have fled away. The individual of dubious appearance saw in this attitude a tacit encouragement, the only language which these creatures of strange sex address to one another. He came nearer to Soran and made some casual remark, as if he wanted to strike up an acquaintance; Jacques replied in monosyllables, but a reply was more than enough. He had a wish to learn about the matter, and so he talked, and the male prostitute's conversation agitated him strangely.

The fellow saw clearly that he had to do with a timid young beginner, and skilfully replied in advance to any objections which he might raise, confining himself, in view of eventualities, to generalities and to vague phrases which could be understood by the initiated alone; Jacques knew what he meant.

He grew more explicit. There would be no danger; there, on a seat behind the Café des Ambassadeurs it was very quiet. Even the policeman on his beat went a little out of his way so as not to disturb the people of good position who were in the habit of going there; and, with interested civility, he pointed out to Jacques an old gentleman who was hiding and waiting.

'He is an officer of the Legion of Honour,' he said, 'but he takes off his ribbon when he comes here.'

Jacques listened with unwholesome pleasure.

'And do you only come here?' he said in a careless way.

'This is the place I prefer; but I sometimes go to the neighbourhood of the Grand Hotel; that's a good part because of the rich foreigners; or to the Palais Royal, or to the Tuileries.'

'And,' persisted Jacques, 'have you many regular customers?'

'Oh yes!' he replied; and as though to prove it and tired of carrying on a useless conversation, he turned to go away. Jacques then felt himself seized with an insurmountable desire.

'Do you know of any less dangerous place?' he said.

The fellow smiled in a satisfied way; he had gained his ends. They both passed along through quiet streets. Jacques blushed as though he were ashamed of being seen in such company. Not far from the Rue de la Boétie, they stopped before a house of respectable appearance.

'This is the place,' said his companion. He knocked at the door and gave a slight cough . . . a stout woman received them very amiably and after a few words in slang which Jacques could not understand, they entered a luxuriously furnished apartment. Jacques would now have liked to go away, but he did not dare.

Thick red curtains hung before the windows, through which no sound could penetrate, and all round the room there were divans covered with cushions.

In a heap on the table, Jacques observed nuns' dresses, women's corsets and drawers, peacocks' feathers, pieces of wood shaped like phalli; in one corner, there was a lay-figure; a large dog of savage appearance leapt from an arm-chair and came and fondled him; on the walls were engravings in which a filthy imagination had depicted men in strange postures and contorsions satisfying their lust in monstrous fashion.

Jacques was ill at ease, and when his disgusting companion laid himself out on the sofa for an act of shameless passivity, Jacques Soran felt overcome with horror and loathing, and this filthy creature, unmentionable in any language, shocked him.

At this supreme moment, the past came up before him, and that past which had failed to ruin him, saved him from an ignoble stain. In a moment he thought of the days of his childhood, so good and pure, of his noble aspirations, which had once raised him above the level of man, and blushing at having fallen so low, he fled . . .

From Henri d'Argis, *Sodome*, Paris, 1888. Preface by Verlaine. Excerpt translated by Dr Jacobus X under the heading 'Solicitation by a little Jesus' in the 'Masculine Prostitution' section of *Crossways of Sex: A Study in Eroto-Pathology*, vol. 2, Paris, British Bibliophiles' Society. Privately Issued For The Subscribers 1904.

The Confession of an Ardent Heart

'But enough of poetry! I've shed tears, so please, do let me cry. It may be foolishness at which everyone will laugh, but not you. Your eyes are shining too. Enough of poetry. I want to tell you now about the "insect", about the insect God has endowed with lust.

And lust in lowly insect fires!

I am that insect, old man, and this has been said of me specially. And all of us Karamazovs are the same kind of insect, and that insect lives in you, too, my angel, and raises storms in your blood. I mean storms, for lust is a storm – worse than a storm! Beauty is a fearful and terrifying thing. Fearful because it is indefinable, and it cannot be defined because God sets us nothing but riddles. Here the shores meet, here all contradictions live side by side. I'm a very uneducated fellow, old man, but I've thought a lot about it. There's a fearful lot of mysteries! Too many riddles oppress man on earth. Solve them as you can, but see that you don't get hurt in the process. Beauty! It makes me mad to think that a man of great heart and high intelligence should begin with the ideal of Madonna and end with the ideal of Sodom. What is more terrible is that a man with the ideal of Sodom already in his soul does not renounce the ideal of Madonna, and it sets his heart ablaze, and it is truly, truly ablaze, as in the days of his youth and innocence. Yes, man is wide, too wide, indeed. I would narrow him. I'm hanged if I know what he really is! What appears shameful to the mind, is sheer beauty to the heart. Is there beauty in Sodom? Believe me, for the great majority of people it *is* in Sodom and nowhere else – did you know that secret or not? The awful thing is that beauty is not only a terrible, but also a mysterious, thing. There God and the devil are fighting for mastery, and the battlefield is the heart of man. Still, one can only talk of one's own pain. Listen, now to business.'

Fyodor Dostoyevsky, *The Brothers Karamazov*, book 3, chapter 3, 'The Confession of an Ardent Heart in Verse'. Translated by David Magarshack.

ROBERT DUNCAN

This Place Rumord To Have Been Sodom

     might have been
Certainly these ashes might have been pleasures.
Pilgrims on their way to the Holy Places remark
this place. Isn't it plain to all
that these mounds were palaces? This was once
a city among men, a gathering together of spirit.
It was measured by the Lord and found wanting.

It was measured by the Lord and found wanting,
destroyd by the angels that inhabit longing.
Surely this is Great Sodom where such cries
as if men were birds flying up from the swamp
ring in our ears, where such fears that were once
desires walk, almost spectacular,
stalking the desolate circles, red eyed.

This place rumord to have been a City surely was,
separated from us by the hand of the Lord.
The devout have laid out gardens in the desert,
drawn water from springs where the light was blighted.
How tenderly they must attend these friendships
or all is lost. All *is* lost.
Only the faithful hold this place green.

Only the faithful hold this place green
where the crown of fiery thorns descends.
Men that once lusted grow listless. A spirit
wrappd in a cloud, ashes more than ashes,
fire more than fire, ascends.
Only these new friends gather joyous here,
where the world like Great Sodom lies under fear.

The world like Great Sodom lies under Love
and knows not the hand of the Lord that moves.
This the friends teach where such cries
as if men were birds fly up from the crowds
gatherd and howling in the heat of the sun.
In the Lord Whom the friends have named at last Love
the images and loves of the friends never die.

Robert Duncan, 'This Place Rumord To Have Been Sodom', *The Opening of the Field: New Directions.*

Sodom: Looking Back

Just a rumour. There is no Sodom, there are only Sodom texts. Pleasures and the ashes of pleasures.

Looking back, like Lot's wife, turning, neck twisted. Looking back, unable to turn away from the stories of Sodom.

I'm more shocked by the violence of the sermon preached before Elizabeth than by Sade's fiction. The preacher's pleasure in the agony of the salt-death, the force of his belief in it. I wonder what Elizabeth made of it. In *Hebrew Myths*, Robert Graves calls Lot's wife Idith. I'd been trying to think of a name for her for months, pleased, at the last minute, to find she had one already.

I'm moved most by Lestey's lament. Or Leslie's or Lesley's, no one seems certain. Sodomites 'choack'd with Smoak . . . burn'd with fire', which comes from an otherwise clumsy verse-play. Moved by that, and the story in Burton of the Brahman and his 'connection with a soldier comrade of low caste'. A connection that, through collisions of class, cultures and attitudes, led to his terrible desire to be hanged, suspended by the feet, so that 'his soul, polluted by exiting "below the waist", would be doomed to endless transmigrations through the lowest forms of life'.

I was surprised and touched by the Dante, the evident love for his Sodomite teachers. And I keep laughing, remembering Huwaay ibn Amr As-Siksiki, whose inkwell all men dipped their pens in.

As to Rochester, he denied writing *Sodom* at all, and in 'To the Author of a Play, called, Sodom', he suggested the work be placed in a public lavatory:

> There bugger wiping Porters when they shite
> And so thy Book itself turn *Sodomite*.

I expect some will wish this book a similar fate.

I've never seen Yeats in the Sodom lists. And yet, looking back over my bookshelves, it's Yeats I remember.

Having spent so much time with parsons, patriarchs, bishops, clerics, popes, scribes, mullahs, missionaries, prophets, rabbis, prelates, learned divines, chaplains, curates, eminences, elders, archbishops, pembertons and andertons . . .

I remember Yeats, and turn to look again at his glorious 'Crazy Jane' poems. She too met with a Bishop.

Crazy Jane Talks with the Bishop

I MET the Bishop on the road
And much said he and I.
'Those breasts are flat and fallen now,
Those veins must soon be dry;
Live in a heavenly mansion,
Not in some foul sty.'

'Fair and foul are near of kin,'
And fair needs foul,' I cried.
'My friends are gone, but that's a truth
Nor grave nor bed denied,
Learned in bodily lowliness
And in the heart's pride.

'A woman can be proud and stiff
When on love intent;
But Love has pitched his mansion in
The place of excrement;
For nothing can be sole or whole
That has not been rent.'

Notes to Introduction and Sodom: A Circuit-Walk/ Looking Back

I was reluctant to clutter memories with footnotes, in spite of a fondness for them. But I have borrowed from many a book, sat through an imagined film season in Sodom. I would like to acknowledge the debts.

Introduction

p. 1   Eusebius Pagit, *A Historie of the Bible, Briefely collected by way of Question and Answer*, London 1627. Thomas Stackhouse, *A New History of the Holy Bible from the Beginning of the World to the Establishment of Christianity with Answers to Most of the Controverted Questions, Dissertations upon the Most Remarkable Passages and a Connection of Prophane History All Along to Which are Added Notes Explaining Difficult Texts, rectifying Mis-Translations, and Reconciling Seeming Contradictions. The Whole Illustrated with Proper Maps*, vol. 2, Edinburgh 1764.

Sodom: A Circuit-Walk

p. 15   Charles Churchill, 'The Times', in *The Poetical Works of Charles Churchill*, James Nichol, Edinburgh 1855.

p. 16   The statements of Messrs Wright, Thickbroom and Swinscow can be found in the papers on the Cleveland Street case in the Public Record Office, London, Ref. DPP I/95/1–7. For a full account of the affair, see H. Montgomery Hyde, *The Cleveland Street Scandal*, W.H. Allen, London 1976.

    'My Lord Gomorrah' appeared anonymously in the *North London Press*, 1889. Quoted in Lewis Chester, David Leitch and Colin Simpson, *The Cleveland Street Affair*, Weidenfeld & Nicolson, London 1976.

p. 17   *The Sins of the Cities of the Plain; or the Recollections of a Mary-Ann with short essays on Sodomy and Tribadism*, London 1881.

p. 19   Garry Wotherspoon, *City of the Plain: History of a Gay-Subculture*, Hale & Iremonger, Sydney 1991. Anon., *Sins of the Cities of the Plain*, A Masquerade 'Badboy' Book, New York 1992.

p. 20   Trials of George Duffus and John Dicks are reported in *Select Trials for Murders, Robberies, Rapes, Sodomy &c at the Sessions House in the Old Bailey . . . 1720–1723*, vol. 1, 2nd edn, London 1742.

    For a full account of molly life see Rictor Norton, *Mother Clap's Molly House: The Gay Subculture in England 1700–1830*, GMP, London 1992. Also watch out for *Mollies*, a short film scripted by Paul Hallam, to be directed by Steve Farrer in 1993/94.

p. 21   *Capital Gay*, *Boyz* and the *Pink Paper* are free gay papers available from gay clubs, cinemas, etc.

    ff is a free monthly magazine. The seizure of *ff* and the 'Rubber Fuck' fuss were widely reported in the gay press. See particularly *Capital Gay*, 23 April 1993.

p. 22   'O how dreadful . . .' Anon., *Proposal for a National Reformation of Manners . . . As also The Black Roll Containing the Names and Crimes of Several Hundred Persons*, London 1694.

p. 23   'Without this care at home . . .' in John Denne, *A Sermon Preached to the Society for the Reformation of Manners*, London 1730.

35th Account of the Progress of the Societies, 1730(?) London. A copy of this, and other SRM pamphlets, can be found in the Guildhall Library, London.

p. 24   On the fortunes of Turnmills, see Alex Kershaw, 'Night Moves' in the *Independent Magazine*, 17 April 1993.
'Many doe so debauch . . .' from D.R.B. in Divin. and Minister of the Gospell, *The Second Part of the Treatise of the Sacrament* bound in with D.R.B.'s *A Practicall Cathechisme*, 2nd edn, London 1633. 'D.R.' identified as Daniel Rogers in the British Library catalogue.

p. 26   Bob Damron's Address Books and Spartacus Gay Guides are guides to the gay haunts of America and the world respectively.

The Heterosexual–Homosexual Rating: Active Incidence scales can be found in Alfred Kinsey, Wardell B. Pomeroy and Clyde B. Martin, *Sexual Behaviour in the Human Male*, W.B. Saunders, Philadelphia and London 1948.
The oft-omitted 'On Sodomy and the Tricks of the Sodomites' chapter of *The Perfumed Garden* can be consulted in Shaykh Nafzawi, *The Glory of the Perfumed Garden*, Neville Spearman, London 1975.

I am much indebted to Joseph Dean for his account of the 'Rex v. Billing' case in the 'Salome and the Black Book' chapter of *Hatred, Ridicule or Contempt: A Book of Libel Cases*, Constable, London 1953.

p. 27   On Oscar Wilde as a posing 'Somdomite' and for the full text of the Marquess of Queensberry's card see Richard Ellmann, *Oscar Wilde*, Hamish Hamilton, London 1987.

p. 28   Anthony Summers, *Official and Confidential: The Secret Life of J. Edgar Hoover*, Gollancz, London 1993.

Many thanks to Martin Duberman for the albeit dubious pleasure of meeting the Countess Waldeck in his *About Time: Exploring the Gay Past*, revised and expanded edition, Meridian/Penguin Books, New York 1991.

p. 32   I'm grateful to Gregory Woods for a footnote in his *Articulate Flesh: Male Homo-Eroticism and Modern Poetry*, Yale University Press, New Haven and London 1987. He drew my attention to a *Gay Sunshine* interview with Allen Ginsberg in which the poet spoke of the gay 'kind of Apostolic succession'. See Winston Leyland, ed., *Gay Sunshine Interviews* 1, San Francisco 1978, where Ginsberg is interviewed by Allen Young.

Right Revd Ashton Oxenden. D.D., *Portraits from The Bible* (Old Testament Series), Hatchard's of Piccadilly 1876.

p. 33   The Rev. J. Paterson Smyth, *The Bible for School and Home: The Book of Genesis*, Sampson Low, Marston & Co., Ltd, London 1894.

p. 35   Living writers of authority, *The Story of the Bible*, Amalgamated Press, London, undated.

K. McLeish, *Stories and Legends from the Bible*, Longman, London 1988.

John Stow, *Surveys of the Cities of London and Westminster and the Borough of Southwark*, London 1598, 'very much enlarged' in 1720 by Johh Strype and sundry 'careful hands'.

p. 37   I am indebted to three scholarly Sodoms: Barry Burg, *Sodomy and the Pirate Tradition: English Sea Rovers in the Seventeenth Century*, New York University Press, New York and London 1984; Gregory W. Bredbeck, *Sodomy and Interpretation: Marlowe to Milton*, Cornell University Press, Ithaca and London 1991; and Jonathan Goldberg, *Sodometries: Renaissance Texts, Modern Sexualities*, Stanford University Press, Stanford, CA 1992.

Michel Foucault discusses 'sodomy, that utterly confused category' in *A History of Sexuality*, Volume 1: *An Introduction*, Allen Lane, London 1979.

p. 38   Thomas Nashe, *The Unfortunate Traveller*, London 1594. Friedrich Engels on those Greeks in *The Origin of the Family, Private Property and the State*, quoted in Jeffrey Weeks, 'Where Engels Feared to Tread', *Gay Left*, 1, autumn 1975.

p. 40   Samuel Laing, revised by Edward Cloud, 'The Historical Element in the Old Testament', in *Human Origins*, Rationalist Press Association, London 1903.

p. 42   Margaret Visser, *Much Depends on Dinner*, Penguin, London 1989. I had begun my ruminations on salt when Antony Peattie referred me to this book. Some of Visser's striking observations wove into mine.

p. 43   Philip Derbyshire drew my attention to the June 1869 letter of Friedrich Engels to Marx in *The Marx–Engels Correspondence*, selected and edited by F.J. Raddatz, translated by Ewald Owens, Weidenfeld & Nicolson, London 1981.

p. 45   John Evelyn, *Fumifugium or the Inconveniencie of the Aer and Smoak of London – With Some Remedies*, London 1661.
'In fact the conceptual vocabulary . . .' from Randal Kincaid, 'Was Marx Anti-Gay?', *Gay Left*, autumn 1976.

p. 46   Louis Ginsberg, *The Legends of the Jews*, vol. 1, translated from the German by Henrietta Szold, the Jewish Publication Society of America, Philadelphia 1908.

Neil Norman, writing under the headline: "The Fear that Stalks the Twilight Zone' in the *Evening Standard*, 25 February 1992.

p. 47   James Anderton's 'cesspit' speech quoted in the *Guardian*, 12 December 1986.

Eighty-nine-year-old grandmother quoted in *Daily Express* editorial, 13 December 1986.

p. 48   August 1992 Scala programme note.
Sodom (Luther Price), 1991.

p. 49   *Sodom and Gomorrah* (Robert Aldrich), 1962.

p. 50   *The Bible . . . in the beginning* (John Huston), 1966.
Zoo Time: children's television programme. Granada TV, 1956.

p. 51   *Salo: or the 120 Days of Sodom* (Pier Paolo Pasolini), 1975.

Seizure of *Salo*. Reported in *Gay News*, 125, 11 August 7 September 1977.
Salo: or the 120 Days of Sodom, the video, 'Now Available': the full-page ad appeared in the *Advocate*, 1 January 1991.

p. 52 *Lot in Sodom* (James Sibley Watson/Melville Webber), 1933. *Cinema Quarterly* quoted in Jack Babuscio, 'Sodom Revisited', *Gay News*, 99, 15–28 July 1976.

p. 53 *Nitrate Kisses* (Barbara Hammer), 1992.

Return to Sodom (David Wilkerson). The film's existence was briefly reported in *Gay News*, 82, 6–19 November 1975.

p. 54 *Sehnsucht nach Sodom* (A Yearning for Sodom) (Kurt Raab, Hanno Baethe, Hans Hirschmüller), 1988.

p. 55 *Last Tango in Paris* (Bernardo Bertolucci), 1972. *Midnight Express* (Alan Parker), 1978. *Querelle* (Rainer Werner Fassbinder), 1982.
Nighthawks (Ron Peck/Paul Hallam), 1978. The 1980 Greek ban by the Second Degree Censor Board was reported in the pamphlet *Greek Gays under Attack: A Short History of the Greek Gay Liberation Movement*, published in support of *Amfi*. *Amfi*, a Greek gay quarterly, was then facing a charge of 'offending public morality' for publishing a poem which contained the word 'prick'. The *Sun* headline, 'CHILDREN TO STAR IN A 'GAY' FILM', appeared in the *Sun*, 3 July 1978.

Caught Looking (Constantine Giannaris), 1991. The medley of viewer complaint is an abstract of viewers' comments, calls noted by the duty officer following the film's late-night transmission on Channel 4, combined with odd words from letters to the Channel and to the Broadcasting Standards Council. The Council's 'Finding' on the film was issued on 14 December 1992.

p.56 Ruff shots in *Male Only*, Pendulum Publications 1970.

p.57 *Gay Times*, a monthly gay magazine published in London. I am indebted to *Gay Times* for much of news-print Sodom.

The story of the raided party in Iran surfaced in *Kayhan* and was taken up by *Gay Times* in October 1992. Earlier events in Iran were reported in *Gay Times*, May 1991 and July 1990.

The Ayatollah Khomeini quotations are from an interview with Oriana Fallaci published in the *Daily Mail*, quoted in *Gay News*, 177, 18–31 October 1979. The same issue of *Gay News* reported on the speech of Pope John Paul II.

p.58 Rapin de Thoyras, *The History of England*, vol. 2, translated into English and with additional notes by N. Tindal, 3rd edn, London 1743.

p. 59 The United Nations' decision to investigate the anti-gay laws of the island of Tasmania is reported in the *Independent*, 27 December 1992.

p. 60 Robert Hughes, *The Fatal Shore*, Knopf, New York 1987.
Madonna, *Sex*, Secker & Warburg, London 1992.

'New "Sodom" is spared' ran the header for an unsigned article in *Gay News*, 87, 29 January–11 February 1976.

p. 61 *Feed Them to the Cannibals* (Fiona Cunningham Reid), 1992.

Garry Wotherspoon, *City of the Plain*, Hale & Iremonger, Sydney 1991.

Robin Maugham quoted in Francis King, 'Of Mountains and Molehills', *Gay Times*, December 1992.

Justinian edicts quoted and examined in Derrick Bailey, *Homosexuality and the Western Christian Tradition*, Longmans, Green & Co., London 1955.

p. 62   'Harvey Milk memorial a "tribute to Sodom"' by Todd Willcox in San Francisco, *Pink Paper*, 23 August 1992. Thanks to the *Pink Paper* for permission to print this and other recent Sodom news.

The *Pink Paper* comment on the 1992 Florida hurricane story appeared in the comment column 'Pink Thinks' under the heading, 'Homosexuality, Earthquakes', 30 August 1992.

p. 63   Blackburn Sodom. *Gay News*, 202, 30 October–12 November 1980.

Nick MacKinnon won champagne for his competition entry in the *Independent Magazine*, 25 July 1992. The Battersea Arts Centre job offer appeared in the 'Creative and Media' columns of the *Guardian*, July 1992.
Discussions on the meanings of 'to know': early Christian attitudes to homosexuality and sodomy laws are extensively discussed in Derrick Bailey, *Homosexuality and the Western Christian Tradition*, Longmans, Green & Co., London 1955; and John Boswell, *Christianity, Social Tolerance and Homosexuality*, University of Chicago Press, Chicago and London 1980.
Derek Rawcliffe, letter to the *Pink Paper*, 18 April 1993.

p. 64   David Keys's front-page report was headed 'Leading archaeologist says Old Testament stories are fiction', *Independent on Sunday*, 28 March 1993.

p. 65   RCA ad for *Hair, it*, 41, 1–17 October 1968.

p. 68   *Theorem* (Pier Paolo Pasolini), 1968.
Oedipus Rex (Pier Paolo Pasolini), 1967.

p. 69   This and all subsequent references to Proust are to the *Sodome et Gomorre* section of *A la recherche . . .*, translated by C.K. Scott Moncrieff as 'Cities of the Plain', Alfred A. Knopf, London 1929.

p. 70   *Women in Love*, London 1921. The D.H. Lawrence Sodom and sodomy trail was an exercise in memory. But I am indebted to Gregory Woods for pointing me to, or reminding me of, specific references.

'Pansies', 'Bawdy Can Be Sane' and the second version of that poem, 'What's Sane and What Isn't' in *The Complete Poems of D.H. Lawrence*, London 1964.

p. 71   *Lady Chatterley's Lover*, Penguin, London 1961.
John Sparrow gives his own account of the give-and-take in *Lady Chatterley's Lover* in his *Controversial Essays*, Faber & Faber, London 1966.
Lawrence on perfect love with a coal-miner: Compton Mackenzie, *My Life and Times, Octave 5*: 1915–1923. London 1966.

p. 73   Della Grace writing in *Quim*, 'for dykes of all sexual persuasions' under the heading 'Smashes and Contrasexuals' and the sub-heading 'Queer as Fuck My Arse', issue 4, London 1992.

Pliny the Elder, *Historia Naturalis*. His remarks on the Esseni are quoted in *Adam International Review: The Image of Jerusalem*, edited by Miron Grindea. This special issue of *Adam* was published by the University of Rochester, New York 1968.

p. 74   William Burkitt, *Expository Notes with Practical Observations on the New-Testament of Our Lord and Saviour Jesus Christ*, 6th edn, London 1751.

p. 75   Thomas Sternhold, John Hopkins and Others, *The Whole Book of Psalmes: Collected into English Meeter*. Numerous London editions.

St Augustine, *The Confessions of Saint Augustine*, Airmont paperback edition, New York 1969. Translation unattributed.

p. 77   *Johnny, Go Home* (John Willis, YTV, 1975).

Schoolboys and Sodom sleaze. Editions and dates refer to paperback editions only: Roger Peyrefitte, *Special Friendships*, Panther, 1964; Eric Jourdan, *Two*, Pyramid Publications, 1963; Angus Stewart, *Sandel*, Panther, 1970; Gerald Tesch, *Never The Same Again*, Pyramid Books, 1958; Fritz Peters, *Finistère*, Panther, 1969; Jay Little, *Somewhere Between the Two*, Paperback Library, 1965. Jay Little also wrote *Maybe Tomorrow*. Deborah Deutsch, *The Flaming Heart*, Swan Edition, 1966; James Barr, *The Occasional Man*, Paperback Library, 1966; Joe Leon Houston, *Desire in the Shadows*, Paperback Library, 1966; George Moor, *The Pole and Whistle*, New English Library, 1966; Edwin Fey, *Summer in Sodom*, Paperback Library, 1965. The morals of public schools were discussed in *New Review*, July 1893. Quoted in Ivan Bloch, *Sexual Life in England Past and Present*, Francis Aldor, London 1938. *If . . .* (Lindsay Anderson), 1968.

p. 79   Louis Ginsberg, *The Legends of the Jews*, vol. 1, translated from the German by Henrietta Szold, the Jewish Publication Society of America, Philadelphia 1908.

p. 82   'I'll Take You Home Again Kathleen' (traditional).

W.B. Yeats, lines from 'Nineteen Hundred and Nineteen' and 'A Dialogue of Self and Soul', in The *Collected Poems of W.B. Yeats*, Macmillan, London 1950.

p. 84   'Sometimes I Feel Like A Motherless Child' (traditional).

Lewis Bayly, *The Practise of Pietie, directing a Christian how to walke that he may please God*, London 1617.

p. 85   A learned Bishop in Ireland, *A Short Treatise on These Heads viz: Of the Sins* of *Sodom*, of *Pride* in *Apparel* and *Contempt* of *God* in his *Judgements*, etc., London 1689.

p. 87   *Les Petits Bougres au manège* (The Little Buggers' Reply) printed in *L'An second du rêve de la liberté*, 'Year Two of the Dream of Liberty' i.e. year two of the French Revolution), *Cahiers GKC*, II, Lille 1989.

Requête et décret (Petition and Decree), a pamphlet which was printed in 'the second year of fuckative regeneration' (*L'An second de la régénération foutative*), Cahiers GKC, II, Lille 1989. The two pamphlets in one volume, introduced by the series editor, Patrick Cardon.

p. 89   The trial of William Brown for 'Sodomitical Practices', July 1726, in *Select Trials for Murders, Robberies, Rapes, Sodomy &c at the Sessions House in the Old Bailey . . . 1720–1723*, 2nd edn, vol. 3, London 1742.
Thomas S. Szasz, *The Manufacture of Madness*, Harper & Row, New York 1970.

p. 90   *Les Enfans de Sodome* (1790), Cahiers GKC, I, Lille 1989. Introduced by the series editor, Patrick Cardon.

p. 91   Henri d'Argis, *Sodome*, Paris 1888. Preface by Paul Verlaine.
Henri d'Argis, *Gomorrhe*, Paris 1889.

p. 94   Neil Bartlett, *Who Was That Man?: A Present for Mr Oscar Wilde*, Serpent's Tail, London 1988.
Oscar Wilde, letter to the Home Secretary, 2 July 1896, in Rupert Hart-Davies, ed., *Selected Letters of Oscar Wilde*, Oxford 1979.

Max Nordau, *Degeneration*, London 1892.

The Gospel According to St. Matthew (Pier Paolo Pasolini), 1964.

p. 96   The Reverend Troy Perry, *The Lord Is My Shepherd and He Knows I'm Gay*, Nash Publishing Corporation, Los Angeles 1972.

Looking Back

p. 275   Robert Graves (with R. Paatei), *The Hebrew Myths*, London 1963.

John Wilmot, Second Earl of Rochester, 'To the Author of a Play, called, Sodom' quoted in Pisanus Fraxi (H. C. Ashbee), *Centuria Librorum Absconditorum* (Bibliography of Prohibited Books), London 1879.

Yeats, 'Crazy Jane Talks with the Bishop', in *The Collected Poems of W.B. Yeats*, Macmillan, London 1950.

The letters from Kathleen Hallam to her son Paul are unpublished. I wonder what she would have made of my use of them.

Anthology Acknowledgements

Thanks are due for permission to reprint the following copyright material in this book.

ANON. 'A perverse custom it is to prefer boys to girls', translated by John Boswell in *Christianity, Social Tolerance and Homosexuality: Gay People in Western Europe from the Beginning of the Christian Era to the Fourteenth Century*, University of Chicago Press, Reprinted by permission of the translator and University of Chicago Press.

ALDO BUSI From *Sodomie in corpo*, © Mondadori 1988, translated as *Sodomies in Elevenpoint*, by Stuart Hood, Faber and Faber, London 1992, © 1992 Faber and Faber Ltd and Grandi & Vitali Associati srl. Reprinted by permission of Faber and Faber and Grandi & Vitali.

PETER CANTOR 'On Sodomy', translated by John Boswell in John Boswell, *Christianity, Social Tolerance and Homosexuality: Gay People in Western Europe from the Beginning of the Christian Era to the Fourteenth Century*, University of Chicago Press, Chicago 1980, © 1980 John Boswell and University of Chicago Press. Reprinted by permission of the translator and University of Chicago Press.

FYODOR DOSTOYEVSKY From *The Brothers Karamazov* (1980), translated by David Magarshack, Penguin Books, Harmondsworth 1958, © 1958 David Magarshack and Penguin Books Ltd. Reprinted by permission of Penguin Books.

ROBERT DUNCAN 'This Place Rumord To Have Been Sodom' from *The Opening of the Field*, New Directions, New York 1960, © 1960 Robert Duncan. Reprinted by permission of New Directions Publishing Corp.

SUE GOLDING 'The Address Book', © 1993 Sue Golding. Printed by permission of the author.

ANDREW LUMSDEN 'A Day-Trip to Sodom' from *Gay News* 252, 26 October–

W.B. YEATS 'Crazy Jane Talks with the Bishop' from Richard J. Finneran, ed., *The Poems of W.B. Yeats: A New Edition*, Macmillan Publishing Company, New York 1933, © 1933 by Macmillan Publishing Company, renewed 1961 by Bertha Georgie Yeats. Reprinted by permission of Macmillan Publishing Company.

THE BIBLE Extracts from the Authorised Version of the Bible (The King James Bible), the rights in which are vested in the Crown, are reproduced by permission of the Crown's Patentee, Cambridge University Press.

Every effort has been made to trace the copyright holders of material included in this book. Verso apologise for any errors or omissions in the above list and would be grateful to be notified of any corrections that should be incorporated in the next edition of this book.

Index to Anthology